99

Uphill All The Way

Also by John Hawkridge

Sticks and Stones

Uphill All The Way

John Hawkridge

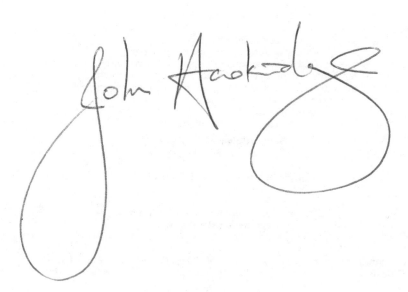

Michael Joseph
LONDON

MICHAEL JOSEPH LTD
Published by the Penguin Group
Penguin Books Ltd, 27 Wrights Lane, London w8 5TZ, England
Viking Penguin, a division of Penguin Books USA Inc.
375 Hudson Street, New York, New York 10014, USA
Penguin Books Australia Ltd, Ringwood, Victoria, Australia
Penguin Books Canada Ltd, 2801 John Street, Markham, Ontario, Canada L3R 1B4
Penguin Books (NZ) Ltd, 182–190 Wairau Road, Auckland 10, New Zealand

Penguin Books Ltd, Registered Offices: Harmondsworth, Middlesex, England

First published in Great Britain January 1991
Second impression before publication
Third impression February 1991

Printed in England by Clays Ltd, St Ives plc
Filmset in Monophoto Plantin Light

A CIP catalogue record for this book is available
from the British Library
ISBN 0 7181 3469 9

The extract on page 230–1 from *Journey Through Nepal* by Mohamed Amin, Duncan
Willetts and Brian Tetley is reproduced by kind permission of The Bodley Head

Uphill All The Way is dedicated to the following people, whose help and encouragement proved invaluable when I was about to make some of the boldest moves of my life:

Marjorie Godley, who from an early age helped fashion my attitude towards life, endeavouring always to support me through both good and bad times;

Betty Clark, who brought to fruition my early camping aspirations and initiated an interest in nature;

Molly Lefebure, without whose persistent encouragement, mostly tempered by a deep understanding, the more personal side to this book would not have been written;

and Chris Bonington, who inspired, encouraged and helped me to fulfil my ultimate mountain ambition and quest for Himalayan adventure.

Author's Note

Spellings of Himalayan place names vary enormously from source to source; every book or map I consulted was different. I have therefore chosen these versions I felt were closest to those we saw and used while we were actually there, and have tried to be as consistent as possible.

Contents

	List of Illustrations	ix
	Introduction	1
1	Lambs to Slaughter	4
2	The Home Front	18
3	Back to School	28
4	A Date with Destiny	35
5	Living under the Shadow of the Knife	44
6	Learning to Live	58
7	Headfirst into Society	67
8	Gone Fishing	72
9	An Uphill Struggle	91
10	New Horizons	106
11	Reaching the Heights	124
12	Distance the Challenge	136
13	The Challenge Gone?	157
14	The Way to Everest	173
15	To Everest the Hardest Way	192
16	The Ultimate Adventure	201
17	After Everest	229
	Postscript: Philosophy and Reality	235
	Index	243

Illustrations

Black and white section

'My condition went unnoticed until I did not make the
  usual progression from crawling to walking'
My first caravan holiday, with my father
Boating with my father and Uncle Gordon
On my tricycle, aged two, with my cousin Sandra
In my car, being pushed by my brother Robert
Robert, Aunt Madge and myself, Filey, summer 1955
Robert and I try rock climbing, Ilkley, June 1955
School outing to the seaside
With Robert and my sister, Christine, 1956
At Larchfield School, wearing the detested callipers
With Robert McLellan and the gardeners at Larchfield
A proud cub
The 19th North Leeds Wolf Cub Pack
Aged ten, just before my first operation
In plaster at Thorp Arch hospital
I taught myself to walk again, eventually progressing to
  walking sticks
Last outing before Everest, on Pillar in the Lake
  District
Reaching Kala Pattar, the fulfilment of a dream

Colour section

Fishing on the River Suck, Ballinasloe, Ireland
Learning to sail
Sea Cadets on Harrison Stickle
My first summit, Helvellyn

Scafell and Scafell Pike from Wasdale Head
Ben Nevis
On the summit of Ben Nevis, June 1974
On the summit of Ben Nevis with Chris Bonington, July
    1987
Kathmandu street scene
Crossing the Dudh Kosi
Namche Bazaar
The trail from Namche Bazaar to Tengboche
The film crew
Ama Dablam
The last tea house before Everest
Kala Pattar
Yonden Sherpa and myself on the summit of Kala Pattar

All photographs courtesy of John Hawkridge

Map of the Himalayas on page 203 showing route to Kala
Pattar by Neil Hyslop

Introduction

This book is about my life as a spastic from my earliest recollections; about my upbringing, schooling, education and family life; about my fears, motivations and innermost thoughts. The purpose of it is to show that being severely disabled or handicapped does not have to mean being severely restricted or inactive. Further, it is to show how my life was shaped and why I had to live it in the way I have done.

I have always known what my aims and ambitions are, and what I intend to achieve through the various activities I undertake. Since the age of fourteen, in so far as it is possible, I have dictated the course which my life has followed. That is to say, I have had full control and accepted complete responsibility for what I have done, whilst always being aware that others are individuals and no matter what I may think, say or do will ultimately exercise their power of free will. That is what living in a democratic society is about – free will – and disabled people need to exercise it just as much as anyone else.

Although the whole of my body is affected by my condition I am fortunate that it is only the permanent and constant tension on my muscles which results in the twisting and awkwardness of limbs. I am never able to relax, although I am able to enjoy long periods of physical inactivity, probably in a similar way to which a physically normal person would relax. I am also fortunate in having all my mental faculties and am therefore, like everyone else, able to make my own decisions and live an otherwise normal life. As a young child I could walk, run, skip and jump quite happily, albeit rather awkwardly, but I was singled out for experimental surgery and after that everything changed. I left hospital in a wheelchair and had to learn to walk all over again. Several years after his retirement I spoke to the surgeon who had performed the operations on my legs. In fact he had done more than just operate. He had shaped the course of my well-being and development from the time my condition was diagnosed at around my first birthday until he retired some twenty years later. I had, however, only seen him once since I had left school, a month before I was fifteen, obligatory monitoring of progress and treatment by government authorities apparently ceasing with the leaving of school. He informed me that I was in 'his book' but that of course I was not mentioned by name. He had been an eminent professor and as such the first thing he had done on retirement was to record his work and achievements.

I ought to make it clear that we got on together very well. I had known him for as long as I could remember and in some ways I had a lot of respect for his concern for me, even though his attentions towards improving my lot were unwelcome. I needed his experience, knowledge and understanding of my disability but could have done without him physically using me to further them. You could say that we had a mutual interest, although we viewed it from different standpoints. 'The hunter and the hunted' might accurately describe our relationship.

He was obviously sufficiently well satisfied with the work he had done on me to feel it warranted a place among his memoirs, but privately had enough reservations not to believe that I was now climbing mountains as a result of any related improvement. In fact we both knew the truth of the matter and in all honesty he was a little embarrassed by the situation. He found some difficulty in facing me, but to his credit he did and furthermore was still concerned for my well-being. I held no grudge against him or what had happened in my childhood but neither would I be party to any public proclamation of anything other than what I believed to be the truth, hence a deafening silence.

I gave his book considerable thought. He had pointed out that there would be nothing in it of interest to me. He was probably right. I did not understand the technicalities of what was wrong with me or the so-called corrective surgery performed. What I did know and intimately understand was my physical status and how to exploit it to the full. I was resolute in everything that I committed myself to. I knew myself. I was my own best friend and that was my key to a happy and successful life.

I have continued to think about his book. Medical science has advanced at such a fantastic rate since World War II that perhaps his biography has become a standard work covering the medical development made during the 1950s and 60s. Progress has ensured that this period is now history, a history faithfully recorded by the authorities of the time. This book is intended in part to be a social history of what it was really like to be a severely handicapped child during that period and then later an adult. I fear that if I do not record my trials, tribulations and joys, which were probably commonplace, then tomorrow's academics may well have an incomplete and rather one-sided picture of our yesteryears.

Although the book remains faithful to the facts as I remember them I sincerely hope that you will not think them all to be doom and gloom for they were most certainly not. When one door closes another inevitably opens. Sometimes, however, we must find and open the door for ourselves. I have no intention of seeking sympathy or depressing anyone but you must remember that there has to be darkness before there can be light; you must set off on the journey in order to arrive. Perhaps many of the events had a beneficial effect in the long term although the results could never have been foreseen at the time. The experiences which shape our lives are not always undergone with joy, many are thrust upon us greatly against our wishes or better judgment, but at the end of the day we are a living testimony to their effect, for better or worse, and here the choice is often our own. As the saying goes, wisdom is born of suffering.

Handicapped or not, life has its share of funny moments and the sooner we can appreciate the lighter side of things the happier we will be. Having said that, enjoying life and making it worthwhile and rewarding has always been a serious business and the most important thing of all to me. I hope this book will not only show my attitude towards life but also how it was formed.

ONE

Lambs to Slaughter

I was born on 19 August 1948, a spastic, most probably the result of a clumsily executed forceps delivery. I was a fairly normal baby, so I am told, and the condition went unnoticed until I did not make the usual progression from crawling to walking. I did walk but was reluctant to let go of the furniture I clung to for support. The condition was diagnosed and I began to attend the health authority's clinic for physiotherapy. What the treatment achieved, if anything, is now impossible to assess but what it did do was to get me used to being mauled about by all and sundry and give the authorities whose charge I was in the opportunity to keep me under close scrutiny.

Visits, as I recollect, consisted of routine exercises, a lot of questions to answer, a check on physical development and periodic appearances before doctors and a surgeon who was just referred to as 'the specialist'. It also made me acutely aware that there was something wrong. I had a brother sixteen months younger than I, and whenever he came with me I could not understand how he survived the visits unscathed. They were giving me an unusual amount of attention that I felt I could well do without, all that limb twisting and stretching accompanied by lots of questions. What was it all in aid of? I would ask myself.

I found out soon enough. At four years of age I was sent to Larchfield School in Harrogate, a Leeds Education Authority residential school for spastic children. The school opened early in 1953 and I was one of the first pupils. There were places for twenty children and I actually started in the second week when the number attending was increased from five to ten as the operation slowly got under way. We resided from Monday to Saturday, being despatched home around mid-morning on Saturday and returning early the following Monday. I suppose the shortness of the break had the advantage of not letting you become accustomed to the pleasant life enjoyed with your family. The reprieve may have been minimal but Monday morning departures were a difficult time for both children and their mothers.

4

Pupils were transported to and from school by ambulance. The type of vehicle varied according to what the general service could spare. Often on a Monday it would be a fully equipped emergency vehicle complete with stretchers and very dark, small one-way vision windows. The ambulance crews used all sorts of ploys to take our minds off the fact that we were being wrenched from our families. There would be organized singing, 'I spy' games and, as the number of children to be collected warranted the use of two vehicles, the ambulances would often meet up on the outskirts of Leeds from which point a cat and mouse chase would ensue. I suppose that wanting to be the first to arrive and thus win the race at least took your mind off the fact that you did not really want to go at all. The radio contact between the vehicles also added to the atmosphere and we took a great interest in the make, type and code name of the ambulances we used.

Sometimes a child would be so distressed that the ambulance crew would refuse to take them on board for fear of upsetting the others already in their care, especially if they were in the latter stages of their round. I was always very upset at leaving for school but my mother knew how to handle the situation. In the event of any mysterious feeling of illness suddenly occurring a Junior Aspirin would be administered, together with a few words of reassurance. She was a loving and caring person, but never said much and I could sense that my departures really hurt her even more than they did me. As far as possible I went quietly for her sake and, besides, no one benefited from tears and tantrums. However, the 'hysterical' act worked for me once. I was five years old, my mother had gone into hospital to have my sister, and I was staying with my grandparents. I was upset at being deprived of my mother, although staying with my grandparents was no hardship. That particular Monday morning I decided to take advantage of the situation and my grandmother's inexperience and feelings. I managed, due mainly I believe to the fact that everyone including the school accepted the extenuating circumstances, through crying and creating, to get the week off. I had never tried this ploy before and since you still had, with increased difficulty, to go the following week, I never tried it again. As time passed and I got older, although leaving for school was never pleasant, it became a way of life. There was always the return home to look forward to and, however bad the time at school, it was reassuring to know that Saturday would eventually arrive and your parents be delighted to have you back home.

Miss Hogarth was in charge of the school and discipline was her speciality. She had a commanding voice and a stature to match. Her discipline reigned throughout the school from top to bottom: teachers, house mothers, gardeners, pupils, cleaners and cooks. No one escaped her direct supervision and everyone feared her wrath. She did, however, have one soft spot, her feline friends. We also loved her family of cats, especially tiger-striped Timothy, and this did at least give us some common ground.

Larchfield had been a residence of the Rowntree family, I think, and it was a very elegant large house set in quite spacious well-kept grounds. I believe it had been used by the telecommunications department of the Post Office during the war and shortly afterwards given to the Leeds Education Authority. The ground-floor accommodation consisted of a large classroom which also doubled as a playroom at break times and in the evening, boys' and girls' toilets, physiotherapy room, a second classroom, entrance hall, dining room, kitchen, staffroom, and the head's office conveniently placed in a remote corner. On the first floor were three bedrooms, boys' and girls' bathrooms and toilets, and staff accommodation. A lift went to the first floor but there was also a very reasonable stairway which we were encouraged to use whenever convenient.

Most of the windows were ornately leaded and many of the rooms decorated with fine wood panelling. Leading from one of the bedrooms was a large iron fire escape and it was considered to be a very big event when a practice was held. At the side of the building was a balustraded terrace and this was our general play area. There was also a rose garden complete with summer house, an upper and lower lawn, rose-covered pergola and a woodland area. To the front of the school was a large overgrown pond with a surrounding swampy area. At the rear of the house and walled from the main garden were some greenhouses, a potting shed and a large vegetable plot. Around the house and throughout the garden were many flower beds and borders.

For whatever reasons there were always developments under way and changes taking place. At one stage the drive, which had been covered roughly with loose stones, was tarmacked and we were allowed, from a safe distance, to watch the men and their machinery at work. Seeing and being near to such a large, dangerous and complicated machine together with the accompanying heat and smell was something we found oddly exciting. The subsequent result also greatly increased the ease with which we could use the drive.

Life at the school was not all bad. The underlying problem was that you lived constantly in fear of reprimand and at four years of age that will get to your soul unless you are a prospective delinquent and challenge all authority anyway. When you live away at that age there is no respite from any aggravation, real or imagined, no feeling of the safety of being at home or parents to go running to should you be hurt, either physically or emotionally. Disability or not, you were on your own, and the only answer was to conform, while trying not to submit to the wishes of those for whom you lacked respect any more than was absolutely necessary. Not that to do as you are told is wrong, but it is definitely not a good thing when your every move is being dictated or supervised – and that is how it seemed to me. I considered myself to be respectful of authority but lacking in respect for many of the individuals who were exercising it. They were often dictatorial and over-zealous in their attitude and approach when a greater degree of sensitivity and understanding would have achieved much better results.

Meal times were often a traumatic experience as no one was allowed to dislike anything that was served or, at least, disliking something was not a good enough reason for not eating it. Everything served had to be devoured although slightly reduced portions of certain foods could be had where it was known that the final result would be vomiting. As if to emphasize the degree of control they had over us and as a last defiant gesture the meal which the majority of pupils detested, fish cakes, was served on a Saturday morning. The volume of tears shed often outweighed the small splash of tomato ketchup you were allowed to assist with the partaking of the despised food.

If you failed to eat a meal then you were either deemed to be ill, which meant being sent to bed, having a routine medical and perhaps a doctor called, or you sat there until you did eat it with the eventual prospect of further meals accumulating in front of you. It was very rare, but not completely unknown, for someone to get to that stage. Should any item be regurgitated and the act judged to be voluntary then that item had to be reconsumed. On one occasion a fellow classmate and close friend, Robert McLellan, was forced to eat his breakfast several times before they eventually decided he was ill. Later that day he was taken to hospital where he had his appendix removed.

Days were never boring, because you had to be constantly alert to the ever-present dangers of the staff. There were four house mothers, each of whom was assigned five children and, together with the physiotherapist and gardeners, these were our only allies, the few people to whom we could speak in confidence. Those whose food phobias were minimal could also risk speaking to the cook and fortunately I came under this category, my main dislike being the milk which we had to drink each morning at break time, which was outside her jurisdiction. There were many other food-stuffs I would have preferred to avoid, but admitting to them would have made the problem much worse, so I just used to force it down while looking for any possible way to get rid of any offending items. My main dislikes were cakes but no one seemed to take too much notice if you quietly avoided them, provided you ate healthy sized portions of the staple foods.

Looking back, it was not that there was much wrong with the food itself, but the menu was almost too varied, with such vegetables as parsnips, marrow and pumpkin, which most of us had never seen before, in addition to the more common ones. With items such as fish the parsley sauce would not be optional and other meals were served with similar traditional accompaniments. The plain wholesome food we all enjoyed so much at home was often no longer recognizable when cooked to an imaginative recipe, more probably designed to arouse the adult palate than a child's. There was always something which the average child would dislike. The simple fact was that you either made mealtimes a misery or came to terms with the situation and got on with the ultimately necessary business of eating.

Although the school was not academically orientated we did have lessons and great emphasis was placed on learning to read and write. Neatness and tidiness were of the utmost importance in all we did. Being constructive or artistic always took second place to presentation. This suited me fine as I enjoyed exercising the basic skills we were being taught. Writing was either neat and tidy or it was scrawled or illegible, arithmetic was either right or it was wrong, there was no biased individual acting as judge and jury as to its merits, it was there for all to see clearly. Whenever the weather was fine lessons were, as far as was practical, held out of doors.

The playing of musical instruments – I nearly always used to end up with the triangle – and singing was a frequent occurrence and I detested this since I could not understand how it had any significance in life, and to make matters worse it was supposed to be a pleasurable and joyous occasion. I fared little better at drawing and painting. I was a perfectionist and one would have had to have a rare talent to produce good results at such an early age. I was never satisfied with the approximation of reality that I could achieve and had much too cold, stiff and calculating a mind ever to improve without an understanding and enlightening teacher. On the other hand, however, I excelled at the more practical creative things such as needlework and model building.

I had a good level of general knowledge but this was mainly attributable to my grandfather with whom I spent a lot of time. He suffered severely from rheumatism and was also slightly deaf, but he was a confirmed believer in the benefits of learning and answered my questions with endless patience. I was an inquisitive child and I suppose my non-stop questioning was quite wearing for many of the folks around me. Although he died when I was only eight years old I can still remember many of our conversations very clearly. He was probably self-educated but he enjoyed doing crosswords and similar puzzles and was very knowledgeable and interested in sport. His advanced years and long-standing disability must have given him a mature and philosophical outlook and understanding of life. Whatever the case, it proved to be to my advantage as I was a child content to operate at his impaired physical level while being bright enough to converse sensibly with him. After his death my grandmother took over from where he left off and continued to encourage my mental development and skill at crafts in every way she possibly could.

When I was learning to read I can remember that on successfully completing your first book you were sent to the head teacher to demonstrate your newly acquired ability. I left the classroom and was immediately called back as I had apparently forgotten my book. To this I replied that I no longer needed the book as I now knew it word for word. Needless to say this did not go down too well with my teacher but at least proved that, whether or not I could read, I did have a good memory!

If there is such a thing as natural talent then mine was the ability to apply myself to a clearly defined logical problem, preferably numerical. I also knew how to use the physical attributes I did have to the full and was dedicated enough when practising any self-chosen physical co-ordination to continue until I got it right. I had a very strong will to succeed and win but was not inventive or an initiator. I followed in the wake of others, content to try and realize my full potential and perhaps beating them at their own game along the way. I was never a child prodigy and had very little time or respect for those individuals who were. I have always been happy when alone and prepared to withdraw from power struggles if I did not like what was going on.

Apart from being bored with music and painting I have few painful memories of my initial learning experiences. In fact when I progressed to the second class I thoroughly enjoyed the lessons and was able to establish a good understanding with the teacher, Miss Donnelly, something which I had not previously been able to do. I believe that the staff in the first class were concerned with both our physical and academic development whereas on moving up they left us much more to our own devices physically – and I have to admit that I was a rather awkward subject in this sensitive area.

Since my earliest recollection I have objected to being told how I should walk and quietly ignored all instructions given. I never made any great fuss about this, I just inwardly believed that they were my legs and the end result that they achieved was my problem and, as I was not an undue burden upon others, this justified my course of action. I could run, skip and jump, even if I did appear rather odd or unstable to the onlooker. The simple fact is that when you can do something more than adequately but are perhaps under some pressure you don't question how you do it, you just absorb yourself in the activity and get on with it – and if you are totally absorbed by and committed to what you are success-fully doing, why on earth should you take any notice of what you are being told?

Around the age of six I was fitted with a pair of metal callipers. I was told that these were for my own good. I suppose that when people were taken to the Tower of London in the Middle Ages and put on the rack – a similar experience, I would imagine – they were told the same thing. I could not see what they were supposed to achieve other than torture me. What I did know was that they were a living hell. The only good thing about them was the fantastic feeling of relief when they were taken off. The experiments had started and I was on the receiving end. Whatever my personal feelings were on this matter they were now of little consequence.

Perhaps I ought to explain that a calliper is a metal splint with leather fittings designed in such a way that it bends at the knee but locks when it is in the straight position. My legs did not and would not quite straighten. In fact, every joint in my body was the same. The tension on muscles and guiders was too great and I was not able to relax this in any way. Apart from this one abnormality which ran throughout the whole of my body I was quite normal. I was physically complete; everything functioned soundly, just not as efficiently and speedily as it might have done. The callipers were put on your legs while in the unlocked position and then forced straight until the lock clicked and the unrelieved agony began.

I wore them each day from the time I got up until the early evening, when I was sometimes allowed a short period of respite before going to bed. One or two other children were also fitted with them, and I suppose it was a healthier position to be in than having surgery, which a couple of the other children had by now been subjected to. I had no fear whatsoever of surgery ever happening to me; I was far too mobile and physically efficient to feel threatened by such drastic action. The ones who had been operated on could not previously walk at all and at least they could now manage a few steps – although with some difficulty – if they tried very hard. A short while later I was fitted with ankle splints which were to be worn throughout the night as I slept. These were more uncomfortable than painful but severely curtailed my already precious few hours of respite. They also made it impossible for me to walk should I ever wish to get out of bed while I was wearing them. I was now no longer allowed to go to bed or sleep in peace and was beginning to feel quite dejected by the situation.

I felt very strongly that there was really little wrong with me and the severity of my disability was only apparent when I viewed myself in a full-length mirror as I walked. I could do most of the things that other children could do, just not on a competitive basis. What did that matter? I tended to have more than my share of tumbles but all children are prone to falling through carelessness and the older they become the less they fall. Life is a marathon, not a short sprint, and other factors begin to play a more important role as the distance increases. I was extremely competitive mentally and this seemed to get me by in the world when I was at home. As far as I was concerned I was purely the human guinea pig in some foolish experiment and sooner or later my beliefs would be confirmed and I would be released from these crazy, hideous shackles.

We crammed all the excitement we could into our spare-time activities. There were several tricycles and I really enjoyed exercising the required skill and the feeling of exhilaration at riding the one which had a fixed-wheel pedal system. Somehow you had much more control over what was happening and could cycle at both your and the bike's limits, experiencing the thrill and elation without getting the same feeling of danger that you got on the freewheel system. Often we raced and, while doing so, sometimes negotiated complicated courses with ramps, tight bends and narrow paths. Accidents and falls from the bikes were not uncommon as we sped around the school grounds. The newly tarmacked drive considerably increased the scope for a safe, smooth and fast ride.

We played football and cricket. I remember well the first time I caught and bowled someone. The ball was of the hard sponge type and the return came so fast I just put my hands in the way and somehow managed to hold on to it. It was in the late afternoon, we were on the terrace and I was wearing my callipers at the time. Prior to taking the catch I can clearly remember thinking that not only was I handicapped by my disability but here I was being forced to play games while painfully burdened with these additional trappings. Perhaps cricketers feel the same way when they are padded up at the crease but at least they do not have to bowl and field with their protective restriction.

Throughout the summer our favourite evening pastime was building dens in a small clearing in the wooded area. I was one of the instigators of this activity and also one of the few who was both fit and strong enough to collect and drag the dead branches and other materials necessary for their construction. The main advantage and thrill of den building was that it got us away from direct supervision and provided a limited amount of freedom. We never actually spent much time in our outdoor hideaways but many extremely pleasurable hours passed as we built them and they were always an interesting talking point on other occasions. To add to the excitement the gardeners, Mr Wilkinson and Mr Bell, who, incidentally, were our heroes, made us a totem pole which was erected in the centre of the small clearing. The den building was a sort of childhood magic, the realization of a very strong inner instinct. Maybe the deep sense of freedom and satisfaction gained from a simple exercise was the meaning of life that awaited everyone in adulthood. It gave me space to dream about what my life in the future might hold, once I had thrown off the constraints of childhood.

We were interested in the wildlife of the gardens and used to look for birds' nests, although I cannot recall ever finding one close enough to the ground to see really properly. Many different species of birds inhabited the grounds and in the spring we would see them collecting nesting materials. We too used to collect nesting materials and build our own birds' nests, usually in a wall by the rose garden which was covered with a very thick growth of ivy.

Throughout the darker months, when we were confined indoors in the evenings, we played with construction toys and other games, and were encouraged to read comics. The only comic which appealed to me was the *Eagle*, in particular the centre page spread which explained how some technical thing or other worked and was illustrated with a large cut-away picture. To me this was the real world. Sometimes the Head would organize special events which she obviously felt would help our development: a trip on foot to the local shops, which were quite a distance away, or involving us in collecting or cooking something. The main thing which came out of her evening involvement was that she was much less formal, although still not to be crossed in any way, and we got to know her as a caring person with a sense of humour. Additionally, the teachers who took lessons throughout the day were never present in the evening and their absence made for a much more relaxed atmosphere.

One year, as part of the school curriculum, we were each allocated a small strip of garden and a weekly period set aside during which we were to tend it. We brought our own seeds, watering cans and other accessories from home. The plot was situated at the foot of a north-east facing wall with several large trees to the south-east, which did not exactly make it an ideal place to bring our crops along quickly. In retrospect I suppose that was why the gardeners so readily surrendered what otherwise looked like a prime piece of garden. The exercise advanced our territory and interests despite its low level of productivity, but I think that we must have broken up for our summer holiday before the fruits of our labour were ready for tasting – if in fact a crop was obtained at all.

The school was designed to cater for children between the ages of four and eleven, but pupils moved on when the authorities felt it was the best time for them to do so. In the early years the age range was fairly limited as I suppose it would have been difficult to take children who had already started attending school on a daily basis and place them residentially. There were a few children slightly older than myself, perhaps even two or three years older, but most were around the same age. As the years passed, however, the majority of replacements were just starting their school days and eventually there were pupils throughout the full age range.

We were a diverse bunch from a wide variety of backgrounds, but we all suffered from cerebral palsy and all came from Leeds. Our sense of comradeship was high. World War II had only been over eight years and the feeling that we were fighting for a common cause was still very strong. We were proud of the parts our parents and other relatives had played in those uncertain times. Many of our fathers had either been on active service or conscripted in the period that ensued. Our community spirit was probably strengthened by the general feeling of the country at large.

A small number of the boys formed a secret society of which I was a member, a sort of self-help group. This was a very secretive affair, although we ultimately became known to the staff as the 'rebels'. We likened the school to a prisoner-of-war camp and planned escapes, resistance plots and cover-ups. I do not know quite what we expected to achieve but it was an outlet for our resentment at being detained against our will. Escapes did actually take place and on a couple of occasions after suffering some distress I remember secretly making my way through the woods and arriving at the entrance to the outside world. This, however, was as far as I ever got, as somehow the prospect of going any further seemed much worse than returning to the devil I knew. I still had the problem of getting back and making my absence, if it had been noticed, fit in with what I should have been doing. Nobody ever did effect a complete escape nor was anyone ever unfortunate enough to get caught in the act. Perhaps the staff really knew what was going on and chose to turn a blind eye and thus encourage enterprise, or maybe it really was all top secret.

Throughout my days at Larchfield I had two close friends, Robert McLellan and Ian Gardiner, and generally cared little for anyone else. The older boys did not impress me even if they did have more physical strength in the early days. Even in those days I lived my life by firm principles and was not prepared to compromise for anyone. Whether or not they were right or wrong is not for me to judge but I would not waver from them and always walked away from a situation I felt unworthy of my attention. I have never been impressed by talk, bravado or bullying; it is action, achievement and sincerity which gains my respect.

We were openly encouraged to fight amongst ourselves so long as a degree of discipline was maintained and the situation did not get too heated. The occasions when it did get out of hand were few and far between and it relieved a lot of tension while sorting out some of the problems of childhood. Many of the hard lessons of life were learned while entangled on the lawn or floor with a fellow pupil. I never relished the prospect of fighting but was never prepared to let any bully or upstart have the better of me, and I rarely came off worst from such encounters. Such aggressive activity, it was no doubt hoped, would aid our overall development and teach us to stand up for ourselves.

There were several highlights in the annual calendar and one of the most enjoyable was Bonfire Night (a moveable feast – if 5 November fell on a weekend, we would celebrate it on the nearest Thursday). The gardeners always built a large fire and a Guy Fawkes was placed on the top. We would be seated at a safe distance and the two men would systematically set off the fireworks, though towards the end those of a nervous disposition were removed before any fireworks likely to go off with a loud report were ignited. It was an occasion where everyone thoroughly enjoyed themselves.

The most feared event was the annual visit of the dentist when few children escaped a much dreaded extraction under the gas anaesthetic. The bathroom was converted into a temporary surgery where the plier-happy dentist could do his worst. It was not uncommon to have anything up to four teeth removed even when you thought that there was nothing wrong; in fact there *was* nothing wrong, but teeth were being taken out to allow second ones an easy passage. In my five years at the school I avoided treatment on only one of his visits and I was terrified by the very thought of his arrival. It was the administration of the gas which I could not come to terms with rather than the actual extractions or any pain.

The annual day trip to the coast in my later years was also an event which brought great excitement and anticipation. At Christmas we always performed a play and parents were invited to attend. In the summer an open day when parents were once again invited was also looked forward to with great eagerness. Having lived away from home for so much of the time you felt that it gave you a chance to show your parents where and how you suffered when you were not with them. They probably did not believe us when they immersed themselves in such pleasant surroundings but it relieved us to think that they understood and, besides, they were allowed to take us home as they left. There would have been a lot of broken hearts on their departure otherwise.

Periodically the specialist and doctors visited the school to check on our progress. On one occasion the furniture was removed from the dining room and floodlighting installed as selected individuals were filmed for posterity. I remember being filmed either naked or almost naked, walking barefoot and then running. I could not understand why all examinations had to be done barefoot as this greatly exaggerated any problems. Normally I wore boots; I could wear shoes but I tended to walk out of them as my heels did not touch the ground. I understand that the film was made for training purposes as the professor also lectured on his work in the field of cerebral palsy.

I still felt that I had more than my share of ironware and, given the option, I believe I would have gone the whole way and swapped the callipers for a wheelchair, but the choice was not mine and the specialist persisted in his belief that they were doing me some good. Or perhaps he thought that they were doing me no harm physically and was not prepared to consider the pain and emotional distress they were causing. I never wore them at home and it was a relief if they ever went for repair or to be modified.

As often as possible I used to arrange for something to go wrong with them deliberately. I would sever one of the leather straps, lose a screw or break one of the weaker pieces of metal. I clearly remember one Friday afternoon when, in severe pain and somewhat distressed, I decided that I had suffered for long enough. I went up to the bedroom and, making sure that no one was about, I took them off. I hated these mobile iron torture chambers and in disgust, anger and frustration put one of them over my knee and deliberately broke it. As I applied all the pressure I could muster the metal slowly began to bend and then suddenly it cracked. The damage was done and there was nothing I could do to reverse it even if I had wanted to. In the lonely silence a cold shiver ran through my body. What had I just done? I felt no remorse, just fear that I might be severely reprimanded if found out. For the moment though I was free. Free to walk and run without pain or restraint and in whatever manner I wanted. I remember stealing out into the grounds and going for a long run. I was so glad to be released and nothing was going to stop me from enjoying my liberty to the full. I ran, skipped, jumped, and leapt. I did everything I wanted to do. They would repair the damage but at least for the time being I was free.

I nervously explained away the break by saying that I had fallen and that the calliper must have accidentally broken as I had crashed to the ground, a very plausible and commonplace event. Luckily I had remained unscathed, I cautiously added. I suspect that they knew otherwise, for steel does not break quite so easily and the break showed the stress marks of first being bent. My explanation, however, was accepted without concern. The freedom I enjoyed that afternoon as I ran through the school grounds is one of the most physically exhilarating and memorable experiences of my whole life.

Physiotherapy, which was always known simply as exercises, was never any great ordeal although I could not understand what exactly it was meant to achieve. In the early days I remember being put through exercises to music, such as 'The Teddy Bears' Picnic', played on a wind-up HMV gramophone which regularly required the needle changing. My first physiotherapist was Mrs Hill and I got along famously with her. Mr Smart, a Scotsman, later took over and this was my first dealings with a man. On special occasions such as St Andrew's Day he wore his kilt and full regalia. We were especially fascinated by his sporran and *sgian dubh*, the small ornamental dagger he carried tucked down the top of one of his stockings. We were convinced that were we not to do as we were told he would use it.

My house mother was Miss Parkinson, a very pleasant young lady. It was her job to make sure that her charges were clean, presentably dressed and looked after. She was also my last line of defence in case of an emotional emergency. All the house mothers were reasonable but each was drawn towards their own allocated group of children. There was also Miss Thackwray, who was greatly admired for her good looks, Miss Airton and Mrs Nettleton, who was a prolific finder of four-leaf clovers and accomplished maker of daisy chains.

On arrival each Monday morning our hair was rigorously inspected with a fine-tooth comb – not a very pleasant welcome back to school. Rarely was anything found but I suppose it was better to be safe than sorry and the pupils did come from diverse backgrounds.

Apart from your clothes, each of which had to have your name sewn in, nothing except a teddy bear or similar toy could be taken for your own personal use. Everything was to be shared. I was not a teddy bear child but in this lonely, restrictive climate began to place a good deal of importance on my handkerchiefs. They were my one personal possession and I treasured them above all else. Usually they were presents from my grandmother Hawkridge and had little pictures of motorcyclists racing or horses showjumping on them. The way other children lost handkerchiefs or other items of clothing as if they had no value secretly grieved me.

At the Easter of 1957, aged just over 8½ years, I left and moved to Potternewton Mansion School, a special school in Leeds where pupils attended on a daily basis. One evening during the week before I left, as a special treat, Miss Parkinson took me into Harrogate. We had tea, went shopping and she bought the book *Robinson Crusoe* and wrote in the front of it to me. I still treasure it to this day. I was pleased to be rejoining my family, but a little sad to be leaving the people around whom my life had revolved for the past four years and extremely apprehensive about how I was going to cope at a much larger school where the ages of pupils ranged from four to sixteen years and the disabilities were just as diverse. At least it was a step in the right direction, I thought, and it could hardly be a harder existence than the one I had so far experienced – and I would have the support of my home and family.

TWO

The Home Front

My earliest recollections of home are of times spent at my grand-parents, both sets, and visits to the clinic for checks on my development and for physiotherapy. My parents lived with my mother's family at the time of my birth, there being a shortage of housing immediately following the war. My father had only recently completed his National Service and resumed his work as an engineer. My mother had three sisters and one, Marjorie (Madge), was currently living at home after the recent loss of her husband to leukaemia. She was like a second mother and looked after me much of the time. I vaguely remember my brother Robert arriving on the scene when I was sixteen months old and I have fleeting memories of some of my first toys and where I sat to play with them.

I was a fairly well-behaved child and quickly learned to feed myself in an orderly manner, so I am told. After my brother was born we went to live with my father's parents for a while before being allocated our own council house in Moortown. The house, which was new and prefabricated, was adjacent to Adel Woods in Leeds and had a medium-sized garden. I remember the weekly pram and then later pushchair trip to the local post office from where my mother obtained her Family Allowance. It was some distance away and en route we passed a site where the new local primary school was being built. My grandfather, Sam Hawkridge, was a foreman labourer on the site and he would come over and talk to us if we could attract his attention as we went by. Shortly afterwards, in March 1953, he died and this is my clearest memory of him.

Visits to the clinic involved journeying into the city centre and I remember on one occasion when I was with my mother and Aunt Madge we lost a wheel off my pushchair. Fortunately we were passing the loading bay at the rear of Marks & Spencer and a helpful man from within rectified the problem. I remember thinking with some concern that I was going to have to walk if we did not get something done about it. Luckily my mother was not on her own and her sister was much more capable of dealing with such emergencies.

Once in our new home we visited my mother's parents religiously every Saturday. If the weather was wet we caught two buses, if it was fine we walked the distance covered by the first bus, my father carrying me on his shoulders when I got tired. The return journey was by a different route and involved catching a tram into the city centre and a bus the rest of the way home. My father always spent the afternoon following the horse racing at a betting office and in the evening met some of his friends at the local pub. Saturday at my grandparents was a meeting point for the family, a sort of weekly reunion. My mother's sister, Madge, had now remarried but another sister, Gwen, had returned home after working away for some time. I always looked forward to seeing my Aunt Madge, or Auntie Margie as I then called her, for she was full of good ideas about things to do, whether trips out, learning or playing games. She had great vigour and radiated enthusiasm, excitement and fun.

The most eagerly awaited annual events were our summer holiday and Christmas, although Easter, the Feast (fairground) on Armley Moor (spring and autumn), Bonfire Night and a visit to Billy Smart's Circus were also excitedly anticipated. At eleven months I spent my first holiday at Sewerby near Bridlington on the east coast of Yorkshire. My parents and grandparents took a caravan for the duration of their one week's annual leave from work. In subsequent years we returned to caravans at Sewerby and Flamborough. Around 1950–53, I believe, annual holidays were increased from one to two weeks.

Memories of holidays are fairly confused. Although I can remember certain events quite clearly I am unable to put them into any sort of sequence. Possibly when I was four and my mother was expecting my sister we did not stay in a caravan but instead had weekly rover tickets for the railway. We went to a different coastal resort each day, and travelling by rail third class was an adventure in itself. It was every child's ambition to be an engine driver when he grew up and I was no different. The noise and smell of a real 'live' steam engine was as near as any youngster ever got to real industrial engineering. And what an important job the wheel-tapper had; the train could never depart until his work was complete. He often flitted from platform to line and back with his long-handled iron hammer, apparently oblivious to the danger.

Then we discovered the delights of Primrose Valley, a large caravan park near Filey, and holidays took on a whole new dimension. Or more likely it was that my brother and I were now old enough properly to understand and appreciate the implications of having a holiday by the sea. Our grandparents continued to accompany us on our annual sojourns and one day I opted to sit on the cliff top with my grandfather, who as I have said was severely disabled with rheumatism, while the rest of the family went for some sort of walk. He was also partially deaf and you had to shout at him to have a conversation but, as children will, we talked. He had suffered since his mid-twenties and he explained to me how to enjoy the peace and tranquillity of just sitting in pleasant surroundings. Time was so unimportant in such a situation. He talked about how to fix your expectations from life on the attainable and not on what you supposed other people were getting. His words have remained with me ever since and as I grew older they began to have a much greater significance.

As soon as we were old enough my father had us playing games on the beach nearly every afternoon: cricket (where I think he tried to emulate Donald Bradman with the sixes he hit), tennis and football. The cricket often evolved into a full scale affair as visiting relatives or other folk who we knew (or sometimes did not know) joined in. This worked both ways as sometimes we joined in other people's games. There were miles of golden sands and we and everyone else made the best of them. Building massive sandcastles and trying to defend them against the incoming tide was my favourite pastime, along with trying to dig through to Australia but usually discovering water before the hole got really deep. Finding water was rewarding enough though . . .

Holidays brought us close together as a family and they were a time when we could enjoy ourselves in an idyllic environment. My brother and I nurtured plans from the end of each holiday throughout the forthcoming year until we could attempt to bring them to fruition the following summer. We dreamt up schemes which we thought would enrich our quest for excitement, knowledge and fulfilment – most of which, I might add, did not meet with our parents' approval. Beach games were great, but only for so long; the spirit of adventure had to surface sooner or later. The pastime we found most satisfying, that we pursued most often, was looking for marine life in rockpools, but you had to venture slightly off the beaten track to do this in popular resorts and that was definitely not my mother's style. My father's interest in this direction was also very limited. Occasionally we scrambled up the cliffs which, if caught, earned us a severe reprimand from our parents.

For lunch we often packed sandwiches, which never failed to have acquired traces of sand by the time we crunchily ate them, and sometimes we ate in cafés, which was a real treat. Holidays were times of feast and plenty, ice creams, sundaes, rock and later shellfish. We would have been saving our pocket money for several months and could now decide exactly how we wished to spend it, decisions which, again, did not always have our parents' blessing.

I had few natural inclinations towards sporting activities and was not very successful when I played, but I was definitely not going to sit around watching others enjoy themselves and I did my best to be as effective as I possibly could. My best was sufficient to get me by although I tired very quickly. Whatever the score was during the day I usually managed to make amends of an evening when we played cards and dominoes. Many happy hours were spent playing cards before the advent of popular television. It was the first thing a child learnt to avert boredom.

Wherever we went or whatever we did, holidays were always the high point of the year. Caravaning was exciting and different and come rain or shine they were on the whole very happy and memorable times.

At bank holidays and occasionally at other times throughout the summer months we went on day trips. Ilkley was the most popular venue. We went either by rail or Sammy Ledgard bus. Once there our routine was a leisurely walk up to White Wells on the moors, a short distance from which stood a hut where pots of tea and other refreshments were served; an excellent point at which to picnic. Sometimes my brother was walked along Rocky Valley to watch the climbers on the Cow and Calf Rocks. It was too long and hazardous a walk for me and I remained at White Wells with my mother. Besides, I was not supposed to be interested in climbing, it was not something I should ever be able to do. In truth, I had great difficulty in walking any distance or crossing stony ground and on these family jaunts I more often than not ended up being carried by my father. In these circumstances it made sense for me to take advantage of the lengthy imposed rest, although in reality I actually resented the fact that I was involuntarily missing out on something. It was all very well others saying that it was not for me when it was obviously all right for everyone else – and to make matters worse my brother usually came back with exciting tales of how far he had managed to climb up the Calf Rock. After leaving the moors we usually went for our tea and then spent some time by the river, perhaps even hiring a rowing boat, before making the return journey home.

Another popular family venue was Knaresborough where we would walk around the old town and market square, visit the castle and then walk alongside the river. I also remember a mystery tour which went to Ripon, and housing estate association trips to Cleethorpes and Blackpool to see the illuminations. On arriving at Blackpool a pushchair was hired as it was anticipated that the walking would be too demanding for me. It squeaked so badly I remember Uncle Cyril having the inspired idea of taking it to a garage to get it oiled. In the afternoon the rain came down in a deluge and we visited the Tower to avoid getting drenched. The big cats in the zoo made Stanley Holloway's then popular monologue of 'Albert and the Lion' seem quite real, the marine aquarium with the cod and large rays was also very exciting. By the evening my brother and I were so tired we struggled to stay awake to see the illuminations as best we could through the badly steamed up windows of the coach. These estate trips also evoke vivid memories of the communal singing of 'Ten green bottles' and 'One man and his dog' during the coach journey.

Adjacent to our house stood Adel Woods and a popular Sunday jaunt was the walk through the woods to Adel itself. This was a spot where people congregated and refreshments were available in a field by a stream. I remember excitedly watching other youngsters catch 'tiddlers' and crayfish from the clear running water. Probably the most thrilling event of all, though, was when we made a small deviation and my father took us across a narrow open-topped aqueduct called the Seven Arches. This was an airy experience and required calm nerves and a head for heights – or so it seemed to children of our age. Such a place is most likely out of bounds to the public these days.

Living next to the woods was very convenient when Bonfire Night came around. Towards the end of the summer holidays some of the older local youths would be allocated two or three trees that had been condemned and felling would begin. As I remember the trees had definitely been singled out for removal because usually a woodman was present as the trees were brought down. Perhaps he should have been doing the work himself but was allowing the boys to do it under his supervision. The communal celebration on 5 November was much bigger than Bonfire Night at Larchfield and equally eagerly anticipated.

Children's Day was held annually on the first Saturday in July at Roundhay Park in Leeds and we always attended. As soon as my brother started school he usually participated in one or other of the sports events and I was keen to follow his progress. Despite the annual downpour, which usually occurred in the late afternoon after the sports had finished, it was a very popular event. It was my introduction to the delights of municipal parks, and in later years a chance to see the anglers fishing on Waterloo Lake.

Playing at home I remember that at a very early age I had a Meccano set which I loved so much I eventually wore it out! Working models of cranes were the things to build. I had a red pedal car as soon as I was old enough to ride one. When I was five my brother and I each received a tricycle for Christmas; a de luxe model with pneumatic tyres, rear boot and a fold-out handle with which one could have assistance on gradients. I assume this latter feature was chosen mainly for my benefit although on occasions my brother's was used to hold him back. He cycled up and down the pavement like the clappers and I did my best to keep up with him. My bike was passed on to my sister years after he had wrecked his.

On starting school my friend Robert McLellan, who was a railway enthusiast, got me interested in electric trains. This was the first toy I ever craved for and Santa Claus duly obliged with a Tri-ang electric train set. My father was not a great believer in lavishing toys on us, but once a year at Christmas he made our dreams come true – and perhaps his own. Not that we had any shortage of toys and games, and he did spend hours playing with us with the ones we did have. I loved to play my father at draughts although it was many years before I actually managed to beat him. While, however, I was receiving train sets, rubber building bricks and the like my brother was equipped with boxing gloves and a punch ball, a football and playing kit and a sledge.

Under the scrupulous guidance of my Aunt Gwen I made my first tapestry while still quite young. I had watched her make one to cover a stool top and decided that I should like to emulate her. She bought me a small canvas depicting a child's castle scene the following Christmas and I began work with my needle and wool. I must have made a mistake because when she saw it she was not happy and unpicked most of what I had done and made me start again. Her remorseless action seemed a little harsh to me at the time but it went some considerable way towards teaching me that if a job was worth doing it was worth doing right. Mistakes never occurred again in any of the tapestries I did, or in fact still do.

Madge and Cyril were the first members of the family to get a television and we had a family get-together at their house on 2 June 1953 to watch the Coronation, soon after I started at Larchfield. Television was the modern miracle and shortly afterwards we got our first black and white set. It made a change from listening to the forever whistling wireless. I saw very little television as I was away at school most of the time but my brother raved about Roy Rogers, the Cisco Kid and similar heroes. Up to this time our source of visual entertainment had been the cinema – the pictures. Going to the picture house was always exciting, especially if it was a children's film like *Snow White and the Seven Dwarfs* or *Tom Thumb*. We always went to the pantomimes at either the Empire or Grand Theatres. My favourite star was Jimmy Clitheroe and I followed his adventures throughout the year on the radio as the Clitheroe Kid. This was second only to *Meet the Huggetts*, the everyday story of a family featuring Jack Warner and Kathleen Harrison.

During school holidays I frequently stayed with my grandparents. My mother's sister, Doris, who had moved to Clitheroe on marrying, now had several children and the eldest, Sandra, who was about nine months my senior, sometimes joined me. On other occasions the second eldest, Linda, would accompany me. I enjoyed staying with my grandmother because she was very patient and tolerant and allowed me to do many things which I would not have been able to at home. I was an enthusiastic assembler of jigsaws and she let me keep these in situ until they were completed, even if this took several weeks. I could also build in peace with my wooden bricks without fear of my brother destroying the structures I created.

In the December of 1956, after the arrival of my sister, we had moved to a new three-bedroomed house on the Cow Close estate on the other side of Leeds. I was eight years old and becoming ever more independent. While living at Moortown our playground had extended no further than the garden and the very edge of the adjacent Adel Woods, and within the confines of the estate one spot had been much the same as another. One had no need to wander in search of different surroundings – there were none. The most exciting adventures had been when we went to meet my father coming home from work and he had given us a ride on the cross bar of his bicycle or when his brother, our Uncle Gordon, had visited us on his motorcycle and given us a pillion ride around the block.

At Moortown I had had no real friends. I spent very little time at home, as I was away at school and part of the holidays were spent away at the coast and with my grandparents, as I have described. Cow Close was a new estate but it was built between the old villages of Lower Wortley, Old Farnley and Stonebridge, each of which was rich with history and tradition. Within the immediate vicinity of our street were several other youngsters around the same age as my brother and I and friendships were soon struck up – as were, I might add, some rivalries.

Our new house was directly opposite a cricket field, an added bonus that provided us with a large flat play area, ideal for any type of game requiring a grass-covered open space. At the far side of the cricket field ran a large fast-flowing beck over which we swung on knotted rope suspended from conveniently overhanging trees and on which we paddled in old metal bathtub-boats. Periodically the beck burst its banks and flooded the cricket field, whereupon we would construct rafts from any available wood or an old oil drum or two and punt around the field using poles. I was greatly into rope swings but had rather too much respect for the water to attempt boating in old receptacles! I occasionally rafted on the flood-water provided proceedings were conducted in what I considered was a safe and sensible manner. I was definitely no daredevil, but provided a situation was treated with respect neither was I just an onlooker.

My first real friend was Stephen Clark, the neighbourhood tough guy. He was not the intimidating type but he knew how to stand his ground and was not afraid of dealing with would-be bullies. We were of a similar intelligence and temperament and had many of the same interests. Being an only child, however, he was indulged a little more than most of us by his parents who, if I remember rightly, both worked. Together we designed and made various weapons such as swords, lances, longbows, crossbows and the like and practised using them whenever possible. We both dreamed of going fishing and during one holiday his father took him. I do not think they actually caught any fish but the stories he told me fuelled my already deep-rooted desire one day to take up angling. Later his father bought him an air rifle and we often went shooting by the beck or fired darts at proper circular targets. He also owned a dart board on which we honed our skills.

In the late summer one of the local pastimes was raiding the apple and pear orchards of Old Farnley. These were far enough away for the owners not to know our identity but not too far for us to walk. The fruit trees grew in an overgrown allotment area, and it was debatable whether the crop being picked was under cultivation or just growing in disused plots, but if caught by anyone in the vicinity then a serious chase was sure to ensue. I assume that some of the allotments were still occupied and the users did not want would-be raiders anywhere near. Because of the risk involved I never went into the danger zone but waited some distance away. If I heard a skirmish or sudden shouts it was time to flee.

Another of our favourite pastimes was building bogies and then riding them down hills. Old pram or pushchair wheels and axles were at a premium, acquiring them like obtaining gold. I cannot remember where they came from but throughout my childhood I owned one complete set, a medium-sized pair for the rear and a small pair for the front, and at different times these were incorporated into various body designs. The most notable was a superlength three-seater which was intended to take my brother, sister and myself. The first time we all used it my sister did not realize that you had to lean as you took bends at speed and she parted company from the contraption at the first fast curve which subsequently caused us to go into a skid before turning over as we endeavoured to save her. I think this minor mishap put her off riding bogies for life as she never joined us again. The ultimate course was a well-worn path crossing rough grassy ground with a bend cambered correctly for speed. It was essential to get the line right for a fast, smooth and safe run. If a wheel got in a rut you were in real trouble.

Bonfire Night became an even bigger event than it had been in Moortown (or Larchfield) and we had our own fire within the confines of the garden until we were too old to bother any more. From the end of the summer holiday until November chumping was a very serious business and we would go anywhere where there was the chance of old timber. The origin of most of the wood we obtained was quite dubious as the pressure from rival local hunters was intense. Old houses being demolished were the biggest single source of fuel since we no longer lived near any woodland where a tree would not be missed. Once procured the wood from a demolition site was not considered stolen property but the actual act of obtaining it was frowned upon by both the demolition company and the law. Removing timbers from such buildings and piles of rubble was fraught with dangers. Rusty nails were in themselves a real hazard, let alone a major collapse of masonry. We took our chances, applied as much common sense as we had and fortunately survived unscathed.

At Old Farnley there was a fish pond and our next-door neighbour, Bob Gaines, who was still a youngster at heart, took us fishing for the indigenous population of sticklebacks. He was a dab hand at netting fish and we soon had several jars full of them. Farnley Fish Pond must have been private property since we had to climb over a wall to get to it. There were some gates but these were always locked. The wall was easily negotiable on the road side but there was a long drop once over the top and this made leaving the site a rather more tricky business. With some help, however, I could just make it. I found catching these small fish totally absorbing but my father would not take us; as far as he was concerned the area was out of bounds. Despite this we did occasionally visit the pond but bringing fish home inevitably gave our game away. I suppose now I can understand why we were not allowed to go there as it was a very dangerous spot for unsupervised children.

Sometime later we discovered that the Farnley Fireclay Company also had a pond. Getting to this was a much longer walk, in fact we organized a mini expedition for our visit. The expanse of water was much greater than our local pond and completely exposed. The stock of fish was plentiful and they were easily seen in the clear water but unfortunately they were all diseased with growths of white fungus. Our mid-summer afternoon sojourn had been pleasant enough, but we returned without spoils since we reckoned it would be unwise to tamper with the diseased fish. I remember feeling very sad and shocked that such a situation could exist in the kingdom of nature. I also remember how strongly I was possessed with the desire to fish seriously.

Although I was keen to learn, I always dreaded the school holidays ending and having to return to school and being under scrutiny again after weeks of freedom from authority.

THREE

Back to School

When the Easter holidays of 1957 were over I moved from Larchfield at Harrogate to Potternewton Mansion School in Leeds. As I have said, I was looking forward to attending school on a daily basis but apprehensive about life at this much larger establishment. By now I was 8½ years old and fully understood that I had been attending Larchfield for the previous four years because it was supposedly to my physical advantage, long-term educational benefit and preferable to being sent directly to a general school for physically handicapped children of all ages. Whatever it was that I was being shielded from, the barrier, for better or worse, was finally about to be removed. In moments of deepest despair and hatred, combined with the utmost resentment at having to reside at Larchfield, I had pleaded with my parents to be sent to a day school, but now the time had come I was filled with trepidation and loneliness at the very thought of it.

Theoretically I could have stayed at Larchfield until I was eleven but the purpose of the early move was to give me the chance of sitting the eleven-plus examination at the appropriate time, the curriculum and education supposedly being much more intense at Potternewton. Two years must have been considered the optimum time for broadening one's knowledge and realizing potential intellect. Even at this early stage it baffled me what was going to happen in the event of my being successful, a question no authority was giving a satisfactory answer to. There were no special High Schools for the handicapped as far as I was aware, and definitely none within daily travelling distance of Leeds. Perhaps the whole exercise was for cosmetic purposes only. The prospect of integration into mainstream education seemed highly unlikely considering the investment the system had already made in me.

The daily journey to school was made by Samuel Ledgard coach. Mr Ledgard, who was a local private bus company proprietor, had left the service as some sort of legacy after his death; I believe that it was inspired by the fact that he was the father of a

28

handicapped daughter. About five coaches were used in all, each collecting from a different area of Leeds. Taxi services were operated for the more severely disabled and those considered too delicate to travel by bus.

The first morning I vaguely remember that it was normal to be accompanied to school by one's mother and this at least went some way towards allaying any unfounded fears and lessening the cultural shock which was in store. Larchfield had always maintained very high social standards and any form of slovenliness or improper behaviour was eradicated immediately. With only twenty specially selected pupils, and the very high staff-to-child ratio, constant monitoring had been practical. There was never any excuse for exercising tolerance. But at Potternewton it was apparent that children of all kinds were often left to their own devices for predetermined periods and, as will happen in such instances, the law of the jungle unfortunately takes over. I say unfortunate because wilfully bad behaviour was something which I did not understand and had no aspirations to be a part of. Yes, I was prepared to be wilful when I thought that I was being hard done by but never just for the sake of it. My father stood no nonsense; either one behaved and followed his orders or suffered the physical consequences, punishment being administered on the spot.

On arriving at school the number of pupils on each coach was carefully counted and a record kept in order that, after taking into account any known discrepancies, the same number could be despatched home in the afternoon. There were often considerable delays as the reconciliation of these figures did not readily occur!

The school was at the opposite side of Leeds to where I lived and my journey therefore was quite lengthy as we circuited the city suburbs. The coach also collected educationally sub-normal children who were set down at another special school along our route. As an alert but physically handicapped child I cannot say that I took too kindly to being lumped together with retarded schoolgoers, some of whom were quite boisterous. The possibility of scuffles breaking out could not be discounted and if reported these were considered a serious offence (as indeed were the all-too-frequent exchanges of insults). The fact that you may be handicapped makes very little difference if you have been wantonly provoked. Children are children whether they be physically sub-normal or slow at learning, and will behave accordingly.

At first sight of the school I cannot say that I was thrilled by what I saw. To start with I had never before seen so many handicapped children in one place and many of them had complaints that I was unable to relate to. Some looked as if there was nothing wrong with them while others were so badly deformed that learning such abnormalities existed gave me, a mere eight-year-old who had led a sheltered life, a considerable shock. However, while all the children I had ever previously seen in wheelchairs were helpless, here a few were propelling themselves around the premises and grounds with a high degree of efficiency. The school was a converted mansion house and equipped as most schools were at that time with furniture and fittings dating back to a much earlier period, perhaps before the war. Whereas Larchfield had been a grand residence equipped with what was then modern furniture, Potternewton seemed well worn and rather antiquated, although in all honesty quite adequate.

Mr Pagdin, the new headmaster, started at the school the same day as I. Other pupils considered me extremely fortunate to avoid the dubious pleasure of the retiring incumbent, the notorious Miss Hayfield, and the change in head of the school proved to be the topic of conversation for some time to come. Perhaps I had timed my move well after all. Although strict I could never fault Mr Pagdin in his attitude and approach, though, as an ex-choirmaster of Leeds Parish Church, he dwelled a bit too much on music and hymn-singing for my tastes. Still, there were many far worse leanings he could have had!

The official formalities of entry to the school over, it was time for my mother to leave and for me to get down to the business of attending lessons. Each class had perhaps fifteen to twenty pupils and it immediately became apparent to me that the teachers' main concern was maintaining discipline and creating an environment where each child could be involved, but at his or her level of ability. Discipline had been taken for granted at Larchfield, there was no such thing as unruly behaviour, and each child had always been taught individually at their own level of educational attainment. I was distressed at losing the personal relationship with my teachers, never having felt remote from them before. Now there was a harshness in the regime that I found hard to take.

A small element of my fellow classmates had delinquent tendencies and a larger proportion were either educationally sub-normal or at least slow when it came to academic subjects. Sometimes these two traits went hand in hand. Initially I found myself struggling educationally, but had no problems with my ability to learn. I did very well at intelligence tests but my education had been restricted by Larchfield's environment, which placed greatest importance on independence as a person. Here the teachers were not really concerned about your physical problems other than how these affected your attendance in class and your ability to carry out the tasks set. I now see that I was taking one step nearer the real world. Larchfield did not exactly shelter you from the harsh realities of life but it did isolate you from the strange ways of the society we live in.

My first teacher was Miss Graham and she was deputy head of the school; a very efficient and solemn, some might say miserable, woman, whose specialist subject was art. Throughout the weekly timetable nearly every teacher in the school took our class for some subject or other, among them Miss Clark for nature study, Mrs Hill for the library, Mr Perry for literature – or perhaps I have illusions of grandeur and it was only a more advanced form of reading. Mr Perry, being an extremely accomplished magician and the popular leader of the school scout troop, was every boy's hero. Much to our dismay he had left the school before I had worked my way up to his class or the boy scouts.

Miss Clark took the class below mine and on the whole her pupils seemed to have such a good time that I always regretted not being assigned to her charge. She was a very firm teacher who stood no nonsense. She knew what she wanted from each child and usually got it. Provided you had done your best you had nothing to fear for she really cared very deeply for the children she worked with. For boys their first encounter with her was usually an invitation to join the school cub pack which she ran. Meetings took place on a Friday lunchtime and continued into the first lesson of the afternoon. A refusal to give it a try was not readily acceptable as an answer, although participating was a very serious decision as this did not exactly endear you to Miss Graham . . . It was a case of either weathering some disharmony in the class or being constantly reminded of what you were missing on the frontiers of life. There really was no choice, any self-respecting lad joined the brotherhood and on 20 June 1957, after completing all the preliminaries, I was officially enrolled as a fully fledged member of the 19th North Leeds Wolf Cub Pack.

The school cub pack played a large part in its members' development. The meetings were lively occasions with the time divided between rituals, games and learning. Miss Clark was ably assisted by her friend Mrs Parker, the two being known respectively as Akela and Racksha. Akela must have been a model of efficiency because each individual was good-humouredly hounded until – as she hoped – he obtained his Leaping Wolf badge before progressing up to the scout troop. Taking proficiency badges was a very serious business and one which I enjoyed very much. As a concession the physical accomplishments of the first and second stars were replaced by subjects within our capabilities. From 11–13 July 1958 the pack attended a camp at Shadwell near Leeds. We were accommodated in the local scout hut with only the most basic facilities, but the camp fire and general atmosphere was an experience that I will never forget. Suddenly and secretly I had discovered the real meaning of life. The leadership was excellent in every respect and the weekend was one of total enjoyment. If I had any choice in the matter this was the direction my life was going. Outdoors. Self-reliant and unfettered.

How on earth the two, even with help from some other friends, dared to take away for the weekend approximately eighteen handicapped children, some quite severely, I will never know. To their credit they did and it probably created more happy memories than they could ever have hoped for. This is what scouting is truly about – service to others and the overcoming of adversity. Miss Clark is the finest example in the scouting world that I have ever had the good fortune to meet. Luckily for me, I knew that at the time.

Further interruptions to the curriculum, where appropriate, were physiotherapy sessions, which I attended at appointed times on two or three occasions a week. Exercises were basically routine although perhaps more demanding than previously. Co-ordination skills were developed through organized ball games and I sensed that a continuous assessment of our physical progress was being made. Exercises were supplemented by a weekly visit to the swimming baths for those wishing to attend. I could not swim but was enthusiastic about learning. I had previously been to the baths with my father and brother and my confidence was slowly building up. I had great hopes that some day swimming would be one physical outlet that I would be really able to enjoy. Robert McLellan, my best friend, was an excellent swimmer and I saw no reason why I could not be also.

I still supposedly wore my callipers but the school had an easy-going attitude towards this. The premises covered quite a large area, had some fairly long corridors and as I got nowhere fast incarcerated in those unnecessary contraptions it suited everyone concerned for me to discard them if agility or haste was required. At first I was merely placed in a wheelchair whenever time was of the essence, but as it became apparent that I was more than competent without them I was encouraged to unshackle myself and get a move on. As far as I was concerned, any command to discard them was music to my ears. Nothing could have delighted me more. However, whilst at home I continued to wear my ankle splints through the night for most of the time. With some help and encouragement my callipers soon fell into a state of disrepair, and I was also outgrowing them. The authorities seemed in no hurry to equip me with a new pair and I was maintaining a deadly silence on the subject. One aspect of my move at least was going well.

Another aspect which, however, was not, was the fact that certain of my fellow pupils were dying. This came as a drastic shock to me. During my period at Larchfield I had seen some very badly disabled children but thankfully I had never seen or known of any who actually succumbed. Potternewton accepted children with all types of ailment and disability and, naturally, a proportion of these had terminal disorders. Returning from school holidays to be informed that a classmate was no longer with us or arriving at the morning assembly to find that it was a memorial service was a depressing state of affairs. Flying the flag at half-mast at the loss of a fellow cub or scout was an equally sombre experience. No one ever explained the different disorders in any depth, maybe it would have been too demoralizing for those who were likely to die, to elucidate on the problems of some of the school population, but to others, those who weren't in such danger, this created hours of unnecessary worry through ignorance. I spent many sleepless nights after the loss of classmates wondering if I or one of my best friends would be the next.

It was not necessarily the actual dying which caused the concern but the fact that it made your own short life seem so miserable and futile. Whatever, it was not a good subject to become obsessed with and it often left me feeling rather morose. Sometimes those whose existence hung precariously lived pretty intense and what seemed like rewarding lives as parents tried to cram as much into the youngsters' days as possible. This created a two-tier system of values within the school: those who were being disciplined for adulthood and those who were spoilt and pampered, having no foreseeable future. The division was not so clearly definable where parents were concerned, as there are always some who will indulge their offspring and a handicapped child is a sitting target for this, especially if he or she is the youngest member of the family, or an only child. Unfortunately I fell under none of these categories and although in no way deprived I was not over-indulged either.

About twelve months after my arrival I had been with Miss

Graham sufficient time for her to be able to assess my educational needs and chances of success in the eleven-plus examination. Personally I was very enthusiastic and totally geared to learning. I was quietly competitive and I knew exactly how I would cope in any given situation. You could say that I knew my limitations and those of others. I could be put down by individual personalities passing verbal judgment but never when tested on paper and judged neutrally. Mostly I was content to keep a low profile and appear to be doing just enough to avoid trouble. Quite honestly, from an early age I had watched those who made much show and noise of everything they did, of what they thought they knew and, worse, what they thought they could do and found that it was not a form of behaviour that pleased me; empty bottles made the most noise. Being out in front or thereabouts at the moment when it mattered most was always my aim and I was usually prepared to work long and hard to achieve this when I thought the objective worthwhile and ultimately attainable.

Passing the eleven-plus examination was now my great goal in life. I was considered to have some chance and began a course of study which involved doing homework and tests during my own time. My mother purchased the prescribed books, Attainment Tests, Intelligence Tests, Arithmetic Tests and some kind of book involving English Language Tests. From the class only a selected few undertook this extra work. Learning became more intense than it had ever previously been in my life but I thoroughly enjoyed the challenge and gave it my total application. Our family did not have a strong history of educational success, though my grandfather had been a noted scholar and his daughter, my aunt Marjorie, had passed the eleven-plus. Her encouragement at this time was extremely helpful, there being no one else I could turn to, with the exception of arithmetic in which my father was competent. In fact it was the only scholastic subject at which he could offer any degree of serious help to the would-be student.

I took the examination and did my best but as it transpired the outcome was of little importance. By the time the results were issued I was in hospital.

FOUR

A Date with Destiny

I had sat the eleven-plus examination, completed my first length at the swimming baths, my callipers had been dispensed with and I was revelling in the freedom this afforded, and I had been awarded the Leaping Wolf badge in the cubs. But now, for better or worse, my life was about to change drastically.

Periodically the doctor and specialist visited the school to check on their charges. Our parents were invited to attend these thorough medical examinations and my mother always accompanied me. Late in 1958 the specialist had decided that the moment for me to meet the knife had arrived, although at this time I was neither informed of his decision nor in any way involved with it. My parents were invited to the education authority's offices for a private meeting with the surgeon, he declared his intentions, displaying in person an example of someone on whom he had already performed the intended operations. In fact she was also a former pupil of Larchfield, and using her as his model he told them what he thought he could achieve with me, and asked my parents to give their consent to the proposed surgery. It was then left up to them to inform me of the impending action.

I did not exactly agree with their decision but the professor's powers of persuasion must have been extremely convincing. A letter arrived through the post; I was scheduled to go into hospital on 1 April 1959. I cannot say that I was thrilled by the prospect; in fact, I was totally shattered and disgusted by the whole affair. Why did they need to change things when I was just beginning to enjoy life? Why did they need to put me through more anguish? My disability was really in the eye of the beholder – it was definitely not in mine. I was no fool, I knew that undergoing surgery involved some degree of suffering. Only an idiot or an extremely vain person would want to bring this kind of thing upon themselves. What if something went wrong? What if something went drastically wrong and I died? I was terrified and traumatized. Did I really have no say whatsoever in my future? My best friend Robert

McLellan had undergone surgery and he was none too impressed by the experience. Other friends had also suffered at the hands of this specialist and they too could not recommend it. This was the news I had most feared since I was about four, when Ronnie Smith had returned to school after a spell in hospital. Some six years had since elapsed and he was still confined to a wheelchair.

My parents believed that if I was to be treated in the most effective way then their only hope was to trust in the knowledge and expertise of those in whose charge I had been placed. It did not please them to see me go for surgery but they felt that to deny the specialist the opportunity to carry out his wishes was to deprive me of modern medicine and the latest in available surgical techniques. My father was a gambling man and from the example he had been shown he reckoned that I had little to lose. I had been acutely aware from an early age of his concern about my long-term future. He feared that I would never become independent or have a normal job of work, and he worried about the day when he would no longer be around or able to take care of me. Although I often felt that his fears were unfounded and grossly exaggerated I do not know how a ten-year-old child even starts to explain this to his father. He was a strong, fit man who came from a family of strong, fit men who had worked hard manually for their living, and because of my physical shortcomings he underestimated my ability to succeed in life. Historically I suppose he had no grounds to do otherwise. My mother did not exactly wish to see me go into hospital but the decision had been made and like it or not the situation had to be faced.

As 1 April drew near I became ever more filled with trepidation at the thought of being carved up, of being encased in plaster for at least six weeks, and of having the plaster and stitches removed, not to mention the inevitable consequences. The hospital was situated at Thorp Arch near Wetherby and I would be away for at least three months, another unenticing prospect. This was what the constant surveillance since infancy had been in aid of. I, a lamb to the slaughter, had my date with destiny. In the past the mere prospect of having dental treatment had been awesome enough, here was a real appointment with fear. I realized that there was no way out. I was finally cornered; this time there was no possibility of rebellion or escape.

A thousand times I searched my soul looking for the logic behind what was about to happen to me, but there were no answers. I was not at all unhappy with the present state of affairs, in fact quite the reverse, I was increasingly becoming satisfied and fully able to cope. None of the children I knew who had already had surgery could boast any real benefit. More often than not, after the side effects had been taken into consideration, the result was the opposite. The therapies and contraptions already administered to me did not exactly instil me with any degree of confidence in those who had charge of me. The truth of the matter was that for the last seven or eight years or so I had been carefully groomed for this event and along the way my parents carefully misled into believing that there was really little alternative if I was to have any chance of living a reasonable life. Professor J. M. P. Clark, M.B.E., F.R.C.S., was about to have his pound of flesh and the final say in all matters connected with my physical future.

The day, 1 April, arrived and my belongings were once again packed for an extended period away from home. Spring was now well upon us and there was a fresh and pleasant feel to the air. Going into hospital required an early start and, accompanied by my mother, I left home around 8.00 a.m. By 8.30 we were in Woolworths shopping for some last-minute items that she thought I may need for the stay (a writing pad, envelopes and a pen, as far as I remember). There may also have been some small treat to take my mind off the forthcoming event.

The journey by West Yorkshire bus with a change en route was quite a lengthy affair for a trip to your 'local hospital'. As each mile passed, I was becoming more and more doom-laden. Earlier I had been enjoying a few last runs in case the worst should happen, but now I was so stiff with fear I could hardly stand up, let alone walk. We arrived at the Marguerite Hepton Orthopaedic Hospital at Thorp Arch, Boston Spa, sometime in the late morning; I was due to have my operation the following morning. My mother left, saying that all being well both she and my father would be there to see me at visiting time on Saturday afternoon.

My first job was to be prepared for surgery and while I was getting ready the sister in charge decided that I was suffering from a chest infection and called a doctor to confirm whether or not it was wise for me to be anaesthetized the next day. He ordered a stay of execution while I fully recovered from the effects of what had been a slight cold. The next available date on which the surgeon could accommodate me was in two weeks' time and I was temporarily reprieved.

The reprieve was more temporary than I anticipated because this was a hospital with a school system and the dreaded Miss Butler was the teacher in charge of the boys' ward. (There were only three wards, a boys', a girls' and a young children's.) For patients encased in plaster, some almost from head to toe, or fastened full length horizontally to metal frames, the majority of whom were suffering some considerable degree of pain, the level of education was pretty intense and uncompromising. As the ages ranged from about eight to fourteen and the class was dispersed over the full length of the ward the teacher was unable to attend to each pupil full time, and thus she constantly demanded initiative. It was not good enough to say (truthfully) that you had dropped your pencil on the floor and were waiting for her to retrieve it for you. In such an event she would rather forcefully demand to know what you had done whilst awaiting the said recovery.

In front of each ward was a veranda and in fine weather beds were wheeled outside. By day you had no option, it was 'one out all out' – unless otherwise medically specified – for the purpose of school, but only the more hardy souls remained outside twenty-four hours a day. If you slept outside you were issued with an extra light quilted cover come nightfall. I was kept indoors in the evening for the first two weeks while they endeavoured to clear my sniffle before the operation.

The time passed and I was duly declared fully fit and ready for the operating table. I was prepared for surgery. My legs were lathered with soap, shaved with a safety razor and then treated with several solutions before being meticulously wrapped in bandages. I was then starved for approximately twenty hours preceding my entry to the theatre.

At this stage it was usual to learn which nurse would be accompanying you throughout your operation. Apart from the sisters in charge of each ward and any staff nurses, the hospital was staffed almost completely by trainee nurses who had arrived straight from school. More than likely it would be their first experience of such an event, perhaps an ordeal. The surgeon arrived in his car, a gleaming new Jaguar, and you knew that your time had come. A pre-med injection was administered and within a few minutes you could not care less what was about to happen. You were warned by other patients who had undergone a similar experience to hold some saliva in your mouth for as long as possible as this would rapidly dry up. The hospital porter arrived, you were loaded on to a stretcher trolley and away you went out of the ward, across the hospital forecourt and into the main building. In those days televised operations were unheard of and public knowledge on such matters was scant, so you peeked into the theatre if possible to survey the scene and catch a glimpse of any equipment about to be used on you. Resigned to the inevitable, you might as well learn as much as you could from the event.

In the theatre anteroom the anesthetist and the surgeon were waiting. I knew the surgeon very well. Until this unforeseen awayday I would even have thought quite highly of him. I still believed that he must know what he was doing – he would not risk wrecking the life of one of his star performers. I was often exhibited before his classes of students. He was still very friendly about the whole affair and we had a chat about what he was going to do. A wad of cotton wool was placed over my face and as the anaesthetist began to drip the ether, I was no longer afraid. Within seconds my senses shut down. In my remote sub-conscious I felt myself being placed on the operating table and then some cuts being made at the back of my legs.

The next thing I knew I was waking up on the ward. I was next to the medical room and the pain in my legs was excruciating, especially in the left one. I put my hands down under the frame which arched across my bed supporting the clothes and I could feel the cold damp plaster reaching to my groin. I screamed in agony. Nurses rushed to attend to me but they were unable to console me as the pain was overwhelming and very shortly I was given an injection which in effect put me back to sleep. This happened repeatedly and I began to dread the sight of the needles. Each time I came to they tried to talk me out of my desperation but the pain was unbelievably intense. This went on for some time until eventually I found that I feared the needle and another four hours of sleep more than the pain, which by now was becoming more of an acute ache. The staff could not understand what my problem was but as soon as I looked at the plaster coverings I knew immediately. My left leg was set slightly past straight, which worried me considerably, as well as being the point from which most of the pain stemmed. Also there was a great deal of pressure on the back of my knees where I had been cut and blood was seeping through the plaster. If I was going to be improved after this little lot then the surgeon must have carried out more than an operation, he had performed a minor miracle.

Having diagnosed the problem I still had much to come to terms with. Would my legs feel like this for the next six weeks or even longer? As soon as I tried to drink or eat I was violently sick. Here I was, propped up in bed unable to move, in agony and throwing up every time anything passed my lips. How long was this going to continue? I asked myself. I was ten years and eight months old, did they really expect me to emerge from this trauma psychologically unscathed and ready for more? My Aunt Marjorie telephoned the hospital to enquire how I was and I suppose the staff thought it might help me if I were to speak to her myself. Her familiar voice was indeed welcome and reinforced my belief that the whole episode was not just a bad dream. I listened to what she had to say but when I tried to reply I could not co-ordinate my thoughts to make sensible conversation. She asked if I knew what day it was and I replied that it was now the day after yesterday – we were in tomorrow. As hard as I tried I could not put my thoughts into logical speech and our talk had to be prematurely terminated.

After the Thursday operating sessions parents were not allowed to visit until the Saturday by which time you would hopefully be in a presentable condition. By Saturday afternoon I was fully co-ordinated but still unable to keep food down. For the full duration of my stay in hospital I was visited by Aunt Marjorie, Uncle Cyril and my parents for the three-hour period every Saturday and my parents again for the two hours on a Sunday. Sometimes if my father was working on nights he came to see me for an hour on a Monday before he went to work or if not my grandmother made the journey. My mother tried to visit for an hour on a Wednesday evening. Throughout my stay a couple of other relatives visited me perhaps once each. Getting to the hospital was a lengthy trip and no doubt visits from my parents were putting a strain on family life at home. Visiting was really discouraged on days other than Wednesday, Saturday and Sunday and I did very well with the numbers I received compared to many of the other children. When visitors arrived on that first Saturday, though, I had no desire to be sociable or optimistic about the ultimate outcome to the week's major event.

Saturday afternoons were usually a time of feast and plenty as visitors descended with sweets and other consumable goodies. The strict hospital regime did not allow them to leave patients with anything edible. Outside visiting times the rigidly enforced code of practice dictated that no one was allowed to possess food or drink of any nature. You were being detained at someone's pleasure (I never did find out whose!) and had no human rights as an individual whatsoever. By the Monday, after being violently ill again during the visiting period on the Sunday, I had recovered my capacity to take food, was back at school and fully expected to get on with my new, totally immobilized, life. The specialist often popped into the hospital on a Sunday morning, I suppose unofficially to take a quick look at any patient who was having his or her progress carefully monitored or in need of his attention. He came on the ward to see me and to check on the difficulties I was experiencing and to look at the angle at which my knee had been set. He dismissed these as being insignificant. Everything was as to be expected and he was not unduly perturbed by the situation.

In all my life I had never been immobilized to this degree and there were many things I needed to get used to; toileting arrangements for one, and the total dependency on others. Bed baths and treatment for the prevention of bed sores were all part of my new routine. Each morning every patient was issued with an alloy metal bowl containing some water, given a piece of soap and a towel with which to get washed and dried. This was accompanied by a small bowl, mug of water and ready pasted toothbrush. Sometimes this activity degenerated into a full scale battle as tablets of soap began to fly across the ward. There is always some idiot who finds life too boring and tries to circumvent this by annoying others or deliberately causing trouble.

The specialist had confirmed that my legs would be encased in plaster for the next six weeks and as each day passed I crossed it off a chart I kept. The time could not pass quickly enough. After the first week or so my legs began to itch quite severely inside the plaster. All one could do was gently to scratch the offending area with a carefully manipulated knitting needle, provided the irritation was not in the vicinity of the stitched cuts. When the full length of your leg is locked in plaster the heat generated around the knee is terrific and this also was a disturbing problem. By about the third week or so my legs were gradually beginning to waste away and, with the resulting small amount of clearance, if I positioned my leg very carefully I could get air almost to reach my knee. The longer the plaster was on the more intense the itching became but as my leg was slowly getting thinner this was easier to deal with. Towards the end of the six weeks I could clearly see inside the plaster and by inserting my hand remove pieces of dark brown dead skin. The heat and distressing level of irritation around the knee increased by the day.

Eventually the fateful day arrived when the plasters were to be removed, a process I greatly feared, but at least it was all downhill from this point. I knew from what I could see and feel that my legs were now only a shadow of their former selves. The plaster was removed by the use of a pair of long-handled snippers, which I can only compare to a pair of stainless steel tree loppers. As the plaster was cut my now very fragile legs were painfully bumped and battered until there only remained the job of prising open the casts and removing my legs. This was the moment I had been eagerly awaiting. As each casing was opened I was stunned as the flesh from my knees came away with them. I was certain that what I was looking at was the bone. The sister in charge immediately told me not to worry, opened a sealed tin and applied a piece of gauze soaked in a vaseline-like substance which I think was penicillin to the deep open wounds.

I sat there and looked at my legs. They were very thin, covered by a layer of dead brown skin and absolutely useless. They began to tremor and this steadily developed until they were shaking uncontrollably. This had nothing to do with fear, it was a purely nervous reaction to the environment in which they now found themselves. They had been released from captivity. I was turned over and the linen stitches were then removed. I felt a small burning sensation as each one came out. It is difficult to say just how many there were but they were numerous and towards the end the feeling became more unpleasant with each cut and pull. Two incisions had been made lengthwise down the back of each knee terminating in an 'L' shaped bend. Hopefully my ordeal was now over and it was just a matter of regaining my old fitness. Presumably an easier and more fulfilling life now awaited me.

I returned to the ward feeling very pleased that this episode was now entering its final stages. Gradually the nerves in my legs got used to the new conditions and the shaking subsided. Besides the hole in each knee the only thing which gave me immediate cause for concern was the fact that the sense of feeling on the inside of each of my shins was drastically changed – if I touched this area it felt partially numbed yet painful. Miraculously the holes on my kneecaps quickly healed up, at least to the point where I no longer worried about them.

Physiotherapy started almost immediately. Initially exercises were administered on the ward just to get things moving again. My enthusiasm was now very high as I was determined to go home at the first opportunity. I had been there long enough. By the following week the physiotherapy had been intensified and I was attempting to stand up again. If they had previously considered my balance to be bad then it was now completely non-existent. They had straightened my legs all right, in fact the left one went slightly past straight and it hurt when I put any weight on it. The basic problem was that in straightening my legs they had moved my centre of balance and I compensated for this by arching my back. I was using my back like a high-wire act uses a pole, and my back being much shorter than a tightrope walker's pole meant it had to work much harder to make the necessary corrections. This action was not happening by instinct, I was conscious of every adjustment that I was making and each time I made an error of judgment my heartbeat would jump with a resounding thud. It was to be hoped that I had no weakness in this direction.

It was obvious that I was not going to be running around for a long time, if indeed ever again. After two weeks I could stand precariously with the aid of a pair of elbow crutches and struggle for a few steps if I had to. I was now really desperate to go home. The specialist came to see me on his Sunday morning visit and I asked him outright if there was any chance of my leaving in the immediate future. He replied, 'Will today be soon enough?' I seized at his offer and most probably had my belongings packed before he had left the ward! I informed my Aunt Marjorie of the decision and she arrived with her car in the early afternoon to take me away.

It was great to be back home, although I was now helpless and my life had changed drastically. My legs were no longer only slightly bent and marginally twisted but otherwise normally proportioned and serviceable, they were now severely damaged, very fragile, painful and useless, and I was in a wheelchair. In the past I had resented and perhaps vandalized the ironware dreamt up for my use but this little lot was going to take some getting rid of. I was now well and truly shackled and probably about to serve a life sentence with no possibility of reprieve or remission for good behaviour. Sixteenth April 1959 was a day I would not be forgetting in a hurry.

FIVE

Living under the Shadow of the Knife

I was out of hospital but straight back to school as there was still another month before the end of the summer term. Despite the time I had spent studying and the hard work I had put in I was not successful in the eleven-plus examination, or at least I was not offered a place at a High School. This came as no surprise – not that I had not passed, but that I was not offered a place at another educational establishment. In some ways I was disappointed at being abruptly discarded after giving it everything I had, especially when people who were too ready to sit in judgment compared my failure with others' success and pointed out that perhaps I had more enthusiasm than knowledge. What did they know? I knew that life would go on regardless and my circumstances had now totally changed. Secretly, I had always had my reservations about being allowed to transfer to mainstream education – or coping physically if I was – and had resigned myself to the inevitable.

Receiving an education was a long process and the race was far from over, this was only the first hurdle. My ego may have been temporarily dented but my enthusiasm for learning was certainly not dampened. I could see no point whatsoever in attending school if I was not going to do my utmost to be successful. Yes, maybe I did have an uphill and ever-steepening task in front of me but application and tenacity are the name of the game and anyone thinking they could write me off would be in for a nasty shock. I was determined that some day I would catch and overtake many of those who now thought they were leading the way. I had no pretence to brilliance, my aim was solely to realize my potential, whatever that may be. By my reckoning there were far too many people who, through lack of effort, did not do this. The race's front runners were not out of sight yet, perhaps if I worked hard enough I would still be there at the finish.

This was but a minor reverse compared to getting back into

action after the appalling physical setback of my operations. That was a very painful, slow and testing process. I had not been the toughest of children before but in my own way I had sought adventure and found it. I did not take great risks in my quest for entertainment but I had always had all the stimulation I needed. Now I was reduced to a physical wreck, rendered almost helpless.

My progress on elbow crutches was very shaky and uncertain and I spent most of the time in a wheelchair. Physiotherapy sessions were extremely intense as I was forced to walk again. It was as if my legs had been wrecked in an accident and I was being told to pull myself together and make the best of what I had left. I can assure you, however, that there is a big difference in your attitude when the wreck is the result of someone else's lack of foresight and failed experiment. There also hangs the dark cloud that whatever you do, well or not so well, further experiments lurk around every corner. Those concerned with such a decision, mainly the surgeon and your parents, are now in too deep to give up without trying to recoup some of their losses. The people in authority I could trust, if any, were now very thin on the ground. What they had done once they could very easily do again – that is the way of human nature.

The threat of further unnecessary surgery was a constant worry and it was hard to live life without letting this show. I had been too honest about my abilities and disabilities in the past and I regretted where this had now got me. I went to the swimming baths with the school but could no longer manage to swim or float as my legs now sank to the bottom as if weighed down by all my problems. It was not a lack of confidence for I could still swim underwater. My legs trailed helplessly behind sinking as I went, no longer able to play a part in any stroke I tried to do. Swimming underwater had severe limitations but was at least better than being afraid of the water. On one occasion as I was trying to get out of the pool at the end of a session I fell backwards and would have drowned had I not been rescued and given artificial respiration on the pool side. I regained consciousness as my arms were still being pulled back and chest pushed. The water I had taken in was running out of my nose and mouth. I was shocked by what had happened but had faith in those who had saved me. If I ever wished to fulfil my ambition of being able to swim I had to keep going and could not afford to let the incident deter me, although I was very wary of a similar event occurring on future visits.

The holidays were soon upon us and we went to stay in a flat at Bridlington. I was confined to my wheelchair for most of the time, only getting out in places where it was not practicable to use it. The first thing that amazed me about being in a wheelchair was that people gave you money. The occasional passerby would push a two-shilling piece into my hand and wish me well. This was a lot of money in 1959 and on our second to last day one benevolent old lady even gave me a ten-shilling note, saying she hoped it would do me some good. It should have done, for I now had just enough money to buy a fishing rod, a secret ambition of mine ever since our illicit fishing expeditions with our next-door neighbour. Unfortunately my parents were not of the same opinion and I had to save it. I could not understand how such generosity could possibly compensate one for being in a wheelchair. I would have thought myself more worthy had I been struggling along on my elbow crutches and perhaps falling down and picking myself up again every now and then, but, as I learned to my astonishment, that is how the world seems to work. In this respect I did wonder if it would be worthwhile staying in a wheelchair for evermore, or at least retaining one for use in the event of physical or monetary crises . . . and I did have grave doubts as to whether I should ever be independently mobile again. Anyone seeing my legs would have agreed that these doubts were not completely unfounded.

My life now had a new dimension which sooner or later I would have to come to terms with if I wanted to start enjoying myself again – it was a thing called pain. My legs may have previously been slightly twisted and bent and my ankles unable to bend fully but to all intents and purposes they were normal. They were at least a matching pair and although perhaps a little restricted in their performance did not give me any undue trouble or pain. All that had now ended and I had entered a new and irreversible era of my life. I had better accept it and get used to it for nothing was going to change. It was I who would have to do the changing if I was to get back to any sort of normality and have a satisfying existence.

My mother and grandmother had always begged me to take account of my disability and not try to do things which were difficult for me. They had wanted me to live cosseted. I was probably not destined to gain employment and compete with the world at large and the sooner I accepted this the better. My current predicament only added weight to their argument. Whenever I tried to do anything which they thought was beyond what I ought to be doing they pleaded with me to accept my limitations. I knew that my ignoring their calls for what they thought was common sense caused them a great deal of anguish but it was my life and I knew what I expected from it. Besides, they could hardly expect me to comply with their wishes just because they had changed the rules of the game. As far as I was concerned, my mother and father were the ones responsible for my present dilemma. It was they who had given their consent for the operations to be performed. They who had obviously not been satisfied with the way things had been before. Well, why the hell should I play their game by a set of changing rules which were not going in my favour? Did I not already have enough problems without all this? I was rapidly becoming disconsolate and very angry and some day those responsible would have to answer for their deeds.

The operations had put paid to such activities as swinging on a rope across the beck and climbing over walls but I was no less aware of the virtues of sport. I had always wanted to own a tennis racket and the previous year I had bought one. Being able to play, though, was now a different matter and I had to be content with just owning and watching. I was regularly forced to lend it to my father, sister and cousin since only my brother and myself had rackets. I bitterly resented this when I thought of how I had come to arrive in a wheelchair. It was like maiming someone so that you could loot their possessions. Apart from the anonymous donations, which I felt a little guilty about accepting, this was not a particularly happy holiday. Being in a wheelchair put me at the mercy of those pushing and I was impatient, ill tempered and I felt that my status as a child and human being was being abused in every conceivable way. Insult was constantly being added to injury.

Those five weeks of school holiday were of little productive use. From the very early days of school I had looked forward to the summer break even if only as respite from officialdom and authority, but now I was at an age where they meant much more. The seemingly endless days of summer were the time when long-dreamed-about projects could be put into practice. I had established myself as a part of the local child community and was accepted for my qualities of leadership, which were somewhat enhanced by having a fit younger brother in tow and technical knowhow. My peers had prided themselves on integrating me into the adventures and activities described earlier, but now, unable to join in on any level, I was useless. I could no longer swim or play tennis, and I had to abandon all hope of ever riding a bicycle again. My friends Stephen and Robin owned bicycles and they had both been giving me tuition in the art of staying upright on two wheels. My progress was slow but steady and with some help from Stephen's father I had just managed to go a short distance on my own when I went into hospital. Afterwards, with my left leg completely useless and my right little better, that was that. If I wanted to do anything I had to enlist the help and support of my brother and friends. I was fortunate to have them, indeed I would have been lost without them. They understood my plight for they had known me before this latest transformation and did their best to integrate me into group activities. I will always be grateful to Robin who was prepared to take risks with me that many others wouldn't, as when he took me on the back of his bicycle. He was a master at 'saddling' people and it used to amaze me the speed at which we covered distances which normally took me some time to complete on my own. Freewheeling downhill round bends was a never-to-be-forgotten experience – one which tested my nerve and my confidence in Robin's expertise!

I was frustrated and there were days when I could not avoid feeling that I was wasting my life away. Perhaps this was to be the shape of my whole future, who knew? I definitely did not. Apart from periodic visits from my regular physiotherapist, it gave me time to lick my wounds and come to terms with what had happened. There was an uphill struggle in front and my mood swung back and forth, and the question was whether or not I was equal to the task. The clock could not be put back. However much I wished it so, the events of the past few months could not be reversed. Wherever there is realistic ambition and a determined will to succeed there is hope. Maybe many of my dreams lay shattered but I still had hope. There has to be light at the end of every tunnel and however far away the first rays of brightness were every day brought me one step closer. The nightmare, however real, could not go on for ever. In the end, I knew that some day I should have control over my own destiny.

The operations had put paid to much more than my walking. I could now no longer kneel or crawl. Sitting on level ground had always been difficult for me, I had to hold myself upright in a stiff posture which was very tiring and wholly unsatisfactory since I could not do anything whilst remaining in this position. Now if I wished to pursue leisure activities on the floor all I could do was lie horizontally and worm my way around. Was this an unfortunate side effect of the surgery or had it been carefully planned? In fact the side effects were so numerous any sane person would have wondered what the benefits were.

My legs were very fragile and if, when playing with other children or even just going about my everyday life, one of them accidentally received a knock, I was in agony. Living with a

48

brother and sister as I did, knocks were inevitable, and I was often reduced to tears with the sheer physical pain. The smallest of bumps would sometimes cause a swelling around my knee or the scars on the back of my legs to bleed. If anyone jarred my bed or sat on the edge it could be very painful. The circulation of blood in my legs was now so bad that as autumn arrived I was unable to get or maintain any warmth in them when I went to bed and my father, realizing how desperate the situation was, bought me an electric blanket, an idea he would have previously dismissed without a second thought. All this had depleted my appetite for coping with the stress and hardship involved; my mental stamina was at an all-time low, which naturally was not particularly helping matters.

However stringent the discipline imposed at home this did not detract from the fact that I had a stable and happy family background. It was a safe haven from the outside world. My father ruled with a stern voice and firm hand but he was also our hero – provider and protector. His word was final and he stood no nonsense but he was also ready to listen, talk and counsel if he thought it necessary. This, together with the time afforded by the summer break, gave me the chance to recover emotionally and prepare myself for the unknown which lay ahead. I was still alive, perhaps when I returned to school one or two of my classmates would not be. My problems were minuscule beside theirs – or maybe they had just found the ultimate, permanent, if apparently rather drastic, solution.

My phobia of death was causing me problems in more ways than one. When I went to my grandmother's I now had to go in my wheelchair. Normally the journey by foot involved a short section of steep hill but this, unless my father was at the helm in which case he always went direct, could be avoided by making a short detour via a road with a more gradual incline. This other route, however, passed the local undertaker's chapel of rest and in my mixed-up emotional state I found that I could not cope with this prospect. I dreaded making the trip and being pushed slowly past the dimly lit building. I was at an impressionable age and this was one impression that I could not bear. The sooner I got out of the wheelchair and began to walk the better. This would also solve the other main problem I had with being wheeled around – dangerous drivers! There was always some lunatic who believed that travelling at speed was great fun. Well, I certainly did not; it was I who was out there in front and in the event of an accident would bear the full brunt.

I had to walk again. At all costs I had to get myself walking. Life in a wheelchair was definitely not for me. I could not live with the hazards and impositions it entailed. Previously I had accepted whatever physical problems I may have had as being a fact of life. It was just the normal me. Even the fitting of callipers and ankle splints was only a temporary hindrance. There was nothing permanent about these contraptions or the results they were supposed to have. I was ultimately still in control of my very being. But now, suddenly things had drastically changed and I resented the whole situation. I sometimes resented being alive, but I knew that if I accepted what had happened then I would be the loser. I was a bad loser and especially so when my participation in an event was not by my choice. My physical standing may have been reduced but I was on my way back and with more determination than ever to play it my way. I had been forced to listen to other people and look where it had got me. Those responsible for the damage did not even start to comprehend the basic rights of human existence. They were playing a game where they had nothing to lose. The stakes were my life and future and I had to get in there and play for all I was worth. Mentally I disowned my current state. It had nothing to do with me. I was, after all, still the same person and no one was going to change me.

I began to walk with the elbow crutches issued to me and gradually became more and more competent until eventually I could swing along on them at great speed. Officially I was not supposed to use them in this way, they were intended as a walking aid only, and such performances were strictly reserved for personal activities such as playing football. With a lot of practice I discovered that I could kick a football and do many other things which one did not normally associate with someone using such aids to mobility! I was determined to join in whatever games I could and what I lacked in skill and strength I made up for in enthusiasm and commitment.

One day the physiotherapist found out the extent of my ability and adeptness with the elbow crutches and decided that I should progress to walking sticks. The transition is not an easy one as once having removed the arm support your hands shake all over the place when you first put weight on to them. Elbow crutches were great for speed and they took practically all the strain off your legs and transferred it to your shoulders, but if you fell there was an awful lot of awkwardly shaped ironware flying around with which to hurt or injure yourself. Walking sticks required much more strength and expertise but were less of a hazard in the event of a mishap. They took none of the body weight from your legs but instead acted only as stabilizers to assist with maintaining your balance. In effect they provide you with an extra two points of contact with the ground, but these further links being only as reliable and efficient as the arms and shoulders that are handling the sticks. It is one thing for a fit walker to use a stick or sticks for assistance and another when one is completely reliant on them for support. The handles have to be gripped in a vice-like hold and held steady with muscles of steel, two qualities developed only after hours of practice and a lot of hard work. Lightning-quick reactions are called for should a stick slip or fail to get the anticipated hold on the ground. Many skills have to be learned before any degree of competence is acquired and the sticks, ultimately, must become an integral part of the user's body. On two legs one either balances and remains upright or one falls over, but in the quadruped state the question of balance is largely eliminated. Standing becomes more a matter of determination, and strength, with locomotion dependent on skill, concentration, flexibility and self-confidence. You must have a total understanding of precisely what accuracy of movement, range and power you can achieve with each foot and stick and the belief that you can reproduce this form at every attempt.

A normal fit walker does not have to judge each step accurately for much of the time since his speed will usually allow him to recover his stride. More often than not, however, for a person committed to two sticks there is no second chance and the points at which something can go amiss have been doubled. In the early days of use every mistake is harshly punished and even after many years of using sticks recovering from a misjudgment often extracts a high price by way of strained arm or back muscles as one teeters to a halt and wrestles to remain upright. The greater your skill the less likely you are to fall but your chances of getting hurt should you make an error are increased as you instinctively strain to recover or, should this fail, you (by now unprepared) unexpectedly hit the ground. Initially I fell quite often but, apart from once falling on a garden rake and impaling my knee on two of the prongs, I suffered little damage of any consequence as I mastered the art of walking with two sticks.

Slowly I became accustomed to my new lifestyle and began to make the best of what I had. I flattened one metal walking stick by stopping the hard ball with it whilst playing cricket. I was fielding quite close to the batsman and my instinctive intervention with what I now considered a natural or at least essential appendage probably saved four runs but the appliance was badly dented. The aluminium alloy sticks I had been issued with were totally unsuitable and inadequate for my circumstances anyway. They rattled as I walked, had no flexibility which meant they jarred every time they hit the ground, the rubber handles were neither comfortable nor completely secure and most dangerously of all my hands became black at any point where they made contact with the alloy. As a result of this my hands and fingers often went septic where the metal rubbed against sores, usually created by the sticks in the first instance. The only real advantage was that they were adjustable in length which was scant consolation as I nursed the wounds they had created. Eventually my pleas were heard and I was provided with traditional wooden sticks. At the side of the high-tech alloy ones they may have appeared primitive to the issuing authority but to me they were a vast improvement.

At Potternewton I moved from a junior class to a senior one, a progression I had eagerly anticipated since the curriculum would now include woodwork. I was also looking forward to moving up from the wolf cub pack to the boy scout troop, but the edge was rather taken off both these events with my newly impaired mobility and independence. Mr Tempest, the teacher to the next class and scout master after Mr Perry, had also chosen this moment to move to another school, a promotion I assume, and was replaced by, in my opinion, a less effective male teacher. The dynamic leadership qualities of Messrs Tempest and Perry had gone and with them the spirit of the troop. Before they left, however, as a farewell gesture, they did take us on a weekend camp to a farm at Methley and this was where I spent my first night under canvas. This was one dream that being a boy scout did fulfil for me and this initiation into life in the open lived up to my wildest expectations in every way.

As time passed the damage done to my left leg became progressively more apparent as it failed to respond to exercise. My right leg was not all that brilliant but my left was totally useless and showing few signs of improvement. Any sane person could see that it never was going to improve, the tendons had been removed and it had no means of bending other than by outside forces. Although I could straighten it – in fact it sprang straight on its own when any pressure used to retain it was released – the knee was not itself able to generate any degree of power to straighten the leg. The simple truth was that when it was straight, or actually slightly past straight as it happened, it was adequate for providing support for only a very short period, sufficient for me to be able to walk on it if I moved my weight across it quickly, and as a short-term balancing aid if I stood still. If I put too much weight on it or used it for any prolonged period it ached to the depths of every sinew and I needed to rest very often. The ankle would still not quite angle at 90 degrees but this was really the least of any problems I had.

Problem or not it fired the imagination of the surgeon and he decided he would operate on it in an attempt to achieve that elusive 90-degree bend. Once again it was an operation which I did not want but this time my circumstances were different. You cannot steal anything but time and freedom from a man who has nothing and this just about summed up the situation regarding my left leg. I was miserable at the thought of going into hospital again and being put through more unnecessary distress and pain for heaven knew what result. I had been conned once and I now knew without any shadow of doubt that those in authority had no conscience. The black clouds of success or failure which had loomed overhead since my first operations had burst. I was caught in what I called the 'operation trap'. If an operation was a success, then the surgeons were inspired to experiment further and try and 'improve' things yet more. If an operation was a failure then they felt that they might as well do another to put things right. They couldn't make things worse . . . (or could they, was my reaction). Ever since my first operation I had felt like I was in the trenches. The minute I put my head over the top they would notice me and I would come under scrutiny for another possible operation. And so I did. The storm had arrived. The word 'operation' struck terror in the depths of my heart and soul, the thought of it reverberated through my mind, there was no safe retreat, my worst fears had materialized. Would I be able to walk at all when they had eventually finished with me?

As a gesture of goodwill, if there is such a thing in these circumstances, the surgeon decided he would allow me to spend Christmas at home and admit me into hospital in the January of 1961. When the time arrived I bade a sad farewell to my pet mice and made sure that my brother fully understood how he was to look after them in my enforced absence. I knew that it was possible I may never see them again. My mother detested them and there was no love lost on my father's part. It had only been my grand-mother's help that had got me them in the first place, but they were my greatest joy in life. Perhaps my fears of total or unnatural loss were a little unfounded, for my parents knew that what they had agreed to was like sentencing me to be locked up and should anything happen to my mice it would be equivalent to throwing away the key. They had been forced into agreeing to certain courses of action but I always knew that they cared very deeply about me. They were not taking any easy way out, in fact if the truth be known it was probably quite the reverse.

Thorp Arch awaited my return and I duly arrived after my visit to Woolworths and the lengthy bus ride. I was a little less apprehensive this time and not quite so mobile. Maybe my lot would be improved after this visit, such institutions must have some successes in their cosmetic surgery department.

My confidence in being able to deal with the situation this time was quickly shattered. I went to be prepared for surgery and was shocked when both legs were shaved, sterilized and bandaged. In fact I was shaved and treated to the waist. I protested that I was only in for an operation on my left ankle and was extremely distressed when the nurse replied that I could be having operations on both ankles and perhaps on my legs also for all she knew. This was the first I had heard of any such drastic action and I was mentally and emotionally unprepared for this devastating revelation. I demanded that someone find out just what was happening quickly but was told that it was no concern of mine. Maybe I had no say in the matter but all the same I still wanted to know. Surely I had a right to know? I had no wish to come to from the anaesthetic and find myself in a totally unexpected condition. It was the following morning before anyone confirmed that it was only my left ankle which was being operated on.

The routine was much the same as it had been for my first operation. On this occasion I was to be accompanied by Nurse Atkinson and it was her first experience of going to theatre. I fell instantly in love with her, which allayed many of my fears as I held on to her comforting hand. I had never been in love before but I wished that this new feeling could go on for ever. It ended all too quickly when, after my brief talk with the surgeon, the ether began to drip on to the cotton wool placed over my face. As I fell unconscious all I wanted was for her still to be there when I awoke.

I came to back on the ward with a plaster cast on my left leg from immediately below the knee to the base of my toes. An intense ache interpersed by spasms of acute pain centred on my Achilles tendon but I knew that somehow I had to bear it. I could not go through the same ordeal as last time and this damage was not quite so extensive. At the first opportunity I enquired about Nurse Atkinson. I needed to make sure that she was not just a figment of my imagination. I needed to know if she still awakened the same feelings within me. Later that evening she came to see how I was getting on. I could have been dying but I would not have let it show. The feelings were still the same; awe and complete abandonment. To my delight I discovered that we had much in common, she had also kept mice. Over the ensuing weeks our friendship strengthened and I learned that her name was Joan. She did not regularly work on the older boys' ward but sometimes late of an evening when the hardier patients were sleeping outside she would visit me for a moonlight chat. I would have slept outside in any weather to see Joan, the thought of her maintained me through those troubled times. On one occasion when I did not see her for a while she sent me a letter which I treasured greatly.

Discipline among the nurses and patients on the ward was not what it had been on my previous stay and unruly behaviour was not uncommon; mass water-throwing sessions early in the morning when we were supposed to be getting washed and on one occasion a knife-throwing incident. Often nurses were involved and on occasions even provoked the outbursts of stupidity. I dreaded ever being involved in such idiotic escapades and definitely had no wish to fight, but when cornered or bullied the only solution as I saw it was to get stuck in and deal with the offenders in a language they understood – that is, heavy-handedly. On two occasions I was put in solitary confinement, once for a whole week, for refusing to have my possessions abused, or my personal well-being jeopardized. In truth I was much happier with my own company than that of bedridden would-be godfathers and petty hooligans, so apart from the apparent disgrace that such punishment brought and being treated by the staff as a social outcast the sentence imposed inflicted no real hardship.

In all my life I had never before been classed as an awkward child but to my dismay I now was. The problem seemed to stem from the fact that I was strong enough and had the will not to be abused while my attitude and behaviour appeared docile. I did not advertise my strength or the threat that I really was until severely provoked. In the environment that I had previously lived in I had never needed to exhibit danger signs. I had never been tested by the harsh realities of jungle law because standards of behaviour in my world had been carefully regulated. I could cope with the jungle but the jungle could not cope with me.

On my left foot the big toe, which protruded from the plaster cast, became very painful and I was once again classed as being awkward for bringing this to the attention of those in charge.

There were no visible signs of anything being wrong but the pain was almost unbearable. My complaints were dismissed as nonsense but I wanted something done about it. The sister, tired of my continual moaning, decided that she would teach me a lesson by applying a hot kaolin poultice. I was in such agony that this actually came as a relief. Within hours it had drawn a large abscess to the surface and I was acquitted of simply seeking attention. Although frightening it was a great relief when it was lanced. I was held steady while the sister lunged at it with a sharp metal instrument. The ordeal of the mysterious pain was over.

There was an age limit on visitors which often prevented patients from seeing their young brothers and sisters. If minors were brought to the hospital they had to remain at the gate but because of the outdoor aspect of the wards it was possible to sneak a quick exchange. One Sunday my parents brought along my brother to see me and, in what I believe was a surprise to all concerned, he had my mice with him. I was pleased to see them but concerned that they should get back home as safely as they had arrived. Nurse Atkinson was around and I was able to introduce them to her. She handled them expertly and I knew that she had been telling the truth about keeping mice.

I had been ticking off the days on a chart I had drawn to the time when the plaster would be removed. I was not looking forward to the actual removal but it was the first step in my push to get discharged as quickly as possible. At least I already knew how to use elbow crutches and maybe I would be able to keep the weight off my left foot and persuade them to let me go home fairly soon.

The dreaded day arrived, the cast was cut away and the stitches taken out. My ankle was weak and looked very fragile. There was a small lump on my Achilles tendon, presumably where it had been tampered with. It would now bend to an apparently much more normal-looking angle and the magic 90 degrees was for the first time achievable but it was painfully tender and in reality useless. Would it ever recover?

Within a few days I began physiotherapy. Soon I was able to put on a shoe and keen to get away from this institution before they found some other way of making me suffer. I believe that my father was becoming increasingly disillusioned and disgusted by the situation because the moment I was given a hint that I could return home he caught the very next bus to the hospital to collect me. The position regarding my discharge appeared somewhat confused with no one prepared to complete the official formalities. I was not sufficiently mobile to make my own way off the premises and in the absence of an official discharge my father wasted no time. He picked up my possessions, put me over his shoulder and we hastily left before anyone had a chance to change their mind.

On the bus we had a long chat and he told me that he had had enough of being messed around and was pleased that I was coming home. His actions did my morale a power of good and the journey back to Leeds was thoroughly enjoyable. If my respect for him had in any way been dented it was now fully restored. The future had to be much brighter than the darkness I had just been through.

SIX

Learning to Live

I had never been very happy at Potternewton Mansion School but now I was twelve years old, in the much feared Mrs Southern's class and things were looking somewhat brighter. She was brilliant. Mrs Southern, a Scot, was a strict disciplinarian, and this made her either loved or hated. She appreciated effort and could spot talent when confronted by it. Her real strength lay in being able to nurture these positive attributes into genuine ability. Her approach was honest, straightforward and forthright. If you worked hard you did well, if you had other ideas then you had more than likely at last met your come-uppance. Tolerance was not one of her strong points and her manner in dealing with transgressors kept her in complete control.

This was the environment I needed and it had perhaps come at the right time. I thrived on her depth of input and the classroom atmosphere she created. Maybe that was why she was in charge of the middle senior class. The school did not have a class for each specific age group, in fact there were only three classes covering the age ranges from eleven to sixteen. (Being a special school pupils normally attended until the age of sixteen instead of the usual fifteen as it was then for those not taking G.C.E. examinations.) Although age played some part in determining which class you were placed in, academic ability was also an important factor. I had moved up as quickly as was practical and was one of the younger members of the group. This was education as I believed it should be. You went to school to learn, not just to pass the time away until you were sixteen. Mrs Southern not only provided the opportunity but also encouraged and gave credit to those showing endeavour. For those who stayed on the straight and narrow there really was nothing to fear from her.

An important part of the school calendar was the play each class had to put on as part of the Christmas festivities. I now began to get leading roles, and the chance to perform in more exacting parts continued through the next class until my final year at the school.

The most eagerly anticipated event of the year was the annual Christmas party arranged by the pupils of Allerton Girls High School for the top two senior classes of Potternewton. They were splendid, rather lavish affairs with each guest being hosted by one of the school's senior girls, which was what we most looked forward to. It was a chance to mix socially, enjoy good food and participate in fun party games with some very nice young ladies. Incidentally, the girls apparently looked forward to the event as much as we did and because of the large size of their school only a limited number of them were chosen to arrange the party. At the end of the evening one of the guests from Potternewton had the awesome task of taking the stage to give a vote of thanks and at the age of fourteen this somewhat dubious honour fell to me. After visiting a school of such dimensions it brought home to me how sheltered was the environment of the establishment which I was attending – which I used to think was large!

The second most important event in the annual calendar was the day trip to Whitby on the east coast in the summer. The headmaster, Mr Pagdin, was having an early type of *perestroika* and the two most senior classes were now allowed to choose their own venue for the yearly excursion. This greatly increased the social standing and value of the outing. It was a chance to do something which we wanted to do and not just attend an arranged fixture. After some lobbying by individuals who considered themselves to be well informed on the tourist spots of the county the destination was determined by a democratic vote.

Our first choice was a tour of the Yorkshire Dales to be centred on Aysgarth Falls and Burnsall. This was my first real awakening to the beauty of the countryside. I had never before ventured quite so far into such rewarding scenery. We had a packed lunch by the tumbling waters after scrambling as best we could over the rocks at Aysgarth Falls. The struggle to walk over the great flat slabs of stone worn smooth by the flow of water did not really interest me but I was totally absorbed by the splendour that surrounded us. The sun was shining brilliantly, time seemed to be of such little importance and the life span of man a mere fleeting moment in the passage of history at the side of such natural wonders. This piece of countryside had a certain indefinable tranquillity that I had never previously experienced. I knew that it was like a drug. I was hooked on it and I needed more. Perhaps it was just the remedy I needed? After tea at Burnsall we hired rowing boats on the river which proved to be very exciting and a satisfactory conclusion to my introductory day in the Yorkshire Dales.

The following year we went to Hornsea, the highlight of which was a motor-launch trip on the mere. We had hoped to have a go on the go-cart track, which a few of us had previously visited, but those in charge of our day out decided that it would not be a wise move – in retrospect, probably quite rightly. However, to complete the day we did get a conducted tour of Hornsea Pottery and saw glass ornaments being made on the sea front.

Since leaving Larchfield an important annual outing had been the one day a year when ex-pupils traditionally returned to meet the staff and children who were now in residence. This took place on voting day, a Thursday sometime in May, when the local councillors were elected. Potternewton was used as a Polling Station and thus closed to normal business giving the pupils the day off. Not every ex-pupil wished to return to Larchfield but there was a small hardcore of faithful devotees which included myself. Miss Hogarth was most welcoming, and I particularly enjoyed my annual chat with Messrs Wilkinson and Bell, the school's gardeners. It was refreshing to return to such a pleasant setting at such a good time of the year in the knowledge that one was no longer under its jurisdiction.

Early in the morning we would meet up at a bus station in Leeds with a couple of the teachers and make the return journey with them in the late afternoon. The visit served the dual purpose of giving the current batch of pupils a chance to see and discuss the progress made by former ones and also providing the opportunity for those who had left to get into full perspective a situation which at the time they may have found extremely daunting or unpleasant. Through these return visits you learned what you were supposed to have gained by attending the school and this put you in a much better position to capitalize on the grounding it had provided. It amounted to an enjoyable and exciting day out and was most beneficial to all concerned.

Schoolfriends played a very important role in my life while I was at Potternewton, especially Robert McLellan, Chris Sollitt and Peter Connell. Robert had more or less been a lifelong companion and had in fact been a great influence on me. He was the typical youth of the day, following all the latest fads and fashions, and I followed in his wake being fairly indifferent to such matters unless my lack of trendiness was brought to my attention! It was Robert who introduced me to the delights of pop music. He was an ardent fan of the Shadows, Cliff Richard and the Everley Brothers, while I, though if I heard something which I liked then I knew that I liked that particular record, was unaware of the performing artists as groups or individuals. But on hearing the Shadows I knew that I had found my type of music, especially as there was this supporting vocalist called Cliff Richard. The release of the hit single 'Wonderful Land' had a devastating effect on my life. I had discovered a form of escapism from the real world. The Beatle era had yet to be born and music was simplistically innocent. Rock 'n' Roll simply expressed heartfelt emotions in musical form and the satisfaction and inspiration that the music of Cliff and the Shadows has given me over more than twenty-five years has been enormous. The only other performer I took seriously was Elvis Presley.

Robert had a drum kit and his brother Donald accompanied him on his guitar. Although I enjoyed listening to music I had no natural talent or inclination towards playing it, and while I longed to be able to play the guitar, as hard as I tried I just did not have what it took. Peter Connell had a superb electric guitar and amplifier but was limited by his physical condition in the extent to which he could play it. He suffered quite severely from the effects of polio and his existence was extremely precarious. He was fitted with a plastic jacket to support his small, fragile body, but was very talented at most things which he turned his hand to and was encouraged and indulged by his parents and older sisters. He was always happy to let his friends have a go on his very fine instrument, but I soon realized that I completely lacked the manual dexterity and co-ordination such an expensive piece deserved.

Peter's father had a mini-bus and one Sunday he took several of us to Hornsea on the East Coast to go go-cart racing. Peter had been before and loved it, but apart from him none of us had ever driven a motorized vehicle before (albeit only powered by a lawnmower engine) but we were prepared to give it a go provided the proprietors would accept a mini-bus load of handicapped fourteen-year-olds. It seemed to me that if your feet could reach the two pedals and you had the right money the proprietors found you acceptable and away we went. Compared to riding the bogies I had built it was decidedly hairy. The feeling of speed is enhanced considerably by the fact that you are so close to the ground and you had to go pretty fast if you were not to be constantly overtaken. There were both left and right hand bends to negotiate as the track weaved its way around the circuit, and we duelled fiercely, not being prepared to give an inch. It was really do or die stuff. The day out was thrilling and I returned home with the feeling that some day I would be able to drive a car if I ever wished to do so.

Chris Sollitt's fascination in life was guns. He owned three air rifles and a pistol of various calibres and velocities and used his back garden as a shooting range. I had first become friendly with him when I sold him two mice that I had bred. On a couple of occasions I went to his house to stay for the weekend and participated in lengthy shooting sessions. His father, if his medals were anything to go by, must have been a veteran of several war campaigns and very safety conscious with regard to the use and storage of the weapons. Chris was pretty careful and I never felt worried shooting with him.

Visits to friends were often returned and the main interest in our home was my brother's and my good quality Joe Davis quarter-size (six foot by three foot) snooker/billiard table. We had received it as a Christmas present when I was about thirteen and for a couple of years it provided us with a considerable amount of entertainment and gave tremendous pleasure. Our living room temporarily became a sporting arena as some epic battles of nerve and skill were fought out on the green baize!

If I was honest my one big ambition in life was to go fishing. The snooker, drums, guitars, go-carts and guns were all very well but it was a fishing rod that I really longed for. Unfortunately none of my school friends were interested in angling. There had only ever been one lad at school who I knew was interested, Frank Greenfield, and he was a bit older than me. Apart from travelling to school on the same bus I unfortunately had very little to do with him. On one occasion he gave me two small hooks tied to short lengths of nylon and although completely useless on their own they were one of my most treasured and prized possessions. I would sometimes build fishing rods out of pieces of bamboo cane with wooden bobbins used as reels but I never actually got to try any of these minor works of art out. They were usually quite fragile constructions and would probably have been useless, but in my chagrin I could imagine that they were the real thing, just like I had seen in shop windows. Angling was a dream and if those concerned with my upbringing and welfare had their way it would remain so. The school librarian however, Mrs Hill, found me as many books on angling as she could which helped to satisfy my interest. On one occasion she even arranged for me to join a small party of pupils selected to visit the local library to choose books for loan to the school and I was able to commandeer everything they had covering the subject.

Mrs Hill was another superb teacher who privately helped a lot of pupils. She was an extremely understanding and well-balanced person, on whom you could certainly count for support if you were trying to improve yourself. The Branch College of Commerce in Leeds had recently started admitting handicapped students provided they were reasonably intelligent and able to cope with the college facilities. I was determined not to languish at Potternewton until I was sixteen and this seemed like a good move to me. Entry was by examination and Mrs Hill formulated a programme of study and helped me along the way with advice. This was work which she did unofficially in her own time, an inspiring gesture in itself. She had the ability to treat teenagers as young adults and was a truly wonderful woman.

A school draughts tournament was inaugurated and I won the cup together with a small cash prize the first time it was played for. I won it again the third time and thereafter was not permitted to enter the competition but was allowed to play the winner in a special challenge. Once I had finally managed to beat my invincible father at the game I never looked back. I had tried to play chess but I did not enjoy it; draughts was my game. My strength lay in being able to focus my attention on one course of action at once and excluding all else from my mind. So long as I considered the goal worthwhile simplicity of a task neither bored me nor induced complacency, in fact I rather enjoyed giving continuous application to jobs others may well have considered unworthy of such dedication, so long as I felt the ultimate conclusion was satisfactory reward. In truth, if I was going to undertake a course of action of my own free will then I was going to perform to the best of my ability and absolute capacity. There was little point, otherwise, in ever becoming involved in the first place.

The shadow of my operations and further surgery still loomed over me. The one I had recently undergone on my left ankle could hardly be described as successful. Yes, my heel now touched the ground, but my ankle was so weak that it was of little real use. I could stand on it and brace it to kick a football, and that was about all. If it was knocked it immediately swelled up and this caused me many problems. There was no easy solution but I was determined that I was not going to let it stop me doing the things I wanted to do. I wanted to take part in real sport, football and cricket, not just play draughts and other non-physical pastimes. All I could do was battle on regardless of the apparent hopelessness of the situation and what others thought. Every time it swelled up I treated the swelling and then when it went down continued as normal until it swelled up again. My mother used to buy dried poppy heads and these were scalded with boiling water and the swollen part held over the steam. I do not know if they actually did any good but the swelling always went.

At school rumours were rife that they were about to start performing on arms the same operations that I had had done on my legs, and I lived in fear of being the human guinea pig for this little experiment. It had taken the authorities nearly two years from the time of my first operation until they had struck again. In another two years, with a bit of luck and some hard work, I would hopefully be about ready to leave school. Surely they would not pursue me against my will into adulthood? Their limits of power must end somewhere? I was taking no chances and kept as low a profile as possible for this period, head well below the level of the trenches. I would eventually be free of the shackles of childhood, although I had by now already paid a considerable price and the physical so-called benefits were wholly irreversible. There had to be mental scars also but the destiny of those was at least within my own determination. There was only one person who could do anything about healing them and that was myself.

Mr Hyatt now took the most senior class and he brought new ideas to the school. Fretwork and toy-making, printing, classical literature and concern for animal welfare. Woodwork lessons had now been transferred to Elmete Hall, a nearby school for the deaf and related problems, and had lost some of their former appeal when under the auspices of Mr Duxbury at Potternewton. One bench and set of basic tools had been retained and this was now situated within our classroom. A 'Hobbies' treadle fretsaw machine had been obtained and some pupils found this useful. Personally I preferred to use a hand saw although the machine could cope much better with the thicker pieces of wood and was not quite so prone to breaking blades. We made various children's toys, one of which I remember particularly well was a doll's cot, from start to finish.

The printing was done on an Adana hand-levered press and we were able to produce small certificates, cards and tickets for school events. It was great fun setting up the type, clamping it into the holder and then seeing the finished result. We were working with a semi-professional machine and this gave us a degree of mental stimulus.

Another subject which I found illuminating was classical literature. This came in the form of studying and memorizing extracts from Shakespeare. More modern works such as *The Autobiography of a Super-Tramp* were also read and analysed in detail. For me *Macbeth* was the highlight and even with the passage of time I still remember the words I learnt.

Animal welfare came as a new subject. Many of us were already animal owners and interested in their care and well-being. Now we were encouraged to join the RSPCA and take the monthly magazine. An officer from the organization came to the school and gave us a talk on the general care of pets and the aims and structure of the society. Mr Hyatt was a strict vegetarian and sometimes the class would discuss the moral dilemma and necessity of eating meat and the alternatives. Perhaps one could live a much healthier life on a meat-free diet and not be the instigator of inhumane treatment to domesticated animals?

I suffered from several minor ailments and decided that I would give up eating meat to see if this had any effect on the symptoms I was experiencing. I also had to come to terms with the dilemma of eating the animals which graced the countryside. My action met with strong disapproval at home but in general I felt much better for the abstention. It was about two years before I came to terms with the idea of eating meat again and I gradually returned to it. In retrospect I am glad that I made the conscious decision to understand why I eat animal flesh and I also know that I can live perfectly well without it. Incidentally, the symptoms of my ailments did not recur on my reversion from vegetarianism. The food we eat must play a large part in our state of health and this is something which I have always considered to be of the utmost importance in the way I live.

The school had a tank of tropical fish and in my final year I was delighted to be appointed responsible for its maintenance and upkeep. I was also installed as a prefect and subsequently became head boy. These were jobs which I felt should be done in as unauthoritative a manner as possible. In my view previous incumbents had often been guilty of over-zealousness and even abusing their position.

Sport at school now consisted of playing football with a tennis ball in the playground. In summer we sometimes played cricket and this was the first sport I followed publicly. One of the school's physiotherapists, Mr Lewis, was also physio to the touring team from Pakistan when they played at Headingley and he managed to get those pupils interested in attending the Test Match admitted free. This was my introduction to watching professional competitive sport and my brother and I subsequently enjoyed some good days out.

There was an air of excitement each time a pupil left school to take up employment. Visits to prospective employers were arranged and one afternoon several of us went to Heatons, a local furriers. Conditions were reasonable and the work appeared interesting. My best friend, Robert McLellan, decided that the fur trade would suit him and applied for a job. He was successful and soon took up his appointment. Potternewton Mansion School had an excellent record for finding those capable of work gainful and satisfying employment and perhaps for this reason alone it must be considered a very successful establishment. Mr Pagdin did his level best to bring maturity and a sense of responsibility to his older pupils encouraging them in every way he could, treating those who responded positively as adults and equals to himself. No praise is too high for the firm open attitude he adopted and what he ultimately achieved in the personal development of individuals.

With the help of Mrs Hill my progress towards gaining entry to the Branch College of Commerce was coming along nicely. I sat the entrance examination and was accepted. I would have much preferred to have been a carpenter, an electrician or a gardener but such vocations were obviously beyond my physical capabilities and I was realistic about this. I knew several physically fit people who wanted to be policemen and firemen but did not measure up to the required height or physique. I looked at my situation in a similar light. I had to be practical about seeking work and I was in any case inclined towards education and learning. I was not very tall for my age – under five feet – and I was not very heavy either. In July 1963, a month before my fifteenth birthday, I left Potternewton Mansion School and was ready to make my way in the big wide world. I was on my way to the Branch College of Commerce but was still a little uncertain of what the word commerce actually meant. I would soon find out that and a lot more!

For the first time in my life I was actually going to do something which I really wanted to do. Though a little apprehensive as to just exactly what lay ahead, I at least knew that I was totally committed to the situation and determined to succeed. My future was at last under my own control, a moment I had long been waiting for. It was not going to slip by or fizzle out; I had endured too much to lose this one. Those who doubted my ability were about to learn otherwise. I would make every second count and, having given my best, would be satisfied that I could have done no more. Society would know that I was now an integral, competitive and successful part of it. I had reached the watershed of life and was about to journey forth with enthusiasm towards the great plains which lay ahead.

SEVEN

Headfirst into Society

Leaving Potternewton was tinged with a certain sadness. Not only was I going into the unknown but I was also leaving behind all that I knew. My relationship with the headmaster and some of the other staff was like that of personal friends. I had worked my way through the ranks and now commanded the respect of the majority of those in charge. Most of my contemporaries, being a little older than myself, had left; others had died or were now extremely frail and doing well just to cling on to the little remaining life they had. I was left with only a few friends at the school and the time was obviously right for me to go.

Some had their doubts as to how well I would cope integrated with mainstream education, but furthering my education was a prospect which I relished greatly and I had no fears whatsoever. I knew that dedication and a willingness to work will always triumph in the end. I wondered whether or not I would have any unnecessary trouble from fellow students but there was only one way to find out. I had my parents' full backing on this venture. My father would support me at college for as long as I wished to stay as long as I kept achieving satisfactory examination results. He maintained that ultimately I would reap the benefit from whatever studies I chose to undertake. It was good to know that I was never under any sort of pressure from home either to do exceptionally well or leave before I decided that the time was right.

Going to college was a big adventure: I had to catch two buses to get there and back. I felt quite competent at travelling alone on the public transport system but wondered how I would manage to carry my text books and work. This feat did pose a problem but somehow I managed and as time went by it became less of a difficulty as my strength and adeptness improved.

The classroom atmosphere that first morning did not fill me with confidence. The lecturers were strict on discipline and obviously expected results. Incompetence was not tolerated. Previously my classes had always covered the full spectrum of ability, but now

I was a member of a supposedly élite group of students who would all leave the college qualified in the subjects being studied, principally Commerce, Accounting, English and Arithmetic. As far as education went I came bottom in the class hierarchy.

My initiation into mainstream society was both a rapid and alarming experience, but I had no serious worries about my initial status or my future performance. As far as I was concerned my position in the hierarchy was only a temporary one, unless, of course, as was most unlikely, I was in a class of geniuses. I was being given my first educational break in life whereas many of these had already wasted the opportunities which had as a matter of course come their way. To me this fact stood out a mile, and I was going to perform to the best of my ability – something which if the others had done previously would have eliminated their need to be on such a course. It was a mixed class and in fairness many of the girls were studying to become secretaries, their main subjects being Shorthand and Typing, but of the lads an alarming proportion were either failures being given a last chance or foolish boys delaying the inevitable day when they would have to start work.

My main problem was that by appearing to be the weakest member of the group I attracted the attention of those who were actually the weakest. In an effort to draw attention away from themselves such people have to try and make someone else look worse than they are. With my physical disability and general lack of education I was an obvious target. On this occasion they had got it wrong. If they wished to pick on me physically there was very little I could do, but this was a College of Commerce not Physical Education and in the end it was what qualifications you left with that really mattered.

It was only a matter of two or three weeks before I had caught up with the other students and was soon a contender for one of the top five positions. Examinations held no fear for me as I knew that you just had to do your best and be satisfied with the result achieved. Things could go wrong on the day but there was little point in worrying about this until it actually happened. If you had applied yourself conscientiously you would realize your potential, whatever level that was, and you could do no more. It really was as simple as that. Anything less than your best and you were cheating yourself.

I thoroughly enjoyed most of the classes but the disruptive and careless attitude of a number of fellow students saddened me greatly. It was not something I had ever had to deal with before. Was this really the way society worked? Was this – battling against this type of behaviour – the way the rest of my life would have to be lived? If these people were normal and I was supposedly abnormal then all in all I could consider myself fortunate being born with cerebral palsy.

I did not allow my colleagues' attitude to affect my performance. By the end of the first term I finished fourth overall out of a class of twenty-four students and at the end of the year fifth. This was nothing short of a miracle considering that I did not have the manual dexterity to compete with the other students at typing. Throughout the year I had also maintained a 100 per cent attendance record, being in class the full 720½ prescribed hours. Our course tutors, Messrs D. Naylor and T. D. Kilburn, were a pair of very able lecturers who both knew their subjects inside out and commanded the respect of everyone associated with them. On completion of the year-long course, when RSA stage I examinations were taken, those students who had performed reasonably well were invited to apply for admission to a further twelve-month course which would culminate in the sitting of GCE 'O' levels. My aim was to become as well educated as I possibly could so I made every effort to get on this course and was readily accepted, so I began a further year's study.

That year was blighted for a while when I became the target of abuse by a small section of the students, partly because of my serious attitude towards learning and partly because of my disability, or so I assume. I say the latter because had I been physically strong these weak people would not have dared single me out as a target for their loutish behaviour. Their actions were so persistent and upsetting that they were pushing me towards a nervous breakdown and I seriously contemplated leaving the college and looking for a job. Finally, when my personal possessions were defaced by vindictive comments about my disability I decided that enough was enough and made an official complaint. The offender on this occasion, who incidentally was simply an overgrown, over-indulged child, was warned as to his future conduct and the trouble subsided. The strained atmosphere that remained between this person and myself I could cope with.

Throughout this very difficult period only the emotional support of my father had kept me going. As a schoolboy he had been confronted by the school bully, stood his ground and won. He understood the pressure I was suffering. Although I was emotionally fragile and a physical weakling I hoped that I had inherited my father's calm and resolve. He was my one and only hero in life, and some day I wanted to be just like him (minus his self-confessed bad habits!). I felt that if I could apply his strength of character and physical ability to my objectives, dedication and intelligence there was no telling what life had in store for me. I needed to learn how to take the knocks and bounce back even stronger than before. Somehow I had to acquire my father's spirit and inner strength.

The vandalizing incident could have been the final straw had my father not supported me in every way he could. My problem was that faced with such lunatic behaviour one half of me frankly said 'Kill. Get in there and eliminate the cause', while the other half of me was saying that maybe such a measure was a bit drastic . . . and definitely against the law! I may have been emotionally soft but it was as much a worldly naïvety as personal weakness. I could deal with people who were answerable for their behaviour but childishness was another thing altogether. As the year drew to a close I gave serious consideration to my future. I decided that I needed to broaden my education by moving to another college and filling in on the other subjects which I had missed by not attending a normal school. Enquiries showed that the Branch College of Engineering and Science, also near the city centre, ran courses covering the next batch of GCE 'O' levels I wished to pursue. I fixed myself up with an interview, confident that I would be accepted. I may have been a late starter but in the last two years I had proved my ability to learn, complete courses and pass examinations. As I saw it I now had a track record and would be allowed to progress until such time as I felt that I had gone far enough or my results disappointed. The college, however, did not see it this way. The first question I was asked at the interview was which school had I attended, and on giving my reply I was immediately informed that I was an unacceptable candidate as this did not meet with the college's requirements. I questioned such instant judgment in view of my record since leaving Potternewton but was dismissed as wasting the institution's time and asked to leave. If I had passed with a first class notation RSA stage II Commercial Arithmetic why could I not broaden this to GCE 'O' level Mathematics? On being shown the door I realized that the decision was final and, somewhat disillusioned, I left.

My dreams for the future lay in ruins. I had hoped that I would eventually pass perhaps nine or ten GCE 'O' levels in all, progress to 'A' levels and ultimately gain entry to university. Now starkly aware that this was not to be I decided that I would find a job, start work and continue to study at night school and maybe through day release classes also if I was lucky. The thing that grieved me most was that I had not failed in anything that I had taken and yet

I was being turned away while others whom I knew to have failed were being given a second chance. I could have found alternative courses to take had I wished but none would have led me immediately in the direction I wanted to go and would have been, at least in part, a waste of time. That was not my style. I needed to know exactly where I was going.

So the door had been slammed in my face and, if I wished to proceed, I would have to find another. I was coming up to my seventeenth birthday and while I knew that my father would support whatever decision I made I was also well aware that time was not on my side as far as continuing in full time education was concerned, but I had no real idea what I wanted to do workwise, mainly due to the fact that I had set my heart on being an accountant. If I had been successful at university I would also have considered becoming a schoolteacher or college lecturer but these were avenues no longer open to me. I had to be realistic in my approach to getting work and, perhaps against my better judgment, decided to follow the Careers Advice Officer's lead.

He arranged for me to attend an interview with British Rail and I got the job subject to the statutory completion of a medical examination. Apart from my obvious disability I was physically A1 and healthy. The BR Medical Officer confirmed this and a starting date of 6 September 1965 was agreed. Once again I was not particularly looking forward to the great transition about to take place in my life but the decision had been consciously made by me and it had to be faced.

EIGHT

Gone Fishing

The year 1963 had seen one major turning point in my life – my integration into mainstream education as I left Potternewton and went to the Branch College of Commerce. But of equal – perhaps even greater – importance was the second turning point, sparked off by the events of that Christmas 1963.

I had many hobbies and these were centred around the home. Physically, since my operations, I had had to accept that I was not up to many of the outdoor activities participated in by my brother and friends. I did join them when possible, but there came a level beyond which I was unable to keep up with them. However, my mobility and confidence in gradually extending personal limitations increased greatly after I began attending college. Travelling daily to and from the city centre by public transport, carrying my books and work as I went, was in effect putting me through a rigorous training schedule. I was gaining in strength and getting fitter by the week. The prospect of broadening the activities I could pursue was also increasing with each step of progress made. I was now fifteen years old and certain that I was ready to make my own decisions regarding my physical abilities and what I did with my spare time. I accepted that some things were dangerous and others even out of the question but, as far as I was concerned, what I wanted to do did not come under either of these categories. I desperately wanted to go fishing.

From the earliest days of my childhood I had been fascinated by water and thought of the fish which may be living within the depths. This fascination, I suppose, is a basic human instinct, as is the case with fire. There is a certain soothing quality about water, even when it is rushing; it gives a sense of continuity and ceaseless energy, responding predictably to given circumstances but never completely under control. To complete the captivation all that is needed is the elusive and fascinating qualities of fish and the symbiotic balance of nature. A perfect recipe for total mental absorption.

For many years my ambition had been to take up angling. I had read every book I could find on the subject, but my parents were less than keen on the idea, for water is also dangerous. To add to my frustration my father would sometimes recall with obvious happiness his own angling days, which had apparently been curtailed when he was called up to the armed forces and then married. While on our annual fortnight's holiday to the East Coast of Yorkshire I had been sea fishing twice. The first occasion was from Filey Brigg with a handline, although it was more a case of watching my father, and the second was from a boat in Bridlington Bay. On both outings I remember a distinct lack of fish but my enthusiasm was not dampened by such a trivial detail. However, deep down I knew that it was not really sea fishing which interested me but more the gentle art of fresh-water coarse angling. There was something not quite right and too final about killing the fish caught. If it was the pursuit and participation which really brought the enjoyment, then putting the creatures back to fight another day was a more satisfactory and forward-looking conclusion. Besides, we did not live near the coast but there were many fresh waters within reasonable travelling distance of home.

My brother had his fourteenth birthday just before the Christmas and my parents felt, quite rightly, that it was time to get him interested in fishing. For Christmas he was given a complete fishing outfit while I received some tools with which to pursue my interest in woodwork. They had obviously not anticipated the intensity with which I would react. Here they were encouraging him to do the only thing which I really wanted to do when he did not have the same enthusiasm as I, while I was being discouraged from doing it. There comes a time in every adolescent's life when he realizes that there are limits to which parental control can be tolerated. And when he has been brought up to know what is right and what is wrong, he fights with all the courage of his convictions when he believes, without any shadow of doubt, that he is right.

Despite the fact that I had previously looked on with indifference as he received football outfits, a toboggan and various other activity equipment while I was kept interested in electric train sets and model-making, I found the situation now intolerable. Watching the fishing tackle repeatedly taken out of the box only to be carefully returned, as he periodically admired his new acquisition, was like some never-ending nightmare. In fairness I must admit that up to then I had often benefited from his activity equipment in the long term. I had played with his football and ridden his sledge whenever the opportunity had arisen, so perhaps the picture was not quite so black as it seemed. I also knew that he was on my side and that I could always rely on his support should I wish to challenge our parents.

The first Sunday in January he was away fishing on a nearby river with his friends and I was left at home wondering just what I had done to be placed in such a terrible position. I spent a lot of time studying at home to satisfy my thirst for knowledge, and I was therefore making very good progress at college but I was getting very little from life as a whole. My parents encouraged me and gave as much support as they were capable of but felt (especially my mother) that they could control what I did. They could not understand my need to pursue recreational activities of my choice. They did not keep nearly such a close eye on my brother's activities, but then he was physically fit and well. I was making every effort to live a normal life and was in fact in many ways achieving more success than he was. Why should I be singled out for special treatment? I knew what I wanted from life and I was not getting it. Nor could I be manipulated into believing that I was. The arguments I was having with my mother were increasing in intensity with each confrontation. She was pleased that I was doing well at college. Pleased that I had achieved some degree of independence physically, but she still wanted to dictate to me over very simple personal issues. Going fishing, as I saw it, was a very simple matter. It was similar to attending college except that you went to a stretch of water and you leisurely enjoyed yourself instead of sitting in a classroom. There really were no complications unless your imagination ran riot with itself.

The Sunday was thoroughly miserable. I went through absolute agony at being denied the simple pleasure of going fishing. I felt like I was being kicked when I was down and I intended to get back up and fight back, whatever the consequences. I was suffering and I was determined not to suffer alone. I made everyone else's life a misery. Why should I put everything into achieving what other people wanted me to achieve and not be able to do the things which would give me satisfaction and pleasure? Was there something wrong with wanting to go fishing? Life seemed so unfair and I had taken about as much of this unfairness as I was going to take. Something had to give and it was not going to be me.

So my mother and I were on a collision course. We were living on the edge of a very unstable emotional volcano and it was about to erupt. As a child I had been very close to her, perhaps closer than my brother and sister, but now I hated her and everything that she stood for. I had always held my father in great esteem, but now I had lost all respect for him too, for he supported her decisions.

I suppose that basically, the problems that I had with my parents were twofold. My mother was unable to accept the fact that I was quickly growing up, which is not too difficult to understand when you bear in mind that I was quite small for my age and that my physical condition had previously warranted some degree of protection from what could be a very cruel world. I was still only 4 feet 10 inches tall, although I continued to grow until I was about 20 or 21 eventually attaining a height of 5 feet 6 inches, and like most mothers it was difficult for her to let go.

My father's view of the situation was different. We were totally dissimilar in nature and he lacked faith in my ability to overcome the odds which were so heavily stacked against me. I believe he had serious doubts as to whether I would ever become self-supporting and was afraid of the day when he would no longer be around to look after me. I had ambitious plans and an optimistic outlook on the future, but he would constantly dismiss my ideas as impractical or impossible. As far as he was concerned I was living in a world of make-believe and parents do not like to see their children get hurt. In fact, because I lacked the normal masculine stature he probably thought that I was and possibly always would be a complete physical nonentity. I gave him plenty of reasons for adopting the attitude he did, for I was physically soft and at times I must have appeared emotionally very weak. I was an extremely sparing and choosy eater. He had carried me around for most of my life and picked me up or helped me whenever I fell or came up against any obstacles. Why should he reason any differently from the way he did? Besides, his first loyalties were to my mother and he did not want to see her getting distressed over me.

Weakling or not, however, I was determined that I was going fishing and, by the following weekend, after much heartache for everyone concerned, my parents had relented, on the understanding that various conditions were met; my brother had enough fishing tackle for the two of us and he was to look after me; if there were any difficulties then I would not be allowed to go again. This was just the opening I needed and I was absolutely certain of one thing. There would be no difficulties, at least as far as they were concerned. I was going fishing and this was to be my new beginning. I was at last about to enjoy the simple pleasures of being alive.

It is one thing reading about a subject, quite another putting the theory into practice, especially where considerable skill is involved. To begin with I was frightened of maggots, and neither was I keen on the idea of handling worms, but these fears had to be overcome before I could even get started. I had to take the plunge and get stuck in.

There were a lot of preparations to be made: where to go; what times did the buses run; what to wear for a day sitting on a riverbank in January; what should we take to eat and how would we fish. No detail was too small to be considered. The suspense and anticipation all added to the excitement, in fact in those early days it was probably more important than the fishing itself! I recollect that the weather that winter was kind and we went to the River Wharfe at Collingham, near Wetherby, every Sunday until the season closed at the end of February.

You have to be very keen to keep going at that time of the year. In all those weeks neither of us had so much as a bite, never mind a fish. But for that matter I cannot remember anyone else catching one either! For me the way to the river was strewn with obstacles. First I had to climb over a wall, then cross a field and negotiate a rather awkward stile before walking a little further to the riverbank. Having got there I then had to find a reasonable spot from which to fish. The water level fluctuated according to the weather and riverbanks can be muddy and slippery places at the best of times. It also goes without saying that the water was constantly waiting, cold and merciless, to punish any mistakes. We persevered with Collingham in the knowledge that we knew we could manage, and that no further major planning was required. However I was on the lookout for different venues, possibly where the fish would be not quite so elusive.

I enjoyed those first weeks immensely, although I spent most of the time untangling line and trying to keep warm. The tangled line problem is one which is best sorted out, without interference from anyone else, by the individual responsible. It is only through making mistakes and dealing with the consequences that the skill to do it right is acquired, and fishing is very much a lone pastime; one man, a rod and line. In angling terms things were not going too well for us, but since the experience as a whole was rewarding, time was not being wasted. Surely we would eventually start to catch fish? There were plenty of people around telling stories about those they had caught, or the ones that had got away. I think my brother would have given up had it not been for the pressure he was under from me to continue our weekly outings.

The trout season opened in mid-March and we started once again at Collingham. Then I heard of a good spot on the River Nidd at Knaresborough and in early April, at a little extra expense, we decided to venture a bit further afield and give it a try. The walk from the bus was along a lane and the bank was extremely easy compared with that which we had previously encountered. The water was pleasant, flowing very gently. Around midday I caught my first fish, a dace approximately ten inches in length. My heart pounded as I carefully played it in. I had never handled a fish before and the flapping frightened me as shakily I unhooked it and returned it to the river. Knaresborough, we decided, was the place to be and we returned the following Saturday. I fished from the same spot and caught a trout about twelve inches long. I returned it to the water where it lay momentarily dazed as it regained its balance before disappearing with one flick of its sturdy tail back to where it belonged. Life had never seemed so good. After the long dark, cold and often gloomy winter months there is nothing finer than to be out in the fresh and clear bracing April air and at peace with the world.

I now had my own fishing tackle and each new piece of equipment helped to bring my dream to fruition. After the first couple of outings back in January I had sold my electric train set and part of my stamp collection in order to purchase my own equipment. My outfit consisted of a fixed spool reel and a 10 foot 6 inch split-cane rod which, at that time, suited my needs perfectly. All good rods were made of split cane, hollow glass having only recently appeared on the market. With the use of my woodworking tools I made my own box which turned out to be a bit on the large side for my requirements and was very awkward to carry. However, I learned from my mistakes and I soon produced an improved version which I have continued to use until today.

Many a happy hour was spent at home making floats, tying hooks, renovating worn-out items and generally producing anything which might be of use on the riverbank. There are many different techniques involved in angling and methods were not quite so refined in those days as they are today. There was room for ingenuity and it all added to the pleasure if you caught fish with the help of some homemade piece of equipment. There were trips to be planned, new waters to be found and, like most sports, lots to be talked about.

My skill in handling a rod and line was improving and, with each fish caught, my confidence grew. It was now not so much a case of whether or not fish would be caught, but how many and of what species. Dace and trout were the most common, followed by chub and grayling. A visit to a lake produced roach and perch. The suspense of hooking and then playing a fish, not knowing what it was until it was ready for the net, was tremendously exciting and comparatively small fish, if hooked in fast-flowing water or at long range, were capable of giving a worthy account of themselves.

By the Whitsun holiday fishing had become a serious business and was now playing a large part in my life. My parents accepted that it was here to stay and, as long as I could be seen to be taking care, they put no pressure on me to give it up. In the early days the fact that we were not catching fish had often been used as a reason why I was foolish to want to waste my time going, but that was now all in the past. In fact I think they were beginning to see the benefit I was deriving from it. My brother and I wanted to be fishing as often as possible, and the main restriction was financial. The logical answer was to buy a tent and extend our visits over several days for a not much greater outlay.

For almost as long as I had wanted to fish, I had harboured a strong desire to go camping. There seemed something so very real and right in synchronizing with the wild and living next to nature. Was it the removal of constraints, independence, freedom, sense of timelessness, or perhaps even the feeling of inner peace? I did not exactly know what it was but I knew that I wanted it. Remembering my delight at my first night under canvas as a cub, throughout the long warm summer weeks I had set my sights on it as my ultimate goal. The idea of looking after myself and being responsible for my own actions and well-being really appealed to me. Surely this was what life was all about? And the fishing would usefully fill in the time by an exciting and enjoyable means!

Our parents' resistance was minimal, their main argument being that it would be rather uncomfortable and perhaps I would not be up to such a hard way of life. I cannot remember how we raised the money but our first tent cost 35/- (£1.75). It was a simple white canvas ridge tent measuring 6 feet × 4 feet × 3 feet with 6-inch walls. I suppose it was little more than a children's play tent, but with the addition of a rubberized canvas groundsheet it became our mobile home. We cooked on a tin-can-type methylated spirit stove. The tent had no fly sheet nor was capable of taking one, should our finances ever permit, so when it rained we had to be very careful not to touch the inside of the material. Our equipment was completed with the purchase of two kapok-filled sleeping bags. We were fully equipped for about £4 and ready to go.

The fishing at Knaresborough adjoined a camp site, which I think must have given us the idea to combine the two in the first place, and this was where we went. Our parents were right. Life in our tent was hard, but never miserable, rather an exciting adventure and (in our opinion!) a fight for survival. Through the night our fishing tackle had to stand outside the tent under whatever protection we could afford it. The nights were often very damp even inside the tent and I am surprised the bends of my walking stick handles did not begin to straighten out. On our first week that Whitsuntide we developed routines which made life run smoothly. I did all the cooking and organized the food, and my brother did the washing up and looked after the equipment. Our team effort worked very well and to our mutual satisfaction. Whatever the weather – and it snowed the following Easter – we always stayed the full duration of our holiday.

I had not thought match fishing practical in my circumstances, but while waiting in a bus station on our way home one day, we began talking to a fellow angler and he invited us to join the Farnley Loco Angling Club. They fished about eight matches a year and were a reasonably friendly bunch. The big attraction to us was that they hired a coach and went to waters which we could only read about. Despite the possible extra cost, it was too good an opportunity to be missed and we joined. They really looked after me. They helped carry my tackle and I was always given the option of having the first peg, which I usually took, not wishing to walk any further than was absolutely necessary.

The first match was at Hunters Lodge on the River Ouse and I finished third with a catch of two small fish, a bleak and a roach. They weighed 3½ ounces and I was helped by the fact that most of the other competitors failed to catch a fish at all. Later in the season on the club's annual match, fished at Rillington on the River Derwent, I finished second, runner-up to my brother who did not normally do so well. We both produced good weights of gudgeon and roach and he beat me by about four ounces.

During the summer I was fishing in a match at Beningborough on the River Ouse when it began to rain and then thunder and lightning. Suddenly, and without warning, a crack appeared in the bank behind me and I was stranded on a small island which was rapidly disappearing into the river. I was fishing on the bottom at a depth of about twelve feet and I was, therefore, horrified at the prospect of what was about to happen. The island slipped further and then collapsed, launching me headlong into the river. Since my operations I could no longer swim although I was not afraid of actually going underwater, so long as I knew that I could put my feet on the bottom and stand up if I so wished.

I floated while my wellington boots slowly filled with water and then the weight from them dragged me feet-first towards the riverbed. It seemed like an eternity as I descended into the murky depths of the river, and I thought, 'Well, this is it.' For some unknown reason, however, I did not panic but was completely calm, accepting what I thought was the inevitable as if it did not really matter. I felt my feet touch the bottom and I crouched before pushing upwards with all the strength and air I had left. Much to my amazement I started to ascend through the warm water. I surfaced, a voice shouted, 'Thank God' and, as I splashed my way towards the bank, a hand very quickly grabbed me before I had time to go under again.

I have never been so relieved in my life and I do not think that the chap at next peg, who had saved me, had either. He said that I had been under for such a long time that he had almost given up hope of ever seeing me alive again. I had been very lucky, and the fact that the water was warm had contributed considerably to my survival. Unsurprisingly, I retired from the match. Fortunately the farmer whose land we were on had some old clothes, which I believe he had put to one side for a scarecrow, and he lent them to me. To complete the day (and make me the envy of my fellow anglers, most of whom had not caught anything and were almost as wet as I had been), three young ladies took pity on me and invited me to their nearby caravan for refreshment and to get dried and changed while the match ended.

My mother was horrified when I explained the reason for the wet clothes and my tramp-like appearance, and put an immediate stop to my fishing. My father, however, intervened, saying that if I could not do what I wanted to with my life – and going fishing was not an unreasonable expectation – then I might as well not be alive anyway. He had by now realized I *could* cope. She reluctantly accepted his philosophy and never again challenged my right to make my own decisions. She still tried to persuade me not to undertake certain activities, but she left the final reckoning to me. Our truce became less and less uneasy. I had nearly lost my life, and through no particular fault of my own, but indirectly some good had come of it. My life might be my own but I was now acutely aware of how easily it could come to an accidental and premature end.

In the late autumn, following a severe overnight frost, I won my first match at Spennithorne on the River Ure and I was the only competitor to catch a fish, a twelve-ounce perch. I won another match after that and was placed in several more. Competing, and on equal terms, helped to give me self-respect and I always enjoyed the prospect of arriving at some water that I had never fished before intent on doing my best against other, often highly respected, anglers. That is what sport is all about; there is no guarantee that even the best will catch fish every time, and they are there to be beaten.

By the summer of 1965 as I was finishing my time at college camping and fishing had become a way of life. During the Whitsuntide holiday, while camping at Knaresborough, I was blown on to a barbed wire fence by strong winds and almost severed the thumb from my left hand. Fortunately my brother managed to find the farmer fairly quickly and he rushed me to Harrogate hospital where they were able to repair the wound and prevent infection. Luckily I escaped without any permanent damage.

Back home accidents of this nature were no reason for a crisis; at the age of seven my hand had become impaled on a nail protruding from the underside of a table and at twelve I had fallen on a garden rake and two of the prongs had deeply penetrated my knee. There was no cause for alarm, I had suffered as many cuts and bruises as any child: I had once been knocked down by a bicycle on a newly gravelled road, another time I had fallen down the stairs and through a window of the front door. Accidents were a fact of life and were just as, if not more, likely to occur at home than while I was out.

My ambition now was to catch a barbel and aim for larger fish. I was inspired weekly by Dick Walker's column in the *Angling Times* and he, together with fellow columnist Fred Taylor, always gave me plenty to think about. They were anglers with the true spirit of the game. Everyone needs heroes. As a child mine had been my father but now I had my share in most of the activities I followed. They provided me with goals to be aimed for, standards to be achieved and rules to be played by. Even though I may never attain the same degree of skill or proficiency I could still apply the qualities which helped them become outstanding in their chosen field.

So with barbel and larger fish in mind we went to Topcliffe on the River Swale for our annual holiday, the last two weeks in July. We had bought a slightly larger tent, six inches longer, wider and higher than the previous one and it had nine-inch walls. A few days before we were due to leave my father bought us a fly sheet for added protection. The tent was made of a heavily waxed green canvas and was so stiff that any creases were almost permanent. Our old white tent, which had given much faithful service, was also taken along to house the stores and equipment. We had by this time invested in a gas stove: camping in luxury!

Topcliffe was further than we had previously travelled alone on public transport and we would probably have had considerable difficulty in getting there with all the camping equipment and fishing tackle had not my mother's sister and her husband, Madge and Cyril Godley, offered to transport us in their car, and return to collect us two weeks later. We arrived at Topcliffe in the middle of the horse fair and men were running horses up and down the main street. The Angel Hotel had fishing rights on a good length of the river and we were granted permission to camp in the orchard at the rear of the pub and fish the river. The hotel was owned and run by the Siggsworth family, two elderly sisters, one wheelchair-bound, and their brother. They admired our adventurous spirit and determination and we were allowed to camp and fish for a nominal charge, which to our surprise they returned to us at the end of our stay, when we were also invited to return free of charge at any time.

The holiday was a sheer delight. I caught four barbel among many more fish. The shoals of dace were obliging and I returned a catch of sixty fish in approximately one hour one morning before changing tactics and going in pursuit of the larger quarry. We spent a day in nearby Thirsk, a day fishing the Cod Beck, my first experience of small-stream fishing, and, on another day, met our parents in Scarborough, where they took us for a good meal. Life was still carefree and innocent and summer days were there to be enjoyed. I had wished to take full advantage of my last long holiday before I started work in September 1965 at the District Engineer's office of British Rail.

Although I had spent two years at college I was naïve about what 'going out to work' involved, about the complicated ways of working adults, the games people played in their everyday struggle for power or survival. I believed that one simply went to work to do a job to the best of one's ability. Work hard and be honest and truthful in dealing with others and you would eventually be rewarded by the fruits of your labour. Yes, I most certainly did have a lot to learn. There was also the matter of the well-known corporate theory which said that anyone who pushed hard enough would likely be promoted to one level higher than that at which they could efficiently perform. I was determined from the onset that this would never happen to me. How could it if you were straightforward in your dealings? What sort of conscience could live with such a situation? Definitely not mine. That was for sure.

The office, furniture, equipment and systems at British Rail were antiquated. In fact the whole set-up appeared to have changed very little since its foundation. The staff all had their private piece of territory both physically and jobwise and woe betide anyone who intruded on it. This made life as a newcomer extremely frustrating. The only good thing was that at the end of the week you were paid; in my case the sum of £5.12s. (£5.60). Those with five GCE 'O' levels including English Language and Mathematics moved, I believe, three points along the increment scale which amounted to roughly another £3 per week. Day release was given to attend further education in approved subjects and I quickly enrolled at the college which I had just left for 'O' level Mathematics in order to qualify for this hefty pay increase. Another benefit was the free travel – five free tickets a year – and the cheap fare employees pass for general use.

The following spring, with our finances improved, my brother and I bought a much larger modern ridge tent complete with sewn-in ground sheet and integral extending flysheet. The only problem was that, at twenty-three pounds, it was on the heavy and bulky side. However, we now had rucksacks and my brother was a big strong lad and well able to carry it, together with most of the other heavier items of equipment. I carried the lighter items as these were all I could manage. At Whitsuntide we ventured to Topcliffe, using public transport, for a trial run. It was a success except for the fact that while we slept on the first night, mice chewed a hole through the tent in order to get to our food supplies, one problem which we had not previously encountered.

I was now becoming enthralled by the adventure of travel and for our summer holiday we headed west to Ireland where the fishing was reputedly first-class. We travelled by rail, of course, taking the train from Leeds to Holyhead then the ferry to Dun Laoghaire, where we had to spend our first night alone in a waiting room on Dublin Railway Station. They normally turn everyone out at night since there are no trains and the station is closed but, to our relief, they made an exception in our case. We had arrived in Ireland with only £20 each and a guidebook to the country's fishing. Our destination was wherever we could reach by local transport. We worried about today, thought about tomorrow and gave little concern to the days thereafter; travel at its best.

In Ireland the carriage doors of trains were locked by guards between destinations and we arrived at Mullingar to find that the platform was built on a curve and the doors at either end of the carriage not only were locked but were also some distance from the platform itself. This could only happen in Ireland. We panicked but eventually a guard arrived and opened a door. I disembarked with a quick prayer and a hopeful leap.

We had chosen a lake renowned for its carp and tench fishing near Mullingar, which is midway across country directly west of

Dublin. The lake was a mass of weed and holes had to be dragged with a rake head attached to a length of rope before we could get started. We had never caught carp or tench or for that matter dragged holes in weed before. The places we normally fished were all popular haunts. The early morning tench fishing was superb and the only pity was that you had to use a stout rod with a heavy line and heave like mad when you hooked a fish in order to keep it from the surrounding weed. It was unbelievable. The bites were positive and we never caught a fish under $2\frac{1}{2}$ pounds on the two mornings we fished. The only problem was that the weather was very hot and by mid-morning there were swarms of large flies pestering us, some of the largest we had ever seen before or since. For the remainder of the day we had to take refuge in the tent. We could see the large carp basking in the sun but fishing for them with so much weed would have been futile. We contented ourselves with just observing their majestic beauty at such close quarters. We had never seen fish like this before, and in such a small water.

The lake was in the grounds of a large house some way from the town and, apart from fishing, there were few other diversions. We decided to move on to Athlone and called a taxi to take us back to the railway station.

We used taxis regularly as most of the places we wished to visit were not accessible by any other form of public transport. We were always careful to obtain an estimate of the cost in advance, although I think the drivers were very honest, and were definitely good at imparting their local knowledge. After a good meal in Athlone we went to Coosan Point on Lough Ree on the advice of the taxi driver. It was a remote place having only a public bar and boats for hire. Handling the small rowing boats on such a large expanse of water turned out to be more exciting than the fishing. We caught only small perch, but the bar with its draught Guinness and local people who sang, played the spoons and danced every evening, made up for whatever the fishing lacked.

We continued our journey westward to Ballinasloe, a small town on the River Suck, once again on the advice of our now regular taxi driver and at a very reasonable negotiated cost. Ballinasloe is a typical small Irish town, many of the shops having bars at the back where local men – and it was only men – would congregate each evening to watch the World Cup on television. The fishing was quite good and we caught small pike and bream. Our tent was pitched on a narrow strip of land between the end of a building and the riverbank. While we were erecting it we were not aware that we were sharing the field with a large carthorse. Suddenly there was the sound of galloping hooves and, as we looked up, we were horrified to see this great hulk of an animal heading towards us. It narrowly missed us before it turned around and came back, once again nearly taking the tent and us with it. This exercise continued until the owner, appreciating our predicament, removed the animal to another field.

As England progressed towards the final of the World Cup the weather was glorious and we journeyed back stopping at Hudson Bay, a small holiday resort on the Western shore of Lough Ree, for a few days' relaxation, since it was much too warm to bother about fishing. Within two days I was suffering with second-degree burns as a result of too much exposure to the rays of the sun, and the journey home was extremely painful as my body began to break out in blisters, then scab and bleed. We arrived home just in time to watch the World Cup Final on television and England's victory was a fitting climax to an exciting two weeks.

By the following year my brother was more interested in girls than in fishing and I was going off with other friends or alone, having now become reasonably proficient at coping with my fishing tackle on public transport. I fished with my next door neighbour and good friend, Robin Rogers, and with another friend who lived only a few houses away, Les Jones. That summer Les and I made another trip to Ireland, omitting only the stay at Mullingar – and the distinct possibility of giant flying insects – from our itinerary. The highlight of the holiday was undoubtedly a night fishing session for the monster bream of the River Suck at Ballinasloe where, incidentally, the horse was no longer in the same residence.

I had also become interested in photography and, with my first decent camera, was taking photographs of the places visited and some of the fish we caught.

By now I was not fishing quite so often and when I did it was usually alone. Being an employee of British Rail I travelled by train as often as possible where this was practical, and it was on a lone visit to Topcliffe that I finally conquered boredom. The journey involved catching a bus to Leeds, a train to Ripon and from there another bus to Topcliffe. The timing of the connections was tight but just possible and I made the trip several times without a hitch. Then one day, as I was returning home, I missed the train at Ripon by a matter of only a few seconds. I positioned my box on the platform and sat there fuming. The next train would be another three hours and I was in no mood to sit for three hours with nothing to do but keep my bottom free from cramp. I sat there and began to think. Why on earth should I let a three-hour wait worry me? True, I had eaten all my sandwiches and there were no facilities to purchase further refreshments on or anywhere near the station, but at least there was another train due that evening and the time would eventually pass. The more I could switch off from thinking about the time the quicker it would seem to pass, and there was never any doubt that it would pass. I developed a technique for slowing down my mind and just enjoying being alive. Since then I have never been bored, at least when alone.

I had other sporting interests; I was an ardent follower of Leeds United, even if I did not actually go to matches. I first went to Elland Road to see them play against Liverpool at Christmas 1965. The crowd limit at that time was probably in the region of 50,000 and the ground was full to capacity. I think that they must have allowed people in until the ground would hold no more, or that was how it seemed. I spent most of the match struggling to keep upright, saw very little of the game itself, and missed the only goal, by which Leeds lost. In fact to be honest, as I left the ground I was still unsure of the score or result. I might not have seen the game but I was impressed by the atmosphere and ready to give it another try at some future time, hopefully positioning myself in a much safer part of the ground.

Our neighbour Brian Gaines (son of the stickleback-netter extraordinaire!) played Rugby League as a second row forward with Keighley. Some friends had a relative who was a referee and they were going to watch him handle the Dewsbury v. Keighley pre-season Friendly. They invited me along as they knew I was keen to see Brian in action. He had played for the England Under-24 Team and I wondered just how good he was. It was a pleasure to watch him. He was a quiet, hard-working gentleman of a player and I continued to support Keighley throughout the 1966/67 season, never missing a game. I travelled to both home and away matches by rail, often alongside the players, which was as much a part of the enjoyment as was watching the game, where a seat could be easily obtained at most grounds.

At work things were not going so well. I passed my 'O' level Mathematics and moved four points along the pay scale (being due a further increment by virtue of age at the same time). I also learned another lesson about life. With a class of twenty-plus students at the start of the nine months' course I had never imagined that by the end I would be receiving individual tuition. I was unable to comprehend how anyone attending college on day release

(RIGHT) 'My condition went unnoticed until I did not make the usual progression from crawling to walking. I did walk, but was reluctant to let go of the furniture I clung to for support.'

My first caravan holiday at Sewerby on the east coast of Yorkshire, July 1949, though at eleven months I was a little young to appreciate it! (ABOVE RIGHT) With my father and (LEFT) with him and my uncle Gordon Hawkridge (*right*), boating at Bridlington.

I was soon as mobile as possible, (TOP) on my tricycle at Moortown aged two, with my cousin Sandra, and (ABOVE) in my beloved car, being pushed by my brother Robert.

Robert (*left*), Aunt Madge and myself by the sea at Filey, summer 1955.
Holidays brought us close together as a family as my brother and I fulfilled the
schemes we had been dreaming up all year.

(TOP) Family outings at weekends and bank holidays enlivened the summer. Here Robert (*right*) and I try rock climbing for the first time at Ilkley, June 1955.

(ABOVE) The annual outing from school to the seaside with my classmates was something we all eagerly anticipated. (I am second from left.)

(ABOVE) With Robert and my sister, Christine, 1956.

(LEFT) At Larchfield School, wearing the detested callipers, just before I left in 1957.

(RIGHT) My best friend Robert McLellan (*front left*) and myself (*front right*) at Larchfield with our heroes the gardeners, Mr Wilkinson (*back left*) and Mr Bell (*back right*).

(ABOVE) The 19th North Leeds Wolf Cub Pack, with (LEFT) a very proud new member, 20 June 1957.

OPPOSITE PAGE

(TOP) Aged ten, just before my first operation. 'Earlier I had been enjoying a last few runs in case the worst should happen.'

(BELOW LEFT) After the first operation, in plaster at Thorp Arch hospital with my mother, April 1959.

I had to teach myself to walk again, eventually progressing to walking sticks. (BELOW RIGHT) An adventurous day out with my uncle, Ron Humble, at Guild Hall, York, 10 September 1960, before my second operation.

As I struggled to walk after the operations, little did I think in thirty years' time I would be walking to Kala Pattar in the Himalayas. Here I am nearing the summit of Pillar in the Lake District with James Manchester, my last outing before leaving for Everest. (INSET) Reaching Kala Pattar, the fulfilment of a dream.

from work or from personal choice could give up so easily, especially when the course tutor, Mr Taylor, was so talented. Presumably they wanted to pass GCE 'O' level Mathematics or they would not have enrolled for the course and paid the fee in the first place? Then why pack it in without really trying? Were these the type of people who were being given places on courses where I had been refused? In disgust I have to say that the answer is probably, very likely.

Now earning more than £9 per week I felt much better off and rewarded for the extra years I had spent at college. The chief clerk had other ideas, however, and he began to make life difficult for me. I planned to continue my education through day release and night school for as long as the release facility was available and I felt my knowledge was expanding in worthwhile areas. He had other ideas but, since he was powerless to stop me from applying for day release until I reached the statutory age, put other plans into operation. I was granted permission to study for the Ordinary National Certificate in Business Studies and duly enrolled. The course required attendance on one day and two evenings a week.

I had now worked for British Rail for more than twelve months without any serious shortcomings but suddenly everything I did failed to meet the chief clerk's approval. First I was summoned to his office to discuss my disposition. He had decided that I was much too serious in my outlook and recommended that I smile more often and perhaps occasionally manage a laugh! I had not been aware of any solemnity in my behaviour but I had been told and that was that. Within weeks I was once again summoned to his office to receive his displeasure. He had seen me laugh and was not pleased that I should find time to do this while working for British Rail. What did I find so humorous? Enough was enough and I realized that there was no logical response to him. I politely asked him if he could provide me with a piece of paper so that I could take note of his warning, and on receipt of this I proceeded to write my resignation. I felt that there were so many areas in life where I could be successful that it was foolhardy to pursue one with so unequal odds where I could not.

I spent 7½ months on the dole as I endeavoured to find employment of my own choosing. Within days of handing in my resignation I had responded to an advertisement in my local newspaper for a job with the Inland Revenue but with first the interview and then a stringent medical it was to be another ten months before I was offered a post. After the interview I was informed that subject to my health being satisfactory I would be given a job with the Revenue and on the strength of this I chose not to seek further interviews with prospective employers. After 7½ months, however, my financial position was becoming extremely strained and I joined Exide Batteries. I enjoyed the work but the job had little or no prospects and when I was finally offered a post at the Inland Revenue the decision to accept it and move on, albeit initially for less money, was not a difficult one.

I started my new job on 1 April 1968. The office occupied the eleventh and twelfth floors of what was then a modern high-rise block in the city centre of Leeds. This meant that whenever the lifts were not operational the staff had a long haul to their place of work. Fortunately I could manage stairs with adequate handrails quite well and this was not a serious problem. There was no day release given to those over the age of eighteen and I continued my studies for 'A' level (which I obtained with grade A) and RSA stage III standard in Accounting at night school.

A large percentage of the staff at the newly formed Accounts Office to which I was assigned were school leavers and discipline was stringent. All regulations – time-keeping, holiday cover, eating, personal belongings near your desk, dress etc. – were strictly enforced and there was no talking amongst employees during work hours except about essential matters relating to the job. The office was designed and run for maximum efficiency and so long as there were no problem staff or unusual circumstances things generally went very well. Most people worked diligently and were reasonably happy or at least secure in that they knew exactly where they stood from a work point of view – official regulations made that quite clear!

The pressure at work was intense and the atmosphere far from relaxed but I enjoyed my job because I knew what was required of me and I worked for some knowledgeable, motivating and fair-minded section leaders. However, the mental intensity of work followed by long evenings at night school reaffirmed my need for a physical outlet in life. From my early days at the Branch College when I started going fishing I had felt the need to get away from the pressures of the Monday to Friday routine, away from people and the demands of society. Increasingly I yearned for adventure and a greater knowledge and understanding of the world around me, to escape into the lonely but real world of the countryside where nature is so serene and beautiful yet so cruelly hard and un-forgiving.

Football provided another escape, as I began to attend matches regularly. Leeds United were a formidable force at this time. I had stood on the terracing behind the goal when they beat Arsenal 1-0 in the League Cup Final at Wembley in 1968. I was also behind the goal at Nottingham when the stand burned down. Although I was in no immediate danger from the fire it did get very warm and a few of the Forest fans became a bit unruly afterwards. My hero at Leeds was Norman Hunter, with Johnny Giles running him a very close second. Norman was an inspiration to me, probably the biggest single physical influence there has ever been in my life. He gave everything, was ruthlessly determined while never complaining or disputing decisions, consistently reliable under every situation and much more skilful than many people would give him credit for. He was also extremely modest, a fact which was personally confirmed when in 1983 I was invited to Oakwell, the Barnsley football ground for a kick around on the first team pitch with Norman and his son. Although well past any peak of football fitness I may have ever had, I was never given a chance to display any skill as the ball invariably arrived at my feet and stopped almost dead with every pass, whatever the distance. It was a twenty-year-old dream come true as we each fired in shots at goal, although I must add that Norman and I were each wearing suits and our normal everyday shoes! Nevertheless his fierce competitiveness surfaced as he took a turn in goal. I only managed to beat him once and that was probably once too often for him. For me the whole session was a magical experience that I will never forget.

Football has played a large part in my life. From the moment I came out of hospital in a wheelchair my sole physical aim in life was to kick a football. By the time I was on elbow crutches I was playing football as often as possible. The local lads all knew me well and, although I may not have been competent, they always found a place for me, even if it was only in goal. Football was engrossing and exciting. To succeed it needed courage and commitment and, although I knew I would never have the balance, speed or power to excel, there was no reason why I should not give it everything that I had. Only by giving all would I learn just what I did have.

I spent hour after hour alone just kicking a football against a wall. All I was interested in was placing the ball accurately and taking the return cleanly or volleying it accurately back. I never developed any skill of taking on and beating other players but I did become an extremely confident and accurate passer of the ball. When not in possession I chased everything, even when I had no chance. I was going to be no walkover for anybody, however skilful they were, and it was amazing the number of players who thought they could beat me only to find they had been relieved of the ball in the process. I never tried to beat anybody, instead I looked for unmarked support. There are far too many people who play football, and probably lots of other sports, who do not seem aware of their limitations and nor do they learn from their failures. The game is about finding space and keeping the action simple. On several occasions I have scored very simple goals from within the six-yard box by having gone wide of the action only to find that the ball has come my way. Putting all the practice to good use, the finishing needs only a calm, calculated and accurate touch.

Competitively I have played on very few occasions. While attending college I used to be thrilled to be allowed to make up the number whenever they were short. My brother would lend me his outfit. The boots were a bit on the large side but I managed with extra woollen socks under the normal ones. In one game I played as an unreliable fullback, basically to cover as best I could. The opposition won a corner and I took up my position on the inside of the goal post in an effort to narrow the goal space. The ball came over and the opposition's most lethal player sent in a fierce first time volley. Realizing that I could get my chest behind it if I moved quickly, I launched myself in the right direction. The ball hit me and went over the cross bar leaving my team mates to disentangle me from the back of the net. To my great delight and satisfaction we went on to win 11-10.

On another occasion, I won the ball in midfield and quickly played it away to a team mate who was in open space only to find an upset opponent thundering in on me. I went up in air as he venomously and needlessly followed through. There was a loud crack. He had broken one of my walking sticks! We both had to go hospital, I for a new stick and he for treatment to an injured leg. I learned one thing quickly; if there is a physical challenge it must be met with all you have, or you will definitely be the one who gets hurt.

I followed Leeds United until the end of the 1972/73 season and then decided that crowd trouble was becoming so unpredictable that it was not worth the risk. I was always apprehensive and aware of the dangers involved in being in a crowd but I had witnessed, both in victory and defeat, some great sporting moments. However, with the changes in social standards of behaviour it was time to call it a day. I am not too keen on danger, especially when it is completely beyond my control.

I owed much to football and fishing, they had given me a lot of pleasure and something which no amount of physiotherapy could ever do – a reason for living.

NINE

An Uphill Struggle

In the May of 1968 I began to suffer pains in my thighs and decided to consult the surgeon who had earlier carried out the operations on them. After a thorough examination he concluded that I was suffering from the stress of too much physical activity and suggested that he arrange for me to be supplied with an invalid carriage since he felt the first thing I should do was to stop using public transport. At this time I travelled to work by bus. On the three evenings I attended night school I caught a further bus from work and then two further buses home. I used buses and trains at the weekend to follow sport and go fishing. Come to think of it, I did seem to do an awful lot of travelling on public transport.

I had never had aspirations to drive or to own a vehicle. Public transport had always served me well, even if I did spend a lot of time standing waiting for connections; besides, I was used to it. Travelling by bus had its exciting moments and there was a certain thrill that came with knowing that I could cope along with the rest, even when I had to stand up, or when the bus pulled away before I had got on properly. There had been one occasion when I was on my way home from college and the bus, packed with fellow students, left me hanging on at the back of a crowded platform as it set off. It took the first corner rather quickly and I swung completely around the pole, leaving the platform at one side and returning at the other. Fortunately such hair-raising events were few and far between.

Several friends from my school days drove invalid carriages and the prospect did not really appeal to me. I declined the surgeon's offer. He insisted that it was not just an offer. He was being very serious. If my condition were not to deteriorate further I must take some of the strain out of my life, and this was a step in the right direction. I was not convinced but agreed to his proposal of a trial period of two weeks. After the two weeks I still did not like the vehicle itself but could not bring myself to give it up as I enjoyed the freedom it gave me. I quickly passed my driving test and arranged to take further driving lessons in a four-wheeled car with a hand clutch adaptation. I also began to save to purchase my own vehicle once I could obtain a full driving licence. Operating the hand clutch caused many problems and I was often at the point of despair and ready to give up. Only the instructor's faith and encouragement kept me going through those nerve-racking times. He sat there calmly overriding my mistakes with his dual controls while assuring me that eventually everything would fall into place, and he did not just mean the gears!

Fortunately he was right and after twenty lessons I passed my test first time, despite a slight problem as I did the emergency stop. I had an abscess on the big toe of my left foot and could only wear a slipper, but this made little difference as I did not use it for driving. When a car is fitted with a hand clutch the foot pedal remains in use, thus enabling anyone else to drive it without difficulty. Being servo-assisted the clutch is also very light and, as I pulled up for the emergency stop, the pedal went to the floor, trapping my toe beneath it. I screamed and quickly took the necessary action to release my very painful toe. The examiner remarked quietly that after bringing the vehicle to a halt, I was supposed to remain stationary and not to inch forward, as I had done, until he gave the command to do so . . .

Having received my invalid carriage in the July I ceased to go fishing on a regular basis. Perhaps the challenge of getting there was greater than I had previously been prepared to admit, or maybe just having my own transport gave me the opportunity to do different things in a more relaxed way. Whatever the reasons, my horizons broadened, for the countryside still beckoned. I began to enjoy it just for its own worth. I was interested in geology, archaeology and photography. I visited ancient monuments and enjoyed being free to go as I pleased.

For the first time in my life I chose to go on holiday alone. I had no close friends who I thought would appreciate the type of low-key holiday I was seeking and the invalid carriage did have an 'isolating' effect. Although there was no room for passengers, at least actually getting to my destination would not be a problem. I had once been to the Lake District on a day trip with my parents and the idea of spending a holiday there had remained with me since. Perhaps on my original visit as a thirteen-year-old I had been fascinated by the prospect of so many lakes and the possible fishing. In the September I decided to go to the Lake District for ten days, this being considered long enough for my first lone venture, just to see as much as possible, take colour slides of the views and study the geology of the area. There would be no fishing, but there may be a few short walks to see any points of interest. I had a pair of walking boots which I wore for attending football matches and in the spring I had walked some short distances along the banks of the River Wharfe above Bolton Abbey, simply for the enjoyment of the surroundings and the physical exercise.

I had disliked walking when I had to do it. On fishing trips I had kept any distance to be covered on foot to a minimum, but I was now much stronger and more resolute in physical adversity. While fishing I had spent long periods alone and this had made me reasonably self-sufficient, both physically and emotionally. I had learned to find a way round whatever obstacles had confronted me without too many problems. Climbing up and down awkward riverbanks and carrying my box and rods had helped build up my strength and staying power. I had confidence in my ability yet believed I knew my limitations and was well aware of the dangers to be met in open country, particularly those of the weather.

I chose Keswick as my base and found lodgings via the Tourist Information Office on arrival. Travelling by invalid carriage was slow, very noisy and there was little in the way of comfort, making the 105-mile journey more an expedition than a pleasant drive. I stayed with the Masons of Eskin Street for bed and breakfast. They were very good to me and the family have remained close friends ever since.

I was greatly impressed by the scenery and covered most of the area, buying books and maps for further knowledge as I went. My vehicle did not have the power to climb the upper part of the Wrynose Pass and I was grateful to my fellow motorists who came to my rescue on the steep and narrow road, giving me a push whenever the engine was no longer able to cope with the severe incline. I now knew the car's limitations and realized that any crossing of the Hard Knott Pass was completely out of the question as I contemplated the recurring series of acute angled 'Z' bends and read the warning sign. The Honister Pass, on the other hand, had been no real problem after taking a second run at the steep hill which left Seatoller. But the experience of Wrynose had made me wary of trying any further steep passes with sheer drops. I had cultivated an instant healthy respect for such roads and, to add to the problem, the surface of the road at the summit of the Wrynose had been made up of only loose stones.

I had arrived on the Wednesday and by Saturday was sufficiently captivated by the mountains that I decided to go for a walk uphill the following day. Daily I had looked down Eskin Street and marvelled at the fine view of Skiddaw. I had seen people going off to the hills to walk, and had thought it a waste of time, energy and effort. My opinion was, however, based on my own physical experience and ignorance. I know now that, for the average fit person, little or no distress is involved in ascending most Lakeland Peaks during reasonable weather conditions.

The idea of attempting to climb a mountain seemed impossible, but on the Saturday evening, as I returned from Whitehaven, I gave it some serious thought. Weather permitting I would see what I could do. I would park at Millbeck and head upwards over White Stones towards the summit of Carl Side. Depending on how things went I might be able to go on further and eventually reach the summit of Skiddaw, which, at 3,053 feet, was quite impressive. I had never tackled any venture of this nature before, let alone on my own. Every aspect of the walk would be up to me.

I selected the Carl Side route because of the distance involved. At 2¾ miles it is one of the shortest, though steepest, routes to the summit. I preferred to tackle the incline rather than the greater distance, always bearing in mind that, however far I reached, I had to get back down again. I was not optimistic about my chances of success but had resolved that I would just see how I managed as I progressed upwards, not forgetting that, if I did get into difficulties, there would most likely be no possibility of any assistance being on hand. The main aim of the exercise was to take colour slides of the views and generally enjoy the exhilarating experience. I was under no illusions about the difficulty of the task I had set myself.

It was 15 September 1968 and the weather was fine. I met my first obstacle when I informed the landlady where I was going and what time I intended to return. It is customary to let someone know of your proposed whereabouts when taking to the fells, both for your own safety and that of anyone who could be called out in the event of your not returning. Having done this it is then important that you stick to these plans. The landlady tried her best to convince me that it was not normal to ascend mountains, in fact she had lived below them all her life and they had never attracted her.

At about 10.00 a.m. I left my invalid carriage at Millbeck and, rather pleased that there was no one around to see me, started the ascent to White Stones. The further I ascended the more spectacular the views became. I just kept going and eventually arrived on the shoulder of Carl Side where I met a solitary walker, the only person I saw on the fells all day. We exchanged a few brief words, I got him to take my photograph, then he was gone. The meeting brought home to me the extreme loneliness of the situation but it was something I could cope with, and, come to that, enjoy. It was a relief to be in a tight situation and not to have someone trying to tell me what I should do or which route I should take.

I descended from the 2,400-foot summit of Carl Side to Carlside col and the tarn. The route to the top of Skiddaw, which was clearly visible, went straight up and across the steepening screes ahead. It looked impossible. I was frightened at the thought of climbing it but had come so far, and with only about 700 feet left to the summit, was not about to give up so easily. Although the day was bright the cold wind seemed to be gale force at that altitude. I went forward carefully, climbing about 300 feet up the pro-gressively worsening screes before I lost my footing. I slipped about 20 feet back down, scattering objects from my pockets as I went. All was not well, and there was still a considerable distance to the summit. The track got worse before it got better.

I had suffered no serious damage and I scrambled around on the loose stones gathering my dispersed belongings, having decided that I would go back down while I was still in a fit state to do so. I admitted defeat as, greatly relieved, I came down over Carsleddam. Well, defeat was not quite appropriate for I had enjoyed and photographed breathtaking views of the Solway and Scotland and, in the other direction, Derwentwater and the Scafells. A whole new world had been opened up to me. I would return. This new territory would not be so easily surrendered.

The landlady was pleased to see me despite my blistered hands and sore feet. Further walking expeditions required a good pair of purpose-designed boots and several pairs of woollen socks. Despite the difficulties I had experienced I realized that the giant peaks of England were not invincible, although there would probably be more days of hardship with no positive result before I finally conquered one. I was pleased with the holiday which had served as a basic introduction to the Lake District. I had done much more than I had anticipated ten days earlier as I drove from Leeds in the pouring rain. It had remained fine for eight of the ten days and as I returned home in the rain I remember enjoying the gushing water-falls that cascaded down the hillsides as I drove over Dunmail Raise. I was hooked and would return at the first opportunity.

In November my work took me to Worthing on the South Coast. I left the invalid carriage at home and relied on public transport or on friends who had cars. Working away from home was a new experi-ence and something which I found difficult to get used to. I had too many interests not to miss being at home. I had to get used to watching Leeds United play away matches rather than at home, and studying for the GCE A level was much more difficult in the absence of night-school classes. The course was for two nights a week over two years and I was only in the first year. I would have the chance to make good any deficiency and was fortunate that it was a subject in which I excelled. I worked at Worthing until the end of February and the main thing which came out of it was that I learned that, although I was independent, I still needed my family and home life. They too learned that they had no wish to lose me, and the experience was to our mutual and lasting benefit.

The following Easter it was back to Keswick, only this time with a pair of good boots and an expanded knowledge of the terrain. I had bought a pair of Hawkins 'Scafells' which seemed to suit my requirements ideally. They were heavy, semi-rigid, waterproof and comfortable. They were of a good basic design with no gimmicks that could go wrong. The laces were attached by 'D' rings, an advantage where the foot was used in all sorts of unorthodox positions and where hooks were likely to become jammed and bend or break.

On the Good Friday, which was a glorious day, I ascended the Sty Head Pass from Seathwaite in an attempt to climb Great Gable via the breast route. Now, Great Gable was a mountain which really fired the imagination. I had first been drawn to it when I had gone to Wasdale to see the Scafells. It was the Lake District National Park's emblem and a true mountain in every sense of the word. Although I delighted in the beauty of mountains it was the rocky outcrops and crags that held for me the special interest. I knew that I would never be able to ascend any of the sheer rock faces but I could be in their presence and enjoy the atmosphere they created.

Great Gable is endowed with more than its share of outcrops. The features of the mountain seemed inexhaustible: Napes Ridges, Kern Knotts, Raven Crag, Gable Crag and Westmorland Crag to name but a few. My problem was finding a weakness in such a powerful line of defence. For me the mountain had everything, beauty, charm, magic and mystery, and from the summit I would have magnificent views of the surrounding countryside. Before I started, a visit to the Church at Wasdale Head brought home the dangers of the mountain. It had meant disaster for some and I would have to approach the fell with caution and concern if I was not to join them.

After my failure on Skiddaw I was confident in my ability to keep going, provided I paid proper attention to the conditions underfoot when the going became hazardous. My new boots were an enormous boost to my morale, and one less thing to worry about.

I reached the junction of the breast route at Sty Head and took stock of the situation, being slightly over-awed by the lofty and rugged appearance of the snow-clad peaks in the vicinity. Any attempt at the summit was out of the question and I walked across to Esk Hause in order to obtain better views of my objective. I was excited as I looked at the profile of Gable's West Face. I tried to locate the position of Napes Needle and the many other features of which I had read. It must have been nature's first day of Spring for, as I descended, the hills were alive with the sound of croaking frogs as they spawned in mass.

Once again I had failed, but I had enjoyed some of the finest mountain scenery in Britain, and was undaunted and much happier for the experience. In some respects the walk had gone well; there was no damage to my feet although my hands were beginning to show signs of wear. I was putting a lot of effort into the activity but I was enjoying it, and surely the day when I would stand on a summit was not too far away.

In July I was once again at Keswick, this time camping for a week with my brother, my cousin, Stephen Turner, and three of his friends, Kevin Maynard and Paul and Roy Goodbeer. I convinced them that Great Gable was for them too and a party of four of us left Borrowdale for the Sty Head. By the time we arrived at the Sty Head Tarn there was low cloud and the area was exceedingly damp and unpleasant. We retreated to the safety of the valley and decided that we would make no attempt on any mountain unless the weather was perfect. During the week we did a lowland walk to Scale Force, a 120-foot waterfall near Crummock Water, and I slipped into a stream on one of the wettest paths in England on the return to Buttermere. Fortunately we had taken our swimwear with us and, mine being still dry, I was able to make a quick change from my wet and muddy clothes, comfort being far more important than appearance at such times!

On the last day the weather was fine and I made a snap decision that we should try Helvellyn from Wythburn. The rest agreed and off we went. Helvellyn, at 3,118 feet, is the third highest mountain in England and it would be hard work if I was to make it to the top. I chose that particular mountain partly because of the availability of public transport, since although I was now mobile, the other five members of our party had to take the bus. They had little interest in mountains but were keen to get out and do something during the day before visiting the local hostelries in the evening, and they generally delegated the organization of our daytime programme to me, an arrangement which kept us all happy.

We left Wythburn Church and headed up the massive shoulder of Helvellyn. After five hours of sheer graft I was on the summit, and a dream had come true. There had been no really difficult parts to negotiate, it had been plain hard work, but it was all worthwhile as I stood and surveyed the scene. Below was Striding Edge; Red Tarn looked like the shape of a man's head, and, to complete the picture, there was Swirrel Edge. Although it was breezy we lingered a while on the top enjoying our moment of triumph. I was pleased that I had companions with whom I could share this experience, and especially my brother who had done so much with me.

There still remained the problem of getting back down and we headed for Brown Cove Crags and Thirlspot. Four members of the party descended quickly while Kevin remained with me for safety. Progress down Brown Cove Crags was difficult and suddenly I lost my footing on the loose stones and slid head first downwards. I was out of control and my companion, who had gone slightly ahead, had to brace himself and tackle me rugby fashion as I went past. We slithered to a halt and, apart from a few scratches, I was unhurt. I had slipped down the worst section and we completed the walk without further incident. There was a lesson to be learned from this near disaster. I must always descend by the same route as that by which I had ascended, or by a route which I knew to be safe.

My brother and I decided to have a quiet week camping at Keswick in the September with the aim of consolidating my newly found strength. On the Monday we got to grips with Skiddaw via the tourist path from Gale Road behind Latrigg. It was a steady pull to the summit, which was veiled by low cloud, and ice formed down the windward side of our bodies as we photographed each other by the triangulation point. I was not in bad condition, and that night my thoughts began to turn to the big one. Could I climb Scafell Pike with a ten-mile round walk? We decided that on the first fine day we would make an attempt. It rained all week until the Friday. It was 19 September and the nights were now drawing in quickly. We were late in rising but the sun shone brilliantly, not a cloud was in sight.

This was too good an opportunity to miss. It had to be a late start and an all out effort for a quick ascent. We set a deadline of 4.00 p.m. for reaching the summit as we set off from Seathwaite.

As I was struggling over the loose stones beyond the farmyard we were passed by some other walkers who gave me a peculiar look as if they wondered where I was going. They quickly forged ahead and made their way up Taylor Ghyll towards Sty Head while we followed the valley up through Grains Gill. They passed us again around Esk Hause, only this time their look was one of astonishment. After six hours of extremely hard labour I was on the top of the highest mountain in England. I had climbed the 3,210 feet of Scafell Pike and was feeling very pleased and relieved, if somewhat apprehensive about the return journey. We had the summit to ourselves and I rested while my brother explored the route down to Pikes Crags.

The clouds began to roll in over Scafell, which appeared to be higher than the summit we were on, and we made a hasty retreat to Esk Hause, after which point there was little chance of our getting lost. I had difficulty in placing my sticks as we tried to hurry over the boulder fields of Broad Crag and Ill Crag. It had been difficult but exciting going up, but now the pressure was on, the elation of reaching the summit was passed, I was exhausted, and progress became very slow as we finally reached Esk Hause. The last $1\frac{1}{2}$ miles were completed in darkness and each time I tripped or collapsed, which was often, my brother just stood me up and forced me to carry on.

We arrived back in Keswick shortly before 11.00 p.m. and were able to get a drink and something to eat at the Lake Road Vaults, where by now we had become regulars. I sat on a stool at the bar and, when it was time to leave, I found that I had become locked in that position. Back at the tent I remained in that seated posture for the next twenty-four hours before I was able to move again, but I felt good, and started to wonder what Ben Nevis looked like . . .

I still had some unfinished business on Great Gable and in the September of 1970 my brother and I were back to try again with a new route in mind – an ascent from the Honister Pass. I had now purchased a set of Wainwright guides and was able to study each route up a mountain in detail. This was an enormous improvement over walking with only a map, and a quick look through the pages of any of the volumes never failed to give inspiration for future outings.

Further inspiration came from the books and paintings of W. Heaton Cooper. I had many of the prints of his paintings on my bedroom wall and his ability to capture the essence of rocks and mountains meant a lot to me. I framed the prints myself and was given much encouragement from Richard Hardisty, an employee at Heaton Cooper's studio. He frequently enquired about my latest exploits and was helpful in providing further information when required. It was through Richard that I eventually met Heaton in about 1977 and we have been very good friends since.

On a warm clear day we left Honister and headed up the disused tramway. Reaching the upland plateau I was dismayed to see Great Gable loom large and distant. It looked impossible. Instead I decided to settle for a walk over Haystacks to Gatesgarth. Would I ever conquer Great Gable?

I have to admit that at this period I was becoming increasingly disillusioned with work. I had begun work as an Assistant Collector of Taxes and promotion to Senior Assistant was by way of an examination followed by an interview for those successful in obtaining a satisfactory standard. Alternatively an annual report was prepared on all staff and those consistently recommended for advancement were usually appointed to the next grade. Promotion via this latter method could take several years especially if you were quite young. After completing the necessary qualifying period of service and being of the minimum age I sat the examination and out of several hundred candidates came within the top ten or so. As I went to London for my interview the two section leaders I had worked for thought my chances of promotion were excellent since they had prepared the reports on my performance at work. As far as I was aware the interview went very well and subsequently I was amazed when the results were announced and I was discarded with a rather lowly rating. The people I had personally worked for were so upset that they took the trouble of assuring me that my failure was not a reflection of their reports or my work performance.

You were allowed to sit the examination three times and the following year I once again failed to get promotion. My increasing disappointment was not only in being rejected but in seeing those around me being successful who I knew were not up to the same examination standard as myself and who I strongly felt could not match my enthusiasm or ability to learn and work hard. One can only take so many setbacks before one's attitude towards a situation changes. I realized that my failure was simply due to the interviewing panel drawing conclusions from what they could see when they met me and paying little or no notice either to examination results or work reports. More and more I needed the seclusion of the countryside to hold body and soul together. Mountains are constant and consistent. They can be difficult, even dangerous but they treat everyone alike. No concessions are made for human weaknesses or failings, physical or otherwise, nor is there any discrimination. Treated with respect they are good friends; flouted, they can kill. If the truth be known I suppose it was this latter point which ultimately appealed to me. Climbing mountains took me to my physical limits of skill and endurance. A miscalculation, rash decision or failure to understand my limitations was likely to spell disaster. This was in stark contrast, I felt, to a world where many people made idle talk. It was easy for civil servants, politicians and the like, in fact anyone who did not actually have to bear the consequences, to make decisions affecting others. If your life depends on a series of variable calculated decisions it has a considerably sobering effect on your self-understanding. It forces you to know your limitations while fostering a realistic self-belief and confidence. Hopefully this spills over into your everyday attitude and behaviour.

The Accounts Office system had now been successfully set up by some of the Inland Revenue's best staff and replacements were coming in as those responsible were rewarded with promotion or moved to jobs more in keeping with their personal wishes. The new managers did not always have the integrity of their predecessors and office morale began to suffer badly as some of the new blood took advantage of a few of the female staff. Suddenly there were outgoing young ladies being promoted on the basis of their work reports only. 'Storeroom promotions', as they were commonly known.

I had thoroughly enjoyed my spells working with Richard Puddicombe, Des Swinson and the dynamic young Peter Clark as I had built up a reputation as an efficient reliable worker who got results. It came as a shock when my next section leader took me to one side and told me that my reputation was so good that he was going to go to whatever lengths were necessary to prove it was unjustified. I was forced on to the defensive and eventually suffered a minor nervous breakdown under the relentless pressure. I was nearly twenty-one, and as well as having to cope with this no-win situation many of my schoolfriends were dying. I found the strength to fight back from climbing more mountains. The effort involved, solitude and exhaustion helped me think more clearly and get the things that really mattered in life into perspective. This was not the last time I was deliberately harassed but whenever I felt really down and I fought back I became stronger than the time before until eventually I learned not to succumb but to carry on, simply doing what I knew to be right.

I felt the problem stemmed from the fact that I was a black and white person – things were either right or wrong. I was honest and intensely loyal, at least to those who understood loyalty. My promotion prospects were not being helped by the current situation and I was deeply resenting my previous unfavourable treatment by head office. All was not in fact lost and I was fortunate subsequently to be assigned to the charge of John Concannon and Ken Rogers. At my third attempt I was successful at obtaining promotion to Senior Assistant Collector and then privately informed by a member of the panel of interviewers that previously I had not been seriously considered because of my disability. Shortly the grade of S.A.C. was abolished and I found myself promoted to Collector or in general Civil Service terms, Executive Officer.

On Christmas Day 1970 I was taken ill with epididymitis, a disorder which threatens one's manhood. I lay in bed on my back in agony and barely able to move until February. The doctor visited me three times a week but, despite the different drugs I was taking, my condition did not improve. The doctor arrived one morning and said that he was arranging for me to go into hospital. Fearing the worst, I enquired as to what could be done there that could not be done at home. My worst fears were confirmed when he said that the offending parts would be removed. I asked him what the alternative would be and was shocked to hear that I was very seriously ill and would probably die.

I could not bring myself to consent to the proposed operation and he gave me a day to think about it. It was either surgery or death. I thought long and hard and decided I could not accept the course of treatment being recommended. I could not come to terms with the possibility of losing the motivating force in my life. The doctor had assured me that, since my voice had already broken and I had started shaving, there would be few outward effects. This was scant consolation in the face of such drastic measures.

I had to make up my mind. I did not want to die but I needed to retain the driving forces within me. They made life worthwhile. I was only twenty-two years old and, in spite of my disability, hell bent on living as normal a life as was possible. If this is what the Almighty really intended for me then perhaps he had better get ready to take me back. I declined the offer of surgery and instead chose to pray for help with all the strength I had left. Within a few days the swelling began to decrease and my condition slowly started to improve.

After two months in bed I was so weak that I had to learn how to walk again and as soon as I could get to my car – I had a Mini fitted with a hand clutch by this time – I would go swimming every day until I regained my fitness. At the age of twenty-one, with the help of my childhood friend Robin Rogers, I had once again learnt to swim, albeit with severe limitations. I then progressed to my old football-against-the-wall routine until I thought I was back to my earlier standard. The whole experience had drastically changed my outlook on life. I had been attending night school five nights a week as I studied for part II of the ACCA examination. My two month absence was too much to make up; I had fallen from the crest of the wave, and, besides, I realized that if I could die so easily, what was I doing working so hard for five nights a week together with the extra studying involved at weekends? At best I had lost a year and, to make matters worse, my employers were not prepared to give the certificate which was needed by the examining body to advance beyond the second year, confirming that one was employed in work of an accounting nature, unless I accepted a transfer to London. This seemed a bit odd since two fellow members of staff were studying for the same examination without any such condition. The situation was impossible and I gave up studying for exams altogether. I was already sufficiently well qualified for the work I was doing. I also became aware of the urgent need to get more out of life, I needed to step up the pace a bit. There is really only one way to get more out of life and that is to put more into it. I already had a sense of purpose about what I did, but I now needed to bring some urgency to my plans. The important thing was to try to keep doing something – today; keep it going now, and not wait for it to happen tomorrow. If I wanted for instance to help someone or to express my feelings, then now was the time to do it. Tomorrow could be too late. Things which were of great importance yesterday mattered very little today.

The drive was still there, probably stronger than ever, but it now had to be directed at myself rather than other people. Before, my determination to succeed had made me stand up to everyone, stand up for what I believed in very aggressively. Now I felt, what did it matter what others thought of me? I could not influence other people by force but I could try to gain their respect through my actions and behaviour.

By the Easter of 1971 I was sufficiently recovered to believe that I could now climb Great Gable, and once again I headed for the tramway, this time with one of my cousins, Kenwyn Turner.

Having climbed the Three Peaks of Yorkshire on successive weekends, I was confident that Good Friday was going to be the long-awaited day of reckoning. The weather was glorious and we steadily climbed the tramway and made our way along Moses Trod towards Windy Gap.

As the boulders became more difficult to negotiate, I found myself running out of the necessary mental motivation and succumbing to the physical strain, I resigned myself to yet another failure. After a short sleep in the warm afternoon sun we returned to Honister. This was the first time that I had considered my failure on a mountain to be due to my own personal inadequacy. The will to succeed was not there and I had to either get it back or give up doing this sort of thing. There had never been room in my life for half-heartedness and it was a fact of my existence which I could not and did not wish to change.

At Whitsuntide I went to Coniston alone and in the afternoon climbed the Old Man. I had one nerve-testing moment when it took me more than one attempt to get up a steep stony section near the summit. Initially I climbed up the loose scree only to slide back down again, and I had some doubt as to whether or not a second attempt would be worthwhile or even wise. In this position you can only take stock of the situation honestly and logically and decide whether or not you can surmount the difficulty with extreme care, caution and every ounce of skill and knowhow at your disposal. There is no room for bravado, or sentiment. Wanting to do it is not enough. The only question is, can I or can't I? Once on the summit I was inspired by the view across to the Scafell range and the following day I climbed the 3,162 feet of Scafell, England's second highest mountain, without undue difficulty. Some low cloud around the summit meant that I did not know that I had reached it until I heard the voices of people who were already there. A momentary break in the cloud revealed Scafell Pike, which looked higher, and brought memories of that previous walk flooding back.

A few weeks later I climbed Pavey Ark via Stickle Gill at my second attempt. I was enthralled by Jack's Rake but it was far too difficult for me to consider venturing on to it. Around this time I also climbed Bowfell by the Band with my sister. It was a pleasant walk and we were afforded splendid views of the whole of Lakeland.

In July I was back in Keswick for a weekend and, with renewed determination, I left the Honister Pass with my father, who had never climbed a mountain before. I was beginning to wonder whether it was myself or the difficulty of Great Gable which defeated me. My knowledge of the mountain continued to grow but I was getting no nearer the summit, and I was now making my sixth attempt.

We crossed Green Gable and for the first time I set foot on the mountain proper as we climbed out of Windy Gap. The track disappeared, or, I should say, we lost it. Before long we were climbing a rocky outcrop, which at over 2,000 feet was quite airy, although the angle was quite easy as far as rock climbs go. My father carried my sticks and from below, guided my feet to suitable holds as we quickly ascended the rocks. This was no place to linger and we were soon on the summit ridge making our way up to the summit.

The greatest moment of a climb for me is the point where the summit suddenly becomes attainable, usually on reaching the summit ridge, and that was the case with Great Gable. As my father descended to the Westmorland Cairn I enjoyed a few brief solitary moments at the summit cairn. I looked towards Wasdale and the Scafells and I knew my efforts had been worthwhile. I had recovered from serious illness and once again I was getting what I needed out of life.

At last I had unlocked the mystery of Great Gable and it will always hold a special place among the mountains in my life.

TEN

New Horizons

From the first time I went fishing I had taken a keen interest in the travel side of it. As a child my mother's brother, Ron Humble, had taken me on day trips to London and York to visit the museums and see the famous landmarks. My mother's sister and her husband, Madge and Cyril, who were the only members of the family to own a car, had regularly taken me to the Dales and other parts of Yorkshire for days out, and my parents as I have described had taken us to the East Coast of Yorkshire for our annual holiday. There was undoubtedly something about travel that awakened an inner longing in me. It was something I had to do – for enjoyment and to broaden my horizons.

I had made the two trips to Ireland and enjoyed the consequent widening of my horizons possibly more than the fishing. The Lake District had become my latest playground and while working in Worthing I had taken the opportunity to see as much of that area as possible. There had been weekends at Portsmouth, the Isle of Wight, Brighton and London, days spent wandering around Arundel, Chichester, Bognor Regis, Littlehampton and Lancing.

I had been to London several times on week-long courses connected with my work and I was competent on the rail and underground system. In fact I gained a certain amount of satisfaction from being able to go both up and down the long escalators of the tube system while managing to carry all my needs in a rucksack on my back.

I had a philosophy about travel. I knew lots of folk who went abroad for their holidays and they invariably came back with an enormous amount of enthusiasm for the places they had been to. They always seemed to go to countries which had that special 'something', and they were always keen to persuade everyone else that they should go there too – following in their footsteps as it were. To me, travel was not meant to be that way. It was about deciding what your needs were and tailoring your holiday to suit them.

If the world was so exciting, why did these people find Britain so boring? The answer was simple. Very few of them actually knew very much about their homeland. They had visited coastal resorts, towns of historic interest and beauty spots, but they had never been to the extremities – the islands and the remoter parts of the mainland. Some went abroad for the better weather and some for the drink.

How can you possibly be in a position to know what you are experiencing in another country if your experiences at home have been restricted? It is like trying to speak a foreign language when you can hardly speak your native tongue; you have no base from which to work.

I knew that some day I should like to go abroad, but decided I must see Britain first. In 1970, when I bought my first car, the chance to explore Britain became a reality. I had decided to go to Scotland with my brother in the September, but the car was off the road after I had collided with an articulated lorry. We went to the Lake District instead and camped in Langdale. Gale-force winds forced everyone to retreat. Several chalet tents soared into the sky like box kites, others lay flapping on the ground with broken or bent poles protruding. Our ridge tent suffered the latter fate though fortunately it was repairable. In all the time we had been camping this was the first serious setback we had experienced. Our plans to climb the Langdale Pikes were shelved and instead we consoled ourselves at the Climbers Bar of the Old Dungeon Ghyll Hotel, also one of life's great experiences. Like most of the other campers, we returned home ahead of schedule, in disgust.

The following year my brother was on his way to Spain with his girlfriend and I decided it was time to make a start on the British Isles. I was entitled to three weeks and three days annual leave a year and, if I took most of this in one go, I could make quite an extensive tour. I formulated a plan whereby I could see most of the British Isles in three years.

In the first year, 1971, I would go to Scotland, visit most of the central and western mainland and tour the Hebrides. The following year I would return to Scotland, visiting the northern and eastern mainland and the Orkney and Shetland Isles. In the third year I would go south to the Channel Isles and the Scillies, taking in as much of the southern part of England as possible. Meanwhile I would use other short breaks and Bank Holidays to visit Wales, Northumbria and the less distant and remote areas.

It all sounded so easy when I laid out the plans in my mind, but I had never sailed in rough seas and I would hardly be fortunate enough to avoid them with so much sea travel involved. I had once been out on a pleasure boat from Bridlington when I was about twelve. There had been a heavy swell and I was absolutely terrified. My problem is that, having had operations on my legs, I have no sense of balance. If I close my eyes when I am standing up or am suddenly plunged into darkness, I fall over. My balance is relative to what I can see, and therefore if things around me are moving or unstable, they play havoc with my sense of balance. It was for this reason that I would not consider flying. My fear was that if for any reason I could not cope there was no possibility of cutting the journey short.

I had twice taken the ferry to Ireland without any problems but the weather had been very kind on each occasion. I would just have to set off and hope for the best. I could always change my plans if conditions were not to my liking. After all, the type of holidays I was going to have were not really governed by any predetermined itinerary. It would be more a question of taking advantage of the prevailing local conditions and services. Yes, I could definitely do it. I just needed to be singleminded in my determination to see as much as possible. My most difficult problem was probably that I intended to do it alone.

But having made the decision, carry it out I did, and opened up a new world for myself. I slept in my car when I could (to save money), and I survived some very rough crossings in the Hebrides. On Mull I was privileged to see my first pair of golden eagles, and on Barra I was further privileged to meet and make friends with Nicholas Frayling – 'Vicar Nick' as he became known in Tooting after he was ordained and now rector of Liverpool. I had my first, and last, haggis, and gloried in the diverse birdlife. Life seemed almost as though it was standing still as the summer slowly drew to a close. I needed to draw strength from the experience, enough to carry me through another year and – as it turned out – through a terrible tragedy.

In February, on St Valentine's Day, 1972, my brother was killed in a car crash, the innocent victim of a stray dog and a reckless driver. He was just twenty-two years old and I think that this hurt me more than the fact that he was dead. He had hardly lived. We had been very close. We had shared the same bedroom all our lives. In the early days, seeing him being so active had been the motivating force in my life and he had always been ready to help me achieve my physical goals, even when it meant us both getting into trouble. He was gone and I was still here. For the second time in less than twelve months I resolved that I must live life with more purpose and make sure that his help and inspiration had not been in vain. There were too many good things in life to be waylaid by the bad. I must be even stronger, if this were possible, and concentrate more on putting back into life that which I had received from it.

Shortly before his death I had been organizing a football team for which I arranged only the occasional friendly match. The players were mainly lads I worked with but I also used the team to give some of my friends who wanted a game the chance of a run out. Many of them enjoyed playing but did not want a regular commitment, or were perhaps not considered good enough for their local team.

I had built the team around my brother who played at left half, wearing the No. 6 jersey. He played according to the tactics I dictated and I could rely on his effort and skill to control the game from the back. When I say that, I do not so much mean that I gave him an explicit set of instructions, but rather a set of principles to which I insisted he must adhere. How the team played the game was very much up to the individuals concerned so long as they each remembered that they were playing for one another, and for me.

Although I no longer had any aspirations to play I organized kickabouts for those who did not play regularly and this was my real enjoyment. It gave me a chance to demonstrate my skills, which provided evidence to show that all my fine talk about effort was backed by deeds. The whole thing added up to some exciting games of football on the few occasions that we played and although we sometimes managed only to draw we never lost a match.

When my brother was killed I decided I would wear his shirt the following game. We had previously played a 2–2 draw against the opposition, giving away two silly goals in the dying minutes as the light faded one Sunday afternoon. My first problem was the rock-hard pitch which made conditions under foot very difficult. Although I wore the No. 6 shirt, I really played as an extra centre forward. I instructed my team mates not to pass the ball to me unless they were absolutely desperate and I said I would look after myself while they put in all the effort in an attempt to make up for my serious shortcomings.

The game was played at tremendous pace and I just did the best I could. We won a corner and I took up a position at the far post. My captain, Graham Southam, took it and he had said he would put the ball over on to my head. He did, but by the time it arrived I was on the ground with what felt like eleven pairs of boots on top of me. Fortunately I was unhurt and decided it was time to make my presence felt, if I could.

Since I did not want the ball, the best thing I could do was to mark the deepest defender and shadow him constantly while trying to stay on-side. Defenders are not used to this treatment. It is usually they who are doing the marking and it interferes with their ability to concentrate and read the game. At least this was what I hoped.

Near the end of the first half I was moving towards the edge of their penalty area when a long ball came my way. I was about to put everything into getting the ball under control when I saw a defender racing towards me. I was not afraid of him but I was not going to score either, with both him and the goalkeeper to contend with. I had an inside forward, Nick Garret, coming to my assistance and as he shouted I stepped over the ball letting it go and at the same time doing my best to block the defender's path towards it. Nick cracked the ball straight into the back of the net.

I brought myself off and put on the substitute. We went on to win 1–0 after a nerve-racking second half and I have never played seriously since. My brother was gone, but at least his untimely death did serve to bring my family much closer together.

It was in 1972, after I had completed the second phase of my round-Britain tour (the highlights of which were undoubtedly the ancient monuments on Orkney and the wildlife of the Shetland Isles), and while I was recruiting players for my football team at work, that I met Keith Williamson. Although still in his teens he already had a wife and child and many of the people he worked with felt sorry for him. He received no sympathy from me and I told him straight that he had to be either ready to give everything or I did not want to know.

We quickly became very good friends and one day he explained that he was running a Scout troop and asked me to give them a slide show and talk about my travels. Remembering how, while I was a scout at school, I had enjoyed the theory but the practice had often fallen short of my expectations, I agreed only reluctantly to give the show. I was pleasantly surprised to find the whole thing was taken very seriously and in difficult circumstances. The troop was based at the Church of the Epiphany on the Gipton Estate, one of the less well-disposed areas of Leeds. The members of the group came from a wide cross-section of the community.

My slide show and talk were well received and Keith, knowing that I had a strong interest in outdoor activities, asked me if I would go along and do some of the routine work with him. I agreed and very shortly found that not only was I attending every meeting, but I had become the new scout leader, with Keith assisting when necessary, although I actually had less difficulty when he was not present. Here was another new horizon: not travel, but a new dimension to my life, particularly challenging to my leadership qualities.

I went on a series of training courses for scout leaders, culminating in a week at Gilwell Park, on the edge of Epping Forest. I ran the troop on the principle that they could do what they wanted, but that we would go about doing it in the correct way. On our first outdoor activity outing one lad climbed a tree and fell off. Luckily he was unhurt but I had learned my lesson. You cannot be too careful or safety-conscious when dealing with other people's children. In future any climbing would be done with the precaution of a safety rope.

I took them away camping regularly in groups of four at a time and they accompanied me on many of my travels around the North of England. We followed the full length of Hadrian's Wall by car, stopping at all the points of interest along the way. We went to Alnwick, Bamburgh, Holy Island and the Farne Islands. We often cooked our meals, wrapped in tin foil, on an open fire where this was practical and safe.

We played sports and competed in District events. There was a five-a-side football tournament and, as they were keen to play, we entered a team. My oldest scout was thirteen years old and my team consisted of eleven- to thirteen-year-olds. We arrived at the sports centre to find that we were up against mostly fourteen- and fifteen-year-olds and that we had been drawn in the same league as the favourites to win the competition.

In my team talk I just told them that when we got beaten I did not want to hear complaints about the weaker members of our team. If anyone had enough breath left to talk they would not be playing in the next game since they would not have given all they had. I wanted them to go out and chase everything, and above all else enjoy themselves, even in defeat. There would be no disgrace in being beaten by this lot.

They did not let me down. They chased everything that moved. Throughout the competition we never won a game, and we never came near to scoring a goal, but I was really proud of them. We never conceded a goal either, despite the fact that against the favourites we did not manage to get the ball out of our own half or, come to think about it, I cannot ever remember us having possession. With the help of a good goalkeeper the team just chased and chased and kept the opposition from scoring. We may not have won a single game but we were the only team that did not lose either. We could hold our heads up in defeat.

In 1973 I completed my three-year plan to tour Britain, with a thoroughly enjoyable trip around the Scillies, the Channel Islands and the south of England. I survived the hydrofoil and the Friday night rush hour in the Dartford Tunnel. There was an element of sadness as I reflected on the ambition fulfilled, but it was a rewarding undertaking and certainly my biggest venture thus far.

That same year I went with a combined group of scouts and sea cadets to the boathouse at Great Tower on Lake Windermere for a week. They were not my scouts and I was not in charge but I had been invited along as an extra leader and because of my knowledge of the Lake District. I was to be in control for one day and would lead a mountain climb. Having very little to worry about, except for the one day, suited me fine. From time to time I would probably be put in charge of a small group for certain activities, but this would be no hardship.

Compared to the scouts, the sea cadets were extremely well disciplined for their age, mostly fourteen to fifteen years. From the start we got on famously and their response to my attitude was perfect. They loved fun and had a great sense of humour, which I went along with so long as they knew when to stop. They instinctively knew and I had no problems.

Much of the week was to be spent on the water where we would be canoeing and sailing. When the canoes were out it invariably seemed that capsize drill was the order of the day. Canoeing was a new experience for me and I was not really happy when I had my legs under the decking. I feared I would not be able to exit easily should the canoe capsize, but if nothing else, I did gain confidence on the water.

Sailing was different. The boats were clinker-built and very stable, being almost impossible to capsize. They were slow, but who was bothered? We were in no hurry and I had never sailed before. To create some interest for the cadets a race to the pier at Bowness was arranged and I was assigned to a boat which had a qualified sailing instructor in charge. Progress was slow but we eventually won by just a matter of a few yards.

Returning down the lake to the boathouse I realized how much I was enjoying this leisurely activity. It required a reasonable degree of skill and it had always seemed to me an exciting pastime, though since you have to wear a life jacket there is little danger involved. This new sport was definitely for me, I thought, as I relaxed in the heat of the early summer sunshine, pleasantly cooled by the gentle breeze that wafted us steadily along.

There were rowing boats too and every evening we would form crews and be out on the lake racing. Invariably I coxed my group of well-practised sea cadets to victory. They did not know the meaning of defeat and were perfectly suited to my enthusiastic leadership.

The mountain climb was arranged for the Thursday and the weather turned out to be quite reasonable. I had chosen the Langdale Pikes, having myself previously climbed Pavey Ark. We arrived at the New Dungeon Ghyll Hotel and prepared for the ascent. There were about fourteen lads and only one other leader and myself were prepared to climb, the other leaders deciding that the Hotel was a better prospect.

I had taken my ropes in case there was any difficulty, and everyone was fully equipped for the day out with emergency supplies as well as the normal requisites. I left nothing to chance for any mistake would be on my head. And I still had to engender excitement and enthusiasm or the exercise would not be worthwhile.

I appeared to be receiving very little support for the walk, apart from that of my assistant leader, as I fought off a barrage of moaning youths. Every conceivable excuse was being put forward, mostly by the scouts, as they tried their best to avoid any strenuous effort. I was having none of it and all were eventually ready to go.

By the time we arrived at Stickle Tarn we were all ready for our lunch and we ate. My rate of progress is quite slow and I decided that for those wishing to move on more quickly we should split into two parties, one climbing Pavey Ark, Pike o'Stickle and Harrison Stickle, and the other, which would be led by me, attempting Harrison Stickle direct. It was not too difficult but nevertheless in my case nothing could be taken for granted on a route I had not previously taken and it would be, therefore, only an attempt.

The six sea cadets immediately decided that they were coming with me and the scouts opted to go with the cadet leader. The cadets by this time were getting used to the idea of fellwalking. It was not as bad as they had thought. To add to their excitement we would be needing the rope – for my safety – in certain places on the route ahead.

Being experts at handling equipment, they had already had the rope opened up and recoiled it several times on the way up Stickle Gill. Equipment was for handling. Everything had to be tested, proved to be in working order and then prepared for use should the need arise. The operation was repeated until the whole exercise could be carried out speedily and efficiently. I had never seen such enthusiasm for a rope, or the packing and unpacking of a rucksack before, and it bolstered my confidence considerably to feel that I was in such capable and well practised hands. Well, at least the equipment was!

At 2,403 feet we were not climbing a high mountain but conditions under foot were quite severe as we forced our way up the hillside. We reached a small stony gorge filled with loose scree and had I been alone or without a rope, I would have been unable to proceed further with any degree of safety.

This was the moment they had been waiting for and the rope was ready for action before I could say I needed it. Three of the cadets carefully crossed to the other side and all six anchored themselves against boulders and heaved on the rope in order to provide a handrail by which I could safely cross. I had no wish to be committed to the handrail and instead said that I would pick my way across the scree in my usual manner but that, if they continued to strain on the rope, it would be handy in case of any emergency. This they did as I gingerly started to traverse the loose stones. I got halfway and suddenly everything went from under me. I grabbed at the rope and swung out into mid-air as they held firm with all their strength.

They eased the tension and lowered me gently back to the ground and I made my way, this time using the rope, to the other side. They retrieved my walking sticks as if it had all been part of a normal day's work, and we continued. They were convinced I had slipped and grabbed the rope deliberately to test their reliability, but nothing could have been further from the truth. I can do without any unnecessary risk; there was enough calculated risk in my just being there, let alone trying to perfect a circus act.

We reached the summit where we met up with the other party as planned. As we left for the descent down Dungeon Ghyll, they headed off towards Pike o'Stickle. They should catch us by the time we reached the bottom. In places the drop over the edge of the path was very long and steep and I would not have tackled it alone.

Throughout the walk we had talked a lot and they asked me why I was so different from the other leaders they had known. They were used to being bossed around, never reasoned with or treated like adults. Most of them smoked when their leaders were out of sight. I allowed them to smoke if they wished, since it was only themselves they were abusing, but we discussed the habit sensibly and some subsequently said they very much wanted to give up. I saw them regularly afterwards and I know at least two of them did.

We talked about swearing and other things that were supposedly wrong and I tried to explain that they were not really wrong, it was more a matter of how and when they were used. You must have principles and you have to live by them. It is of little use to pass judgment on other people's behaviour. What really matters is your own.

We had enjoyed an exciting and adventurous day out and they had no regrets about climbing the mountain. In fact they went so far as to say they all thought it was one of the best days out they had had. Once in sight of the Dungeon Ghyll Hotel they spontaneously lifted me aloft and carried me to the end. It was like winning the FA Cup, and I was deeply moved by their action. On arriving at the hotel I bought two pints of beer, one for me and one for the six cadets to share between them, providing they went out of sight behind a wall to drink it.

The walk had firmly moulded us into a team and for a short time we enjoyed the satisfaction that is achieved when a small group unites and operates as one. There had been a purpose, which I think had often been lacking from the activities they were used to, activities where inadequacies did not have serious consequences. With me they had faced a real challenge and proved they were equal to it.

As we prepared to depart at the end of the week I suddenly sensed that something was about to happen. They formed a half circle in front of me and the leader, John Sanderson – there is always a leader in any group – stepped forward, made a short but effective speech and presented me with two small gifts which they wished me to have as a reminder of the day I had climbed Harrison Stickle the hard way.

I was completely overcome by their thoughtfulness. What could I say? That is, had I been able to speak at all. I looked at the mountain-shaped piece of slate with the lone figure of a climber affixed near the top and all I could say was, 'Well this is no good, where are the six men that got me there?' My comment was appreciated and I had to turn away lest I should break down. For the first time I really knew that my services had done some good.

Sailing proved to be another new direction for me, and I recruited the help of the sea cadets who had become such close friends to help me choose a boat, as I knew very little about sailing dinghies. I needed a boat which would give me excitement but which would not be too difficult to handle.

I thought about a Mirror but they decided that what I really needed was an International Enterprise or something similar. We looked through the second-hand boat adverts and there was one Enterprise for sale. I went with one of the cadets and a scout to see the boat. I knew immediately that I must have it.

The owner was emigrating to New Zealand, hence him selling it, and the boat was in very good condition. With the sail up it looked a bit on the fast side, but my man was confident that in no time at all I would be at the helm and perhaps even racing it.

He had put his trust and faith in me that day not so long ago on the mountain. It was now my turn. If I wanted to learn to sail this type of boat I would have to buy my own anyway as no one would be prepared to let me use theirs while I lacked experience. After completing my tour of the British Isles I had bought a new car, a 1300XL Automatic Escort Estate and could fit a towbar. I completed the deal and the boat was mine.

Being a Youth Leader I managed to obtain permission to sail on the Waterloo Lake in Roundhay Park, Leeds. Mind you, I was taking the cadets with me, or rather they were taking me. To be honest I had never seen an Enterprise before and I was horrified as they zipped up and down the lake while I looked on in order to get some idea of what was involved. Even with the set of cruising sails which I was going to learn with, it went far too quickly for my liking.

There was no way out of it. If I did not do as I was told we would practise the capsize drill. Not likely, I thought, it was still only Easter and the water very cold. I did as I was instructed. Up and down the lake we zipped as I sat adjacent to the helmsman. I was supposed to be learning how to control the dinghy but was actually more concerned about keeping the boat upright than interested in what was happening at the helm.

The severe list to starboard was doing me no good at all. In fact, if the truth be known, I was scared stiff. This was nothing compared to what the boat would do with the racing sails, he volunteered. In that case, I replied, we had better get ashore quickly and I would put the dinghy back up for sale.

Realizing I was being perfectly serious they began to make the boat behave much more steadily and I gradually felt more comfortable. Slowly, I learned the techniques for handling the boat, and on our second trip out I took the helm. I have never relinquished it since, except for one occasion several years later, when I sailed with John Leighton, a friend who was a competent helmsman. There was only John, Graham Thackwray, a colleague of mine, and myself sailing and I wished to have a cine film made of my sailing activities. I am only able to helm with a crew of at least another two people besides myself, so I crewed while John helmed and Graham made the film. We had some hair-raising moments as we took in water over the side but he managed to bring the boat back and we remained upright.

The cadets gave me a considerable amount of confidence. They took the boat to its limits, teaching me how to sail it almost on its side. The double chine hull meant that the boat rolled over easily but steadily and was not particularly prone to any sudden capsize. They had complete control and were able to lean the boat over and balance precariously on the top side while it continued its progress forward, the centre board almost leaving the water. They knew my feelings about circus acts. I wished to sail safely and efficiently in order that I might take up racing.

I joined the Derwentwater Boat Club at Portinscale near Keswick and my dream of racing became a reality. I became a reasonably proficient helmsman and have since taken many people sailing, often for their first experience of the sport. I sailed regularly until 1976 when I decided that my boat would have to go, as the maintenance was demanding and the cost too high in relation to the amount of time I was now using it. It was also at this time that I gave up leading scouts and they had formed most of my crews.

I have now found a place where I can hire an Albacore for a reasonable fee and find this is a more practical way to sail. It also means I do not have the problem of looking for crews all the time. However, I would not hesitate to purchase another boat should the occasion ever arise where I could justify owning one.

I was never very successful at racing, but, like running, the field is often large and only one boat can win. It is just a case of doing your best and enjoying the thrill of competition. There are many races which take place within the race itself, between friends – and foes!

I have capsized only once to date and this was the only time I tried to helm with just one crew member, the way the boat ought to be raced. The Greenhows, who ran the Lake Road Vaults in Keswick, were good friends of mine and their son Chris often accompanied me on days out. We would play football, go sailing or go to Carlisle to watch the football there.

One day I decided that since I now had a wet suit I would risk trying to sail the boat with just the two of us aboard. Chris was quite game to try, although I do not think that he had been thrown into a lake before. There was a steady breeze and we sailed briskly out on to the lake. The wind suddenly changed direction and we tried to come about but immediately went into a spin and capsized. I went under the sail and did not have sufficient air in my wet suit life jacket to keep me high up in the water. The freezing cold water shot around inside my suit in an instant, completely taking my breath away as it did so. It was a relief when the suit began to do its job and I began to feel warmer. I managed to get myself clear of the sail and bobbed around in the water gasping and spluttering as I struggled to get more air into the buoyancy aid. We were rescued quite quickly and both were much wiser for the experience. I never tried to sail with just one crew member again. Once I know my limitations I am always fully prepared to accept them.

I also had a small boat which could either be rowed or powered by an outboard motor and I used this for fishing on Derwentwater. In September 1974 I was on the lake near the western shore when a gale suddenly blew up. I wrestled with the outboard motor but I broke the sheer pin as the motor started. I fitted a new one but I was perched precariously over the stern and the wind was now blowing far too strongly for me to be able to exert the power needed to start the motor. I was rapidly being swept out on to the open water.

The waves were enormous' and I feared the boat would be swamped or turn over and sink. With the use of the oars I fought to keep the bow meeting the waves head on. The storm quickly swept me across to the other side of the lake and it was with great relief that I clambered out of the boat, into the shallow water and dragged it as far up the shingle beach as I could.

I was just below Friar's Crag and apparently in someone's garden. I made my way towards the house and was greeted by several children who had seen me 'shipwrecked' at the bottom of their lawn. When I telephoned the boat club to ask for help they were very relieved to hear from me. They had noted I had gone missing out on the lake during the squall and were very concerned. They came out to recover me and the boat immediately. I owed much to Alan, Eve and Tony's (the proprietors of the boat club and their son) confidence in my ability and their willingness to give me help when it was needed, both on the water and ashore.

Of all the outdoor pursuits I have followed, sailing has probably given me the most satisfaction, excitement and the biggest thrills (and pain – I once broke three ribs in gale-force winds on Hornsea Mere!). It is a bit like driving a car with no brakes. You have to turn against the natural forces to slow down or stop, and these forces can change direction and are not always where you would like them to be. Constant awareness is required if you are not to overturn, and the feeling of speed is enhanced by the rush of water and the physical power needed to keep the boat upright.

It is very satisfying to see other members of the crew sharing this excitement knowing that it is only your combined efforts that make it all possible. Each person has a job to do and must do it efficiently if you are to stay afloat.

As a scout leader I had encouraged my group to do outdoor activities, and these included a bit of rock climbing. The safety aspect is most important here, and I insisted that they were always properly roped on. I was interested in rocks and climbing but most rock climbs were beyond my capabilities.

I had purchased a short length of 9 mm rope and carried this when I walked with anyone else in case I should need it. Graham Thackwray and I walked to Scale Force one day, only to find that the ladder up to the first ledge – from which you can obtain a good view of the waterfall – had been broken and taken down. In the interest of safety, out came the length of rope and up I climbed.

Although it was nothing spectacular I enjoyed the feeling it gave me actually to cling on to the rock, find small ledges on to which I could just get the toe of my boot and work my way up. Inspired by my success – albeit extremely modest – I bought another short length of 9 mm rope, some tapes, ironware and a helmet.

Graham accompanied me on several outings to Rocky Valley on Ilkley Moor, Brimham Rocks, and Malham where I explored my capabilities and put my recently acquired equipment into action. John Leighton was a good climber and he had just bought a new rope. He very kindly gave me his old full length 11 mm rope, in which he no longer had complete faith had he fallen any great distance. This was perfectly adequate for my purposes since there was no possibility that I would be running out any long lengths at a time.

My basic problems with rock climbing are firstly that I am frightened of heights, my sense of balance goes haywire when I am exposed to a sheer drop, and secondly my limited range of movement. These however are not deterrents, since climbing is about the exploration of oneself. It tests my ability to remain in complete control in unfavourable and sometimes unpleasant situations. It is a pursuit where no excuses are permissible. You are entirely dependent on your own performance for success. In failure there is little room for self-exoneration.

Initially I practised abseiling down some very steep grassy hillsides until I was confident in handling the rope and figure-of-eight abseiler. I progressed to small rock faces, where I also top-roped for safety. Although the top-rope eliminates most of the danger it does not affect the tension you feel as you step out on to the rock. My legs would still start to shake unless I could remain in complete control of the fear within me.

I did not climb to frighten myself. I got enough frightening moments from sailing. I climbed because I wished to come to terms with fear and wanted to know what my limits were. I was fascinated by rock and interested in all climbs, regardless of whether I could get up them or not. In fact the sort of climb that I could do would be too easy to be described in any modern guide. The thrill, however, of climbing up a rocky outcrop which required the use of hands was tremendous.

In climbing there are certain moves which are considered un-ethical, such as using your knees, but my aim always had to be to get to the top by any means within my physical capabilities. If I had to use my knees, then I would use them. If I had to use friction from my body, then I would use that. If I got absolutely desperate, then I would have the top-rope pulled as tight as possible. I climbed for pleasure and the general experience, not to prove anything. I must add that, if you once get on your knees, it can be very difficult to get off them again and this is one of the reasons why it is not considered to be a good practice.

Once I had learned to abseil I used it only to get back down from the top of climbs. I could gain little satisfaction from it unless it was part of a much wider exercise. The pleasure and sense of achievement was in getting up. The coming down only brought events to a conclusion.

I was never very good at climbing. I often had to search for a long while before I found a climb that I could do, the hand- and footholds having to be fairly regularly spaced out and the incline easy to not quite vertical. My climbing heroes were Dougal Haston, Don Whillans and Chris Bonington. Although they were all good climbers they were more importantly, and without exception, brilliant mountaineers.

Through climbing magazines, television and lectures I followed many of the expeditions to the high Himalayan peaks, including the climbing of the south-west face of Everest, under the outstand-ing leadership of Chris Bonington – the pinnacle of achievement as far as I was concerned. In 1981 I felt greatly honoured when, together with Heaton Cooper who had informed them of my exploits, I was invited to the Boningtons' for lunch. The meeting greatly increased the enormous amount of respect I already had for him and he was very generous in his praise for me. Praise, I might add, of which I felt a little unworthy in his presence.

I had great fun just playing around with my climbing equipment on quite small climbs: swinging in étriers from pitons hammered into mossy and slimy rock that no one had ever previously thought worth climbing (I would never use pitons on a route that some serious climber might want to use); tying myself up as I got into difficulties with my prusiking loops; doing a perfect abseil only to fall over as I stood on the ground; getting in a tangle with the rope as I climbed to the foot of some rock face ... These were all experiences which added to my understanding of the pursuit and life in general.

When my scout-leading activities ceased in 1975 I returned to my old school, Larchfield, at Harrogate, on one night each week to take a small group of children for anything which they might find interesting. My aim was not actually to do anything specific, but instead to create interests which they could follow when alone or which we could all discuss. The most important thing was that to be in my group was a privilege and whatever we discussed never went beyond the four walls of the room in which we held our meetings. This gave the pupils concerned something of their own about which everyone else was inquisitive, and because the children were probably not able to explain just what exactly we did do, it all remained a big secret. The kids thrived on our meetings although the secrecy was probably the greatest reason for their enjoyment.

They questioned me constantly about the way I coped with life. Since I was the same as they were, with the benefit of having already grown up, I suppose my answers gave them hope for the future. I carried on with my activities at Larchfield until 1978, by which time the school, scandalously, was being run down prior to its closure. I had become a School Governor in 1976 and had to deal with this unfortunate aspect as well.

Leeds Education Authority decided it was a luxury they could no longer afford. The level of disability among the children had certainly increased (less severely handicapped children being integrated into mainstream education immediately these days) but the school still did an excellent job as I, from my weekly visits, was well able to see.

The Authority appointed a lady to trim financial spending and she made it her business to steamroller her plans through. As governors we were supposedly 'consulted', in fact we were *informed* of the impending closure. This lady insisted we address her as doctor – though I believe her doctorate was in languages – which was extremely misleading for the handicapped children and their parents. These parents, I must add, had spent twenty years raising money for the school and had finally just had a hydrotherapy pool built. The pupils enjoyed its benefits for only a short time before the school closed. Larchfield is now a private nursing home with a very fine hydrotherapy unit paid for by public subscription.

I have mixed memories of my time at Larchfield but it did achieve results – just not necessarily by the most acceptable means. I wonder what has replaced it to care for the severely disabled children it used to accommodate.

Through returning to Larchfield I met many of the children's parents and they were extremely interested in my activities. They had a Parents Group in Leeds called PACE for anyone with a handicapped child, and I was associated with it until I moved to Bingley in 1982.

In 1980 I was privileged to meet the Banners, Delmar and Josephina, who lived in Little Langdale. They were both artists, Delmar a painter of considerable repute and Josephina an internationally acclaimed sculptress. More importantly, however, they were devoted to helping less fortunate members of society. They had, with the help of others such as Lord Denning, formed charitable trusts and had pioneered Beckstones, an outdoor residential centre for boys in trouble. With the success of this project, and realizing the need for a similar facility for handicapped children, the Harriet Trust had been formed.

The *Harriet*, a vintage fishing trawler from Fleetwood, was purchased and transported to a site on the shores of the Duddon Estuary at Millom. Together with purpose-built accommodation it is now an outdoor centre for handicapped children, accepting the whole family with a handicapped child where appropriate. I was consulted on some of the finer points of the design and, on its opening in 1983, was asked to provide the inaugural group of children and take a hand in the first week of running it.

I was very happy to be involved with the Harriet and, for the first time, I felt that this was one concern that had got it right. The idea, the scale of the operation and its execution, which had all been sorted out before my arrival, were just what was required and it was so fortunate to be situated on the edge of the Lake District. The whole scheme is operated so that groups must organize and help themselves, but they also have the freedom to please themselves just what they do.

On the weeks that I have been involved we have never been at a loss for things to do and the groups have consisted of quite severely handicapped adolescents, both male and female. The help I could give came not so much from what I could actually do, but from the people I had contact with who worked at schools for the physically handicapped, who could put together groups to use in its initial stages.   ·

While working with scouts, sea cadets, Larchfield and other groups I had some very trying moments when I thought that I was getting nowhere and I sometimes, when faced with apathy or delinquency, wondered why I bothered, achieving absolutely nothing. Sometimes I was in total despair, as on the occasion when my walking sticks – I obtained them privately both to suit my needs and because the NHS will issue you with only one pair – disappeared mysteriously as I spoke to a group of scouts in church and were never seen again. Perhaps someone else's need was greater than mine or maybe someone performed only half of a miracle!

However, through voluntary work I expanded my horizons, particularly when dealing with children and youths. I like to think that this learning was a two-way process and that they in turn derived some lasting benefit from my efforts. I was never a 'do-gooder', I wanted results and I was wasting both their time and mine if I did not achieve something positive, however little. It is easy to help the good become better, but helping the not-so-good is what it is all about.

ELEVEN

Reaching the Heights

As I had lain in my tent that night of 19 September 1969, aching and sore from the ascent of Scafell Pike, I had begun to wonder what Ben Nevis looked like. Was the summit an impossible pinnacle or was it a mountain somewhat similar to the one I had just climbed? At what altitude was the nearest road and how far was it to the top? These were the things I wanted to know.

At 4,406 feet it stood considerably higher than the 3,210 feet I had just climbed. Maybe I had no right to think about it, but I wanted to know. I knew people who had been to the summit and they were not prepared to play down its difficulty, but if they could climb it, then perhaps so too could I.

Climbing Scafell Pike had been hard enough. In fact I did not see how I could give any more, but maybe it would be no more difficult and perhaps not quite so dangerous. Anyway, these were all questions I needed answered if I was to have peace of mind.

I was given an old calendar and one of the pictures was of Ben Nevis from Corpach. The mountain looked big but not particularly hazardous. Well, at least I kept trying to convince myself that it looked reasonable, as I studied the picture over and over again.

There was the summit rising above and behind Carn Dearg. If Carn Dearg was 3,961 feet then it did look rather daunting. I began to look for other pictures of the mountain in order to get a different perspective. Perhaps if I kept looking I might find one which showed it to be a much more reasonable prospect.

As I acquired more pictures I suddenly noticed that many of them showed pockets of snow around the summit. The rest of the view looked like a summer's day as there were leaves on the trees. Did the snow ever go, or did it snow up at that altitude in summer? No one I knew had the answers. There were tales that if the snow ever completely disappeared from the mountain, then the ownership of it – or something or other – would change hands. Was this true, and did the snow remain there all year round?

As quickly as I solved one problem, another query would arise, and there were still some questions which remained unanswered. One thing was certain. The mountain held lots of interest. The Lake District was exciting, but this was something else. It was the highest point in Britain and something worth aiming for. If there was any possibility, then I had to climb it. I had to get myself to the summit and back down again!

I continued to climb mountains in the Lake District. Each time I reached another summit I extended myself to the limit of my endurance. On reflection the climbs never seemed so bad, and were extremely enjoyable and rewarding experiences. The problem was that every time I went out it seemed such hard work. There were no such things as easy mountains. Some were more difficult and demanding than others, but none could be taken for granted.

I chose my mountains carefully. I did not just go out for a day's strenuous walking. Each one was a labour of love. I knew what each mountain looked like from most, if not every, angle. I researched the different routes to the summits and I studied their features. They were intimate friends yet I wanted to know them better. Climbing a mountain was like giving a part of myself in exchange for the pleasure it was bestowing upon me. There were no casual affairs – maybe a few flirtations with smaller or less difficult peaks if I had walked too far and was obviously not going to make it to my goal as consolation, but there were definitely no casual affairs. It was real love and appreciation or nothing.

I had fallen in love with Ben Nevis. I was charmed by the beauty and majesty of the massive stone shoulder. Nothing was going to come between me and that mountain. I knew the risk was high, but anything really worth doing in life has its price and I would have to pay whatever it demanded.

I was not being silly about it, just realistic. Every climb was a calculated risk. Sometimes the risk was greater than others. The greater the risk the more calculated I had to be. I had no desire to die, but I had long ago resolved to live and not just opt for an easy existence. To live you have to go out and enjoy life, not simply let life come to you or, even worse, pass you by. Sometimes you have to take it by the scruff of the neck and get a firm grip on your destiny.

When in 1971 I went to Scotland to tour the Hebrides there lurked in my mind the strong possibility that I would also attempt to climb Ben Nevis, weather permitting. I had all the necessary clothing and equipment and I was well read on the area. I had researched the routes as far as possible and knew that any attempt would have to be by the tourist path. I was not anticipating any difficulties underfoot but I was aware that it would be a long hard slog simply because of its height.

I arrived in Fort William on a beautiful sunny day and the Ben was clearly visible, with no cloud or haze at all. It was just like the pictures I had been carefully scrutinizing except for one thing. In reality it looked much higher. I looked again and there it stood in all its glory, looming large and clear, standing there with pride and grace. I drove around to Corpach and along the side of Loch Eil to try to get everything into perspective.

There is something about a photograph that does not do complete justice to rock, and I enjoyed every moment as I surveyed the great mass set against the blue sky. I was over-awed.

Did I really want to climb it? Did I have any hope of climbing it? I was beginning to have doubts. Nevertheless I would go to Glen Nevis and take stock of the situation from there. The path could be clearly seen. It did not look too difficult but as it came out of the Red Burn it just zigzagged up into the sky. The massive shoulder stood completely unrelenting as it curved away towards the summit. It might as well have curved towards eternity, for it was definitely too much for me. If I ever got as far as the disappearing curve I had no doubt that it would still be a long hard pull to the summit. And what if there was any snow?

I resigned myself to giving it a miss as I enjoyed the serenity of the mountain and the glen. I had not told anyone that I was going to climb it, so I would not have to make any excuses. The simple truth was that I was afraid, afraid of the sheer size and constant threat of changing weather conditions. There were no apologies to be made, it was simply beyond my limitations. I had to face reality. This time I had loved and lost, but at least I lived to love another day.

Perhaps I was foolish to think that I could climb it on my own. On the other hand, perhaps if I was to get a party of strong walkers together they may help me achieve my goal?

All was not yet lost. I had never used other people to help me climb a mountain before, but why not? Others had often accompanied me but I had never relied on them, we had been equals if the going got rough. They had done nothing for me which I would not have done for them, and this was the way I had wanted it right from the start. Yes, I had been saved from near disaster once or twice, but perhaps these minor mishaps had resulted from risks that I would not have taken had I been alone.

Later in the holiday I passed Ben Nevis on two further occasions but was relieved to see that it was veiled in a blanket of cloud and I had no soul-searching to do. There was no possibility of my ever considering climbing it with any cloud around. If I ever did get to the top I wanted to enjoy the views, and especially the north-east face. I understood that the summit was only free of cloud between forty and fifty days of the year and that they had closed the weather station, or observatory, near the summit for that very reason.

On returning home I decided that I had been a bit too optimistic in my approach to climbing the mountain. The extra 1,200 feet was just too great a gap to bridge; it was like trying to climb Scafell Pike one and a half times. What I needed was something in between: higher than Scafell Pike but not as high as Ben Nevis.

The answer was Snowdon, the highest mountain in Wales. In July 1972 after my brother's death I took my parents to North Wales for their holidays. I wanted to take a close look at the area and was owed two weeks off work in lieu, because of an overtime arrangement whereby we were granted days off instead of being paid. We needed to spend time together at this difficult period in our lives.

I knew that the track up Snowdon was quite reasonable as there was a mountain railway which ran nearly to the top, and there was a hotel and café at the terminus. It could not be so difficult if enough people could get up there to make a café a viable proposition. On the mountains I had climbed previously there had been very few people on the higher reaches.

Possibly the reason was that, in the Lake District, most of the peaks were popular and hence there were no transport systems up any of them. On the other hand the name Snowdon stood out. Everyone knew that Snowdon was the highest mountain in Wales, but considerably fewer know Scafell Pike. Some thought it was a big fish, a medieval weapon or even a spectacular highboard dive!

We wanted a fine day for the walk and this we got. We started from Llanberis and followed the path which ran parallel to the mountain railway. It was a steady pull and we were able to take advantage of the refreshment hut somewhere near the halfway point.

Although we were climbing to 3,560 feet, the environment, at least by this route, was not hostile. There were many people making the gentle ascent and there was a relaxed holiday atmosphere about the whole thing. The threat of help being far away in the event of an accident or a change in the weather was not present, which unfortunately induced the lack of respect that some had for the mountain. For many this would be their first mountain, a possible reason for them being on the tourist path, and they could easily be lulled into thinking that other mountains were similarly well serviced and maybe attempt a further one without giving it the respect it deserved.

The effort involved in my climbing a mountain is so great that I always choose the easiest route, except if the distance is too far or there is some special feature that I wish to see. I had researched the other routes up Snowdon but was not convinced that any of them were within my capabilities. The Pyg Track looked a bit hazardous as it came out of Llyn Llydaw, around Crib-Goch and up to the summit. I had no wish to face any more danger than was necessary, especially since I had my father with me. He thought the struggle was too great for me when I was quite happy with conditions underfoot; what he would think of me sliding about on loose scree I did not know and, since he would not have been sparing with his words, I did not care to find out.

From the café there was a short but difficult section to the impressive summit. We enjoyed the magnificent views before returning to the café for refreshment in preparation for the long descent. The proprietress of the business came over to speak to me and asked if I had enjoyed the ride up. 'What ride?' I replied. She was amazed that I had walked all that way up and insisted that I take the train down at no charge. They always kept a couple of seats free in case of an emergency and I should have one of them.

She was adamant that I should take up her offer of the ride, although she fully appreciated that I was not an emergency, and, deciding that it had been a long walk to the top and time was getting on, I accepted. I was also curious to know what the journey by rack-and-pinion rail was like, but would have never used it otherwise. For me the descent is much more difficult, although slightly faster, than the ascent, and deep down I was quite pleased that she considered my achievement of reaching the summit by foot (and stick!) worthy of a free ride down.

My father opted for a gentle downhill trot and the further exercise that a descent on foot would give him, no longer having to progress at my laboriously slow pace. I sat back and enjoyed my journey by rail, although I was probably more apprehensive and concerned about my safety on the steam train than I would have been on foot.

Perhaps I should explain here that my mother and I now knew where we stood when it came to my leisure activities. She did not encourage me, she always exhorted me to be careful, but she fully accepted that I would continue to do what I enjoyed. Anyway, whenever I climbed with my father she was quite happy.

*

In September that year I had been ready to make my second tour of Scotland, this time to the Orkney and Shetland Isles. Once again the possibility of climbing Ben Nevis was there. Time had erased the fear that I had felt on my first visit, and I was now a year older and more experienced. And besides, with a bit of luck the cloud would be down, and the question of climbing it would not actually arise. However, should I feel more confident on my second visit, the possibility of making an attempt to climb it was there.

On my way up through Aviemore I could climb the 4,084 feet of Cairn Gorm as training for Ben Nevis, provided, of course, that it did not look too difficult. Cairn Gorm was a civilized place. There were ski lifts and a café near the summit. No doubt you could take your car most of the way.

I arrived at Aviemore and took my car as far as possible before starting to climb. The Ptarmigan Café, the highest in Britain, was a modern building not too far from the summit. The views were phenomenal, and you could see for miles. I decided to save myself and descended by the chairlift. This was more difficult than I anticipated since the chairs never actually stop. You jump on as they are momentarily held back. There is only a seat and a bar for your feet. As the contraption launched into mid-air and down the cable I had not had time to compose myself and, being frightened of heights, I began to shake with fear.

One foot shook loose from the foot-rest and I began to wonder how much longer I could remain in this position or, if I were to fall, how far was the drop? Perhaps I would be able to hang on until the drop was not quite so far. I realized that I was thinking negatively and got a hold on myself so I could enjoy the rest of the journey down.

Perhaps Ben Nevis would not be quite so frightening as the chairlift. On arriving in Glen Nevis at the latter part of my holiday I was dismayed to note that my sentiments were much the same as on the previous year. I was, however, never forced to make a decision, as the weather conditions were unsuitable for an ascent. At times the summit was visible but there was a lot of low cloud about.

I surveyed it carefully. It looked no less fearsome and I knew if ever I wished to climb it then it would be very difficult, very hard work and dangerous if I underestimated any aspect of the walk or if anything went wrong. My love and respect for the mountain were as great as ever but there were many things that I needed to come to terms with before I set foot on it.

In 1974, the previous year having slipped by as I convinced

myself that perhaps the ascent was impossible, I was in a great deal of pain in one of my legs. I had done nothing to cause it, but, however much I rested, it would not go.

I went to see the specialist who had now taken over on the retirement of 'my' surgeon. He was very helpful and arranged for me to have my body and legs X-rayed. He came to the conclusion that the pain was being caused by my spine. I had several bones twisting out of line and they were trapping nerves as they moved. I was fitted with a surgical support but, after several days of wearing it, I decided that it was impossibly restrictive, because it did not fit the curve I have in my back, which is the result of my compensating for having no sense of balance.

I refrained from wearing it and slowly tried to get myself fit by doing more physical exercise than I had been doing lately. There was an alternative; I could spend a long period in hospital on a rack, but this was not my idea of a fun way to spend what could amount to a very long time. From past experience I knew only too well that if they once got me in hospital they might not be prepared to release me until they felt it right for me. I could, as it were, be held prisoner or, even worse, coerced into having some treatment that I did not really want.

I continued to exercise, and the pain subsided. When you are fit the muscles around the spine hold the bones firmly in place; when they are lax the bones can move more easily – hence the pain. I was managing to remain at work, but one day I was summoned to the group leader's office where I was stunned by his announcement. He had decided that I could no longer walk adequately and needed a wheelchair. Who was he to dictate what my medical needs were? If I had taken his attitude I would never have walked in the first place. I flatly refused to consider his directive and immediately earned the tag of being difficult.

In June we had a settled spell of weather and I decided at very short notice to return to Fort William for a serious look at the mountain. At twenty-five I felt that I was now getting old. I knew that of the other people who had undergone the operation I had, most were back in wheelchairs. That was not for me. I could not afford to keep going to just look at the mountain. I must make my mind up one way or the other if the weather remained good.

I left work on the Friday evening and drove up to Fort William. The weather was brilliant and I had to decide whether I should set to and make an immediate attempt, risking the travel weariness catching up with me, or whether I should hope that the weather would hold and make preparations for an attempt on the Sunday.

I had walked after a long drive before and the effects usually started to show around midday. I decided to wait. It would give me that little bit more time to prepare for what was in store.

I bought some new items of equipment in Fort William and reported to the Park Warden what my intentions for the following day were. I drove around to Corpach only to observe that, despite the heat wave, there was snow near the summit. I shut this from my mind, thinking that I would worry about it if and when the problem arose.

I went to the swimming baths for some last-minute exercise and to convince myself that I really was in as good condition as I had ever been. I was fully prepared both mentally and physically. This was going to be the long-awaited day of reckoning. I was either up to it or I was not, and either way I must accept the consequences. If I failed it was doubtful that I had it in me to make a second attempt. I would give everything and more if necessary.

My only ambition, other than to climb the mountain, was to stay alive. Many more people die on British mountains than make the headlines in the national press, though doubtless if anything was to happen to me they would be clamouring for the story. In one year eighteen people died and 126 were injured in the Lake District alone. The figures are staggering, although I suspect that many of the fatalities were due to natural causes since everyone has to die somewhere. Although the route I intended to take up Ben Nevis is known as a tourist path, it had claimed victims and much better physically equipped people than myself. The whole venture needed treating with a lot of respect.

I made my sandwiches and prepared to sleep in my car at the foot of the mountain. I had spoken to the Warden at the Youth Hostel and he had been very helpful in explaining the difficulties of the route and telling me of all the serious casualties he had seen brought down from the tourist path. I got into my sleeping bag and prayed hard. I prayed that I should have the strength to face what was about to come. I prayed not that I should reach the summit but that I should be able to give everything and know when I had given everything, and have the courage and good sense to give up. I prayed for guidance to make rational decisions at all times and remain fully in control. Then I quickly went to sleep.

I awoke at 5.30 a.m. and the weather was perfect. There were few clouds and these were very high in the sky. I could not see the summit but I would have to risk that being clear. By the time I got up there it could so easily have changed. I carefully put on my boots, checked the things I was taking, had my breakfast and at 7.00 a.m. was on my way.

I crossed the footbridge over the river and followed the path along the hillside. There were two metal bridges spanning small gorges and, as I stepped out on to the first, I felt very uncomfortable. I lay on the ground and slowly pulled myself across. This way there was no possibility of my falling off or tripping on the metal surface.

I continued on and round the bend into the Red Burn. All was going well and it was about this time that the first of the walkers started to pass me. Out of the Red Burn and I was soon on to the zigzag path that I had seen heading towards the summit. The summit was, however, nowhere in sight and all I could do was just keep on going.

By early afternoon I was beginning to feel very tired. The time had flown. I did not feel as if I had been walking for so long but my body was exhausted. I sat down to contemplate. I had almost had enough, there were no longer many people passing me and I was still nowhere near the summit. It was beginning to make sense to turn around and forget my desire to climb Ben Nevis. It was just too much for me. The sun shone brightly, making it very warm, and that was not exactly helping matters, although had the weather been cold or windy, that would have been much worse.

I was about to head back down when a man coming up the path stopped to speak to me. He encouraged me to carry on but I insisted that I was ready to go back down. Then I began to think. I felt better for the rest, maybe I was not so far away from the top and perhaps I had not yet given everything.

He offered to carry my haversack and I agreed. Although it was not very heavy this was a great help. After walking some distance with me he said that he was going on to the summit and that he would leave my things there. I told him that there was no certainty that I would get there. In that case, he said, when he got there he would wait for me and if I did not appear, he would pass me on the way down.

This seemed reasonable and away he went, over the rise and out of sight. Once again I was on my own, but my morale had been considerably lifted. I soldiered on as best I could and arrived at the icefield which I had seen the previous day. I made my way up over the frozen snow and the summit came into view. At about 4.00 p.m. I was standing on the summit and, whether or not I got back down safely, nobody was going to take that away from me. I had achieved my ambition and for a while I simply sat there and took it all in.

This was what it was all about. There was the north-east face and all the other features of the summit. The views stretched for miles, and I took the photographs that I wanted. I got the man who had carried my haversack to take some pictures of me before he left. Conditions were perfect. It was Sunday 23 June, midsummer; I was on the top of Ben Nevis.

I remembered my brother who had died, and how much he had helped me in those early days. I wished that he could be there with me but I was alone. Perhaps he knew. I thought of the people in my life who meant so much to me. It was just one month since my group leader had adamantly insisted I should be in a wheelchair.

It was time for one last summit photograph and then I must make my way back down. Suddenly an American chap appeared. He took one look at me and seemed to go berserk. 'I have flogged my . . . guts out getting up here. I am absolutely . . . and I don't know how the . . . hell I'm going to get back down again. And what the . . . hell do I find, a . . . cripple on the summit.'

Having obviously ruined his day, all I could say was, 'Well that makes two of us, I don't know how I'm going to get back down either.' He stormed off in disgust.

I descended towards the icefield. The snow was very deep and with the heat of the day it had softened considerably. My walking sticks sank straight into it and I struggled down over it, keeping the weight on my sticks to an absolute minimum. There was no time for messing about, it had taken me 9 hours to reach the summit and it was already past 4.30 p.m. If it was daylight until 11.00 p.m. I still only had another 6½ hours left.

I progressed steadily downhill, eventually arriving at the zigzagging path. I could see some short cuts between the bends and, fearful of the time and my rapidly diminishing strength, I deviated and headed down the scree. It was much steeper than I had anticipated and very loose. If I was not extremely careful I would not only be heading down but also for disaster. It was treacherous. A young man passed me, he too was obviously in difficulties. What chance did I have if a fit youth was unable to cope?

There I was, over 3,000 feet up, sliding down loose scree with very little control. What was I playing at? I was desperate to get back down as quickly as possible but not this way. I slithered slowly towards the path and was pleased when my feet slid off the scree and on to the firm track. That was another lesson learned. No more short cuts.

Delighted to be back on the path and also at having successfully, if desperately, descended a fair way in a short time, I steadily made my way down. I was by now very tired, my hands were beginning to blister and my feet hurt, but I had to keep going. Suddenly I slipped, falling awkwardly. There was a loud crack. I pulled myself together only to find that I had broken one of my walking sticks. How was I going to continue now? It was hard enough with two sticks. It would be almost impossible with only one.

The stick had broken at an acute angle and I thought it might be possible to lash both pieces together. I had some spare laces for my gaiters in my haversack and I set about whipping them around the stick. I was pleased with the result of my handiwork, but would it hold when I walked with it? I tried it carefully. It wobbled a bit but held firm as I set off back down the track. My hands were now so badly blistered that I was unable to put any more pressure on my sticks than was strictly necessary, so perhaps it would be adequate.

I made it into the Red Burn and felt much more at ease as I started on the final section. I was now at a much safer altitude and all I had to do was just keep going. The only problem was that it was getting dark. A man came down behind me and started to walk alongside. I was greatly relieved that he did not go straight past.

I was in agony and barely able to stand. My feet hurt as they had never hurt before. The blisters on my hands had long since rubbed off and I was using my sticks against the raw flesh. But I had to keep going. The man talked to me, taking my mind off the situation, and I was so elated and satisfied that the pain seemed not to matter.

I was now staggering very badly and how I did keep going I will never know. I was so bad that I did not have the time or the energy even to worry about the metal bridges, I just crossed them. As we finally reached the valley bottom my companion realized that only some unknown force was keeping me going. I was using reserves which I never knew I had and even they were almost exhausted.

I told him that I had nothing left. That was it. I could go no further. I was in a complete state of collapse, but it did not matter; I was very happy. In the dark distance there were some figures coming towards us. Who were they? Had they come to rescue me? If they had, this was not how I wanted the day to end. I dug even deeper into my reserves and found strength to carry on.

There were three men and they had apparently passed me earlier in the day. They had anticipated that it would take me all this time to get back down and they had come straight from the pub to give me a well-earned reception. They were right about one thing, it was well earned, but I was in no fit state for any reception.

Quickly realizing the poor state I was in two of them stood one at either side of me; I leaned on their outstretched arms and was able to walk the last few hundred yards with the pressure taken off my hands. I arrived back at my car at 12.30 a.m. where there were several cans of beer waiting for me.

The problem now was that my hands were too sore to hold a tin and I had to lie on the ground while they gently poured the contents into my mouth. I had just two. I made them drink the rest. You cannot celebrate alone! No wonder my feet were hurting; the sole had worn through on one boot and the nails were firmly holding it to my foot. I braced myself while the boot was carefully removed. They put me into my sleeping bag and left. I had made it – with a little help.

The following day I drove, with some difficulty, past the cloud-capped Ben Nevis to Aberdeen and caught the boat to Shetland where I could relax, recover and practise using my unsteady walking stick. I was in no state to be seen by family or friends. They would not have understood what it meant to me. I had gone to my absolute limits of endurance and I had learned much about myself. There could be no further progress in an upward direction without taking longer than one day, or without going abroad. Not that I ever thought I would.

TWELVE

Distance the Challenge

In the early hours of 24 June 1974 I had achieved my goal. Almost five years after conceiving the idea and many anxious moments I had at last climbed Ben Nevis. It had taken me 17½ hours. I had strained innumerable muscles and joints, my hands and feet were rubbed raw but I was happy. Only one thing bothered me. In terms of climbing mountains I wondered where I should go from there. Everything I had lived for, with regard to climbing mountains, was now in the past.

From my physical state it was apparent that I could make no further progress in climbing alone. My principles on this point were strong and I was not about to change them. If I thought that I could not climb a mountain alone, then I was not prepared to tackle it with someone else.

I had reached my absolute limits of continuous endurance and my immediate reaction was to retire from the fells while I was still winning. There was no pleasure in forcing myself over difficult terrain just for the sake of doing so. I had climbed Ben Nevis alone, with two sticks, and the venture had been the culmination of five years of effort, patience and, finally, calculated risk. For a fit person the ascent is really little more than a strenuous walk and there were people who said they found it impossible to believe that a person of my physical capacity could keep going continuously for 17½ hours. In fact, the real problem, which most people could not get into perspective, was my inability to escape. A fit person could descend quickly and safely in the event of a change in circumstances. My descent would take between three and five times as long, which could put a severe strain on my physical resources, especially if the change had been a break in the weather. Also, I was alone, which even in low cloud, an ever-present hazard, can impose severe mental strain.

However, any decision about my walking would be mine alone. I was summoned to the group leader's office (not the one so concerned with my mode of locomotion, I had by now moved on to a different group) to be told that I must stop fellwalking as I was behaving irresponsibly towards my employers by doing so. I could easily get injured. I was absolutely taken aback to hear this from someone who regularly played football. Had he not considered the possibility that he too could get injured? In fact playing football took his physical destiny beyond his own control. Several members of the office played rugby and he was none too happy when I pointed out that I had as much right as a physically handicapped person to pursue my own choice of activities as he, they or anyone else did. The risk of my getting hurt was perhaps far more calculated than theirs. It is impossible to play football or rugby without sooner or later becoming temporarily immobilized through injury. Why does society think that disabled people do not have the right to suffer the same pain or take the same risks as the physically able do? Once again my reputation for being awkward was being enhanced.

The problem with having a reputation is that there are always those who will prejudge and whatever action you take it will not be right. Many of my problems, I believed, stemmed from not being willing to be a party to deception or dishonesty. Whatever happened I remained true to my own principles. But the situation at work still made it imperative for me to find an escape in my free time.

So, having achieved Ben Nevis, what next? I had completed my tour of the British Isles the previous year and did not wish to start retracing my steps so soon afterwards. I was afraid of going abroad on my own and there was no one with whom I wanted to go. Sitting on a sun-drenched beach drinking excessive amounts of alcohol was not my idea of fun, and I had no wish to go to an alpine resort for a walking holiday.

I needed mental stimulus and something that little bit more demanding. I could see no point in travelling any great distance if I were not going to see and do as much as possible while there. I was frightened of flying and did not speak any foreign languages nor, I must confess, did I have any inclination to do so. I did want to travel abroad, but the prospect was daunting.

However, my negative attitude towards holidays could not continue indefinitely and I decided that I would go to Spain, making the journey by sea and coach at the Easter of 1975. My brother had been to Spain by sea and rail as his girlfriend had also been afraid of flying. Everybody went to Spain, so why not me?

Although I may give the impression that I must have a challenge and do things the average person might not do, this is not really the case. In reality I start something which is fairly straightforward, enjoy it, and then, in pursuit of further enjoyment, try to take it to its ultimate. It is just a natural progression towards my limits and helps eliminate living with the regret of what I might have achieved had I tried.

I had booked my holiday to Spain and was giving an interview for the radio about some of my exploits when the interviewer suddenly put me on the spot. He reeled off things about me which he knew I had done, and ended by asking what I was going to do next. I did not really know what to say, but in a crisis my natural instinct is to be positive and I calmly replied that I was going to go around the world. He was a bit taken aback and, although I did not show it, so was I. What had I just said? He asked no further questions, fortunately.

I would definitely like to travel, but around the world was taking it a little too far. I had not even started yet and here I was professing to have some plan to go around the world. The idea must have been there subconsciously otherwise I would not have said what I had. But what about the problem of flying? How would I do it with only five weeks' holiday a year? And there were certain to be other problems, including those of language and finance.

In fact it was just what I needed, a new purpose, something which would give me adventure, excitement and lasting enjoyment. What was there to worry about? I had served my apprenticeship by travelling around Britain. I was accustomed to travel, even if it was not quite so far. I was used to travelling by land and sea and had learned how to while away the time as I waited for departures or delays. There would probably be little difference.

Being a person who believes in action I went out and booked two further holidays. I would go to Interlaken at the end of July and take a coach tour of Italy at the end of August. Both trips involved travelling across Europe by sea and rail. There were many of Europe's most famous mountains that I wished to see in Switzerland and the archaeological importance of Italy made it a must.

The first major problem that had to be overcome was the way in which I was going to carry all my clothes and other requisites. In the past this had never been a problem when I travelled by car or went on short journeys where I did not need very much. And, should I require any help with my luggage, there would be the language difficulty. Perhaps there would be occasions when I would have to queue for long periods while carrying it, especially at the customs check-outs or while boarding ships.

What I needed was a large modern framed rucksack with lots of outside pockets. This would give me easy access to any items I might need while I was on the journey, besides providing additional space if required. I selected the largest good quality rucksack I could find, an early birthday present from my mother and father, and fitted this to the most comfortable frame with which it was intended to combine. Empty, it weighed very little and I would only have to pack it with as much as I could comfortably carry. The excess space would be there should I wish to take bulky but not too weighty items. This problem solved, I set off for Spain where I spent a successful week at Malgrat de Mar, a coastal resort near Barcelona. I enjoyed my first experience of foreign travel and I awaited with great eagerness my forthcoming trip to Switzerland, which this time was to be by rail.

I headed off to Switzerland with an open mind. The mountains were high and snow-capped, much too difficult for me to consider venturing upon. I wanted to see all the well-known peaks I had seen pictures of and read about and also to travel on some of the mountain railways. Perhaps I could fit in a short walk or two, but I had to remember that I was not in Britain and even a minor injury could prove expensive should I require medical attention or treatment.

I had chosen Interlaken as a base because it was situated in a beautiful area and was overlooked by the Eiger, Mönch and Jungfrau. It was also a good place from which to make daily excursions by rail. I travelled to Grindelwald, Kleine Scheidegg and up to the Jungfraujoch. On arriving I found I was unable to walk. I had to lean against the wall while I became acclimatized to the altitude. After some considerable time I was able to walk, although with as little exertion as possible, and carefully explored the snow-covered area adjacent to the 13,642-feet peak of the Jungfrau. Just being there was a wonderful experience and, as the sun shone brilliantly, I felt no need to do anything more than take it all in. This was the Switzerland I had come to see and, despite the rarefied atmosphere, I enjoyed every moment.

From the train the view of the Eiger North Face was spectacular and I knew instantly what made men want to climb it. To anyone who loves mountains there are just no words to describe the feeling it instils. There it stood like a massive dish; the 'White Spider', the 'Swallows Nest', 'Death Bivouac', the 'Traverse of the Gods', the 'Hinterstoisser Traverse'. I decided that another day I would try to climb to the foot of the face and perhaps make a start on the first icefield to try to get an even better appreciation.

I toured Lakes Brienz and Thun by steamer, leisurely enjoying myself as I went. Later in the week I decided to return to Grindelwald and take the train to Alpiglen from where I would try to walk to the foot of the Eiger. I bought a secondhand ice axe and I already had a pair of crampons. The climb up the steep grassy hillside from Alpiglen was very difficult and, to make matters worse, as I approached the face it began to thunder. It felt as if the whole lot was going to come crashing down. Visibility was almost nil and I lay on the ground and prayed for deliverance. Eventually the banging stopped and the cloud began to thin a little so I could set off again. I arrived at a gully filled with ice and made my way a short distance up before deciding that enough was enough and I returned to the station. I had seen very little of the face itself but I had been terrified by its presence, and now had a greater under-standing of the spell it casts over man.

I wanted to see the Matterhorn, and to do this I travelled to Zermatt and rode up the Gornergrat railway. The vista from the summit station was well worth the journey, but there still remained one special mountain I wished to see, and for this I would have to make the long journey to Chamonix in France. The courier and the hotel staff were sure that it was not possible to make the return journey in one day but I had other ideas. I had enquired about the five trains which I would need to catch if I wished to get there, and it was possible – just! I would have approximately one hour at Chamonix, plenty of time to see Mont Blanc – Europe's highest mountain – providing the weather was favourable.

If I missed a connection then I would not be returning until the following day. I travelled via Thun, Brig, Martigny and Vollorcine to Chamonix. Miraculously, everything went smoothly and the weather obliged. Mont Blanc was just as I had imagined it and I had the added bonus of seeing the Aiguille du Midi and the many other very impressive peaks.

My holiday in Switzerland had been very rewarding and I was much the richer for the experience. Reading about alpine climbs would now have a certain reality about them. They were no longer just places and mountains; I had been and seen them for myself. I would never climb them but I was content with what I had done.

My summer vacation in the Alps had whetted my appetite for more mountain adventure at home. In order to make my next enterprise worthwhile, it would have to be more demanding than anything I had previously undertaken. The only way that this would be possible would be to follow a route for several days, which would also involve carrying enough equipment to cover every eventuality. Distance was now the challenge.

I finally decided on the Three Peaks of Yorkshire walk. It was within reasonable travelling distance of home and I was familiar with the area. I had previously climbed each peak on its own by the easiest routes in 1971.

The Three Peaks are Penyghent (2,273 feet), Whernside (2,419 feet) and Ingleborough (2,373 feet). The walk is about twenty-five miles over rough hills with nearly 5,000 feet of ascent, and is normally completed in a day. It has become a recognized and gruelling test of ability and endurance, recommended for strong walkers only. Many more people start the walk than finish it. This was the sort of challenge I needed. To compensate for the time it would take me, I should have to carry a load of between thirty and forty pounds, no mean feat in itself. It would need skill to navigate the course and tremendous willpower to keep going.

I bought a lightweight mountain tent, goose-down sleeping bag and a Karrimat on which to sleep, together with many other items, such as a torch with a red flashing light, first aid kit and complete change of clothing in case of an emergency. Fully packed, my rucksack weighed about thirty-five pounds. Having had no previous experience of long walks I decided to tackle the walk immediately, which was December, reasoning that since I was only going to walk for about seven hours a day, I would not be restricted by the hours of daylight. The cold weather would also be more conducive to carrying the heavy load for long periods, and, as I considered the safety level to be about 1,500 feet, I would not be spending long periods above this altitude on such modest mountains.

The walk is normally commenced and finished at Horton-in-Ribblesdale and I would do the same. After discussing my plans with Peter and Joyce Bayes at the Pen-y-ghent Café. I left Horton on a glorious December morning and made for Penyghent. I progressed steadily. The weather changed suddenly and before very long it was hailing furiously. I took shelter by a limestone pot and waited for the storm to abate. Within a few minutes I was on my way again.

As I climbed over a limestone outcrop, I slipped on some ice and hit the ground with a thud. My head hit a rock and for a moment I was unsure whether or not I was still alive. The feel of warm blood trickling down my face soon brought me back to my senses. I slipped off the rucksack and assessed the damage.

I had a cut over my right eye, and it hurt. Apart from that I was all right. I wedged a handkerchief under my hat and waited for more than an hour for the bleeding to stop. There being no other people around I felt it safe to leave my rucksack near the point of the incident and I climbed to the summit ridge with only a few emergency items. I then returned to my pack and headed for Whernside.

Although I was not breaking any records, I was making fair progress in the circumstances. Originally, I had not intended to dump my rucksack but this was obviously the thing to do given my situation. My right eye was now swollen and closed, but completely dry. For a short while I sheltered in the lee of a wall as it snowed. The terrain at this stage of the walk is very boggy and, as I descended a gentle slope, I slipped. Part of the rucksack frame embedded itself in the ground and I was trapped beneath it. No amount of struggling would free it and things were looking very black until I found I could just reach one pocket and in this pocket, miraculously, I had a knife.

The freezing water had penetrated my clothing and the feeling was already leaving my arm as I cut myself free. I trembled with fear as I realized what a narrow escape I had just survived, and I was not out of trouble yet.

I had been fortunate that a couple of days before the walk, I had been to the cinema to see *The Eiger Sanction*, a film in which Clint Eastwood had cut himself free as he hung perilously from the Eiger North Face. I had thought it a good idea to take a knife, but I had not really visualized having any serious use for it. The film had indirectly saved my life, although I had been very lucky that the knife had been in the one pocket that I could reach.

I made a new shoulder strap from the waist belt, and realizing that progress was now impossible, I decided to retreat. I descended a few feet and made camp on a grassy ledge above a small stream. I had a good meal and, shocked, slightly wet and cold, I went to sleep not knowing if I would survive the night.

Morning came, and although my drinking water in a bottle at the side of me was frozen solid, I was warm and comfortable. There had been a severe frost and it was 10.00 a.m. before I could fold the tent. I returned to Horton without further incident and, despite a few injuries, extremely happy to be alive. There would be no more lone winter attempts.

I had continued my travels abroad with a Mediterranean cruise that visited Greece, Egypt, Israel, Turkey and Yugoslavia. I still could not bring myself to fly, but the sea no longer held any fears for me. That holiday was such a success that I booked a further one around the Baltic Sea, calling at Holland, Denmark, Poland, Russia, Finland and Sweden. For the second time on my travels I made a good friend, Hazel Bourton, and her company considerably enhanced the trip. But my travels abroad had not dulled my need to climb.

In June 1976 I was back at the Three Peaks again, this time with a different plan. On the first day I climbed Penyghent from Horton with only a light sack and returned in the evening. The day was incident free, apart from the low cloud which descended as I reached the summit, which I shared with a young skylark. On the second day I carried a thirty-pound load in pouring rain six miles along the road to Ribblehead, where I made a base from which to climb Whernside and Ingleborough.

My friend Graham Thackwray arrived that evening and the following day we climbed Whernside. By the fourth day I was in great pain in my right leg, and as the weather was atrocious I decided to retire. I was very worried that it was my spinal problem recurring, but the pain subsided. My approach to the walk had perhaps not been sensible, at least so it now appeared to me, and I decided that any further attempt would have to be by the officially recommended route.

In early July 1976, after a weekend's training in the Lake District to toughen my hands (learning how not to shred my hands as I had on Ben Nevis and other mountains was one of the hardest barriers I have had to overcome) and my soul, I was back, this time with Philip Finch. With spirits high and each carrying his respective load we left Horton for the Three Peaks. After ten hours' walking we had covered only six miles, including Penyghent, and had learned to our dismay that the expected sources of water had fallen victim to that year's extremely fine weather. It looked as if we faced a further three days of hardship as we settled down for the night amidst a swarm of mosquitoes.

With an early start we were at Ribblehead by noon, the only real incidents being one encounter with a bull and another with a river when I accidentally lost control of my rucksack and dropped it. We had arrived at a point where a descent had to be made down a long steep grassy bank to the river. I could not carry my rucksack and as I took it off it slipped out of my hand and cartwheeled down the hillside into the river. Fortunately, by the time it hit the water it was travelling very quickly and it continued on across the river, coming finally to rest on the opposite bank. Phil recovered it and I was greatly relieved to find that the equipment inside, especially my sleeping bag, had remained dry.

Our expected refreshment at the Station Inn failed to materialize since it was 'Closed Until Further Notice – No Water'. We refreshed instead in the River Ribble and at the mobile shop before heading for Whernside.

About 400 feet from the summit, on the hardest section of the whole walk, we were confronted by a ferocious dog. Phil dealt with that problem, relying on his instinct of self-preservation. That evening we enjoyed a hard-earned drink at the Hill Inn, now well positioned for a final assault on Ingleborough.

My back was causing me much concern as it was giving me considerable pain. I was dreading the arrival of morning and the inevitable decision time, but when morning came I was relieved to find the pain had eased. We reached the top of Ingleborough in good time and the Three Peaks were ours.

As we left the summit we were caught in a torrential downpour. With only six miles between us and civilization, the sensible thing to do was keep going. On arriving at Horton I was surprised to be presented with a shield to mark the occasion, and being made an honorary member of the Three Peaks of Yorkshire Club, an honour not previously bestowed on anyone since to be a member you have to have completed the walk in twelve hours.

The walk had taken 57½ hours, about 30 of which had been spent walking. Phil had completed the circuit with me, although for much of the time we had not been together. He had often gone on ahead and then waited for me to catch up.

Having completed the Three Peaks walk at the third attempt, my thoughts turned to Yorkshire's other great route, the Lyke Wake Walk. It seemed a natural progression. If I could walk twenty-five miles over adventurous and exciting terrain in three days, then why not forty-two gentler – though no less adventurous – miles over the North Yorkshire Moors?

Distance poses a far greater problem than terrain, and thus walking forty-two miles seemed a much more daunting prospect than climbing three peaks over a considerably shorter route.

My physical condition at the end of the Three Peaks indicated that I had not yet reached my absolute limits of endurance, but whether or not I could cope with more than half the distance again remained to be seen.

Performing at my capacity I am able to cover about ten miles a day, and in cold weather I am able to maintain a greater degree of consistency. So, with this in mind, I made my first attempt at the Lyke Wake Walk in mid-December 1976. I was once again accompanied by Phil, with Graham taking us and our equipment to the start of the walk.

Although we were prepared for almost every foreseeable even-tuality, which meant carrying a fair amount of equipment and supplies, the conditions became extremely adverse, and after slip-ping and sliding our way over snow-covered ice for a day and a half, we decided that the situation could easily get beyond our control and diverted to Chop Gate, where we retired gracefully.

The main problem with the Lyke Wake Walk is the lack of amenities along the way, though ultimately I suppose this is the main challenge. At least for me it was. The closest you come to civilization is crossing a moors road or railway line or stepping stones over a stream, apart from the refreshment hut at Hasty Bank – if it is open when you pass – and the Youth Hostel at Wheeldale Lodge, for which the same applies.

Although my walking relationship with Phil was good, it was apparent that we could not stand many more failures. We were both independent people. Phil was not used to failure and neither was I, but I was used to waiting for success, for often my successes had been the result of persistence in the face of initial failures. This is something not only Phil but many people cannot fully appreciate, especially when they are a part of an early setback. Nothing had come easily, but perhaps I would not have done them if they had.

We were both keen to make an all-out effort on our next venture and I was attracted to a walk of a completely different nature. The Dales Way, officially an eighty-one-mile jaunt from Ilkley to Bowness on Windermere, for the most part linked Dales villages and was a complete contrast to the potential hostility of the North Yorkshire Moors. It was long but it went through some of my favourite countryside. The distance was the main challenge and with suitable weather it should be most enjoyable.

The second week in July 1977 I left Ilkley with Graham, since Phil was unable to join me until the following day. I enjoyed my walks and outings with Graham but he was not one for continuous periods of hardship. One day at a time was enough for him. Besides, he had recently married and I would certainly not have wished him to stay away from his wife on my account. However he was most accommodating whenever I needed his help and his wife dropped us at Ilkley at about 8.00 a.m., arranging to return to whatever point we reached that day to pick him up in the evening. He would telephone to let her know where we were and she would also bring out the equipment, which meant we did not have to carry it.

Walking was easy for Graham and he would go on ahead and

then sit and wait for me in his usual, unhurried manner. However, as soon as I caught him up and sat down, he would immediately say 'Right, we've had a good rest, let's get moving.' He might well have had a good rest but I had not, and it was really I who needed one. I would protest while he would maintain that we must keep going. Despite his assertions I would rest to my satisfaction before continuing. It was, however, all in good humour. It had to be – I was Graham's manager at work!

I had decided that I should make a cine film of this walk, and locations for shooting clips had to be sought as we went along. Graham's wife filmed us leaving the starting point at Ilkley and from time to time Graham shot short lengths of me as we progressed.

It had rained every day of the previous week but the sun was now at full strength as we walked on. Passing through Addingham we stopped at a house to ask for some water. An elderly lady opened the door, looked at me and asked where we were going. On hearing my reply she maintained that we would need more than water and insisted that we have orange squash and one of her home-made scones.

The path was very muddy and slippery as we descended through the woods near the site where, I believe, Bolton Abbey Railway Station had once been. The path was narrow and there was a steep treacherous drop over the edge. We were slowly descending by the path when suddenly Graham screamed as he lost his footing. Unaware that by now we had passed the drop, he had thought he was about to make a very speedy and unwelcome descent into depths below.

On past Bolton Abbey we came to a place where the road forded a stream. There was a short detour to a bridge but, my boots being reasonably waterproof, I made up my mind to cross direct because I could well do without any unnecessary deviations. As I slowly made my way out across the cobbled bottom I realized that it was extremely slippery for the smooth stones were covered with a very thin layer of algae. By now I was in no position to turn back, I had to keep going, but concentrating hard. Suddenly my walking sticks slipped, and how I managed to remain upright as I wrestled to regain my balance I will never know. I could almost feel the cold water around my body in anticipation of what was about to happen, but fortunately I made it to the other side without disaster, a little wiser for the experience.

After a meal at the Pavilion Café we continued, making steady progress, and eventually arrived at Appletreewick. Graham had driven me on relentlessly and the fifteen miles we covered is probably the greatest distance I have ever walked in one day. The problem was that I still had a long way to go and my hands and feet were already beginning to show serious signs of wear because of the heat and, of course, the extra distance I had covered.

Phil arrived promptly the following lunchtime and caught me up as I was approaching Burnsall. On through Loup Scar, across the suspension bridge and on to Grassington, where we made camp in the late evening. My body had deteriorated further, and walking was becoming a painful business as we pressed on to Kettlewell in time for lunch. Starbotton was a welcome sight in the early evening for further refreshment as we made our way towards Buckden.

I had friends, Bill and Barbara Jones, who lived at Buckden. I had arranged to call on them, and Phil and I spent the night alongside bags of cement and other building materials on the living-room floor of Hartrigg House, which they were in the process of renovating, modernizing and converting into a guest house. Whatever the surroundings, their kind hospitality was very welcome in my well-worn state. My hands were badly blistered and, in places, raw where there had previously been blisters. My feet were also blistering, something which had never happened since I had bought proper walking boots. Before, it had not been a problem since at least if my hands and feet were sore after a mountain climb I did not have to continue the following day, as I now did to tackle the challenge of long-distance walking.

From Bill and Barbara's it was only a short walk to Grange Farm and a visit to some more good friends, Gordon and Angela Falshaw. Stan, the shepherd, and Gordon were in the throes of sheep shearing and we watched for a while before lunching at the George, a few yards down the road at Hubberholme. We had a long haul in front of us before we would reach the next public house. Perhaps two days, if everything went well, as we crossed the watershed at the hamlet of Cam Houses and headed for Dentdale.

Across the river from the George stood the Church of St Oswald dating back to the 12th century, a church I had attended on several occasions. I was now in a desperate state and I needed help. My body was wearing out much too quickly for me to entertain any hope of completing the walk. I had covered only about one-third of the overall distance but my hands and feet were in a total state of disrepair.

There was only one logical thing to do – pack in and give the whole thing up. My friends wondered why and how I kept going, and Phil began to realize that the possibility of completing the walk became more remote as each day passed. I was uncertain about what I should do, but from past experience I knew that life's greatest and most satisfying achievements were not entirely based on logic. I knew that to reach the limits you somehow have to defy all sense of reason while managing to remain in full control of what you are doing.

It was not the walk itself that was the challenge. The real challenge was to take myself to the limits of endurance, both physically and mentally. The walk was only a reasonable and enjoyable way of achieving this. However great the discomfort, it *was* always enjoyable. I loved the countryside and I loved the area and, however bad the pain, love is always enjoyable, although it is perhaps not until you no longer have it that you realize just how enjoyable it was. Nothing can transcend true love and my love for what I was doing was being put to the ultimate test.

The church door was open and I entered. In a strange sort of a way I had looked forward to this moment of tranquillity, solitude and soul-searching. My faith was strong but I was under no illusion about the help I could expect. I sat down in my usual place and prayed. I needed help. A lot of help, and quickly. My dream was falling apart before it had hardly begun. In the cool, dark quietness I questioned my motives for doing the walk and what I hoped to achieve by it. What were my reasons?

Then, for the first time, everything fell into place and I understood fully what my purpose was. A feeling of peace and trust came over me and I knew that, if I was being honest and kept faith, the strength to continue would keep coming. As I left the church I could feel a renewed determination, and was much better able to accept my physical deterioration. Very little in my life had been easy and this would be no different. My few moments of quiet reflection had been well spent and I headed for the stone circle at Yockenthwaite.

We rested at Deepdale for a few minutes and were kindly made a cup of tea by a couple having a picnic by the river. Such acts of consideration lift the spirit much more than the providers probably ever realize. We continued to Oughtershaw before making camp and contemplating the following day's climb over the fell which lay ahead. On the summit there would be the old Roman road, as we crossed the Pennine Way.

By the next day my feet were hurting so much that I had to lay on the ground and brace myself while Phil pulled my boots on for me. I was in agony but I knew that the pain was only superficial, not from deep within, and I felt that the risk of any serious permanent injury was minimal. I walked slowly on, the pain gradually deadening, while Phil folded up the tent and packed the rucksack. I made much faster progress without a rucksack and I had left mine with Bill at Buckden, together with some of the equipment and supplies, as we gambled on the weather remaining fine.

By lunchtime we had crossed the watershed and were on our way to Dent Head. The sun shone relentlessly as it had done all the time, but that day there was no cover as we struggled on in the sweltering conditions. Phil was no longer happy with my rate of progress, probably due to the overbearing heat and the fact that he had run out of cigarettes. He decided that he would leave me and walk on ahead to the Sportsman's Arms in Dentdale. I would have to follow on my own and if I did not arrive that evening he would come out and look for me, but he definitely wanted to terminate the walk. Because of my slow rate of progress Phil was probably under much more pressure mentally than I was. All I had to do was keep going, whereas he had to spend long periods sitting waiting for me. When I rested, it was because I was in desperate need of it, but his enforced breaks amounted to little more than frustrating loitering. This was undoubtedly a good place to pack in, we were on a bus route for both Ingleton and Hawes. However, I had walked a long way and I was – although admittedly with a great amount of difficulty – still walking. So long as I remained on some sort of schedule to complete the walk within the time available I lived with the belief and hope that I would be able to maintain my effort until the end. There was no way that *I* could bring myself to give up unless either my body or mind gave way completely. Yet this was a two-man effort and Phil had just as much right to give up as I did. I told him that I would have no ill feelings should he wish to call it a day, but his pride was, understandably, too strong and he could not accept it. It was my body which had become ragged, not his.

He was quickly out of sight and I struggled on down the road. Presently a farmer in a mini van pulled up alongside me and asked if I would like a lift. I did not really want a lift but I stood there in silence, unable to refuse. He repeated his offer and I had to bring myself to tell him that I was doing a long walk and, as much as I appreciated and appeared to need his offer, I could not bring myself to accept. With a certain amount of disbelief he understood, and I carried on, eventually arriving at the Sportsman's Arms.

Phil had been there quite a while, was well refreshed and pleased to see me. He no longer had any doubts. The walk was on, and we were going to finish it. Provided we could make it to Sedbergh by the next evening we would be still on schedule to complete the walk by the following Sunday, our deadline since we were both due back at work on the Monday.

That evening we enjoyed the luxury of a campsite, and in the morning the farmer informed us that he was going to Sedbergh and would drop our equipment off at a garage there if we wished. We could collect it on our arrival. It was a steady walk to Dent, and Phil went on ahead to take advantage of the freedom.

I was labouring down the road when a party of schoolgirls approached from behind. At the rear of the group were four girls who decided that they preferred to talk to me and walk at my speed. They were on their way to Dent and, so long as they eventually got there, time was unimportant. They were from London and were interested in why I should tackle such a long walk.

Our conversation was very interesting and it lifted my spirits to think that these fourteen- and fifteen-year-old girls should have the time and interest to help me along my way. I maintained as fast a pace as I could in hope that they would not get bored and leave me. We quickly arrived in Dent and I bought them a large bottle of lemonade as a small token of my appreciation.

After lunch, with morale now high, Phil and I were on our way to Sedbergh. Arriving in the early evening we went to the Golden Lion to pass away the remaining hours of daylight before camping on the Grammar School playing fields.

I had passed the crisis point and, although my condition was slowly worsening and there was still some considerable way to go, we both now knew that it was definitely possible. Any emotional strain there may have previously been was now completely gone as we thought only of Bowness and imminent success. Only some unforeseen disaster or total physical collapse could stop us now as we proceeded with a real sense of purpose.

In places the guide book had been difficult to follow, and around Grey Rigg we lost the path, eventually coming out through someone's garden. The occupants of the house appeared and I thought that we would be in trouble, but they were most under-standing. In fact, when the man saw me, he insisted on making some sandwiches for us as he thought I looked ready to lie down and die. Perhaps I could have succumbed to the pain had I not believed so strongly in what I was doing, but it was the genuine faith and honest belief of people such as he who had never previ-ously met me who kept me going.

We eventually made it to Bowness, arriving at lunchtime on the

(ABOVE) A long-term ambition fulfilled, fishing on the River Suck, Ballinasloe, Ireland, 1967.

Scoutleading became a regular and enjoyable pastime; (BELOW) the sea cadets roped up on Harrison Stickle, 1973 (John Sanderson is second from left), and (LEFT) teaching me to sail in Roundhay Park, Leeds, 1974.

(TOP) 'I started to wonder what Ben Nevis looked like . . .'
When in June 1974 I reached the summit of Ben Nevis (ABOVE LEFT) I thought it
would be the limit of my achievements. But when I climbed it again thirteen years
later with Chris Bonington (ABOVE RIGHT), the seeds were sown for an attempt
on a greater mountain.

OPPOSITE PAGE

Tired after ten hard hours climbing Scafell Pike from Wasdale Head, 1975.

(INSET) I was glad that my brother, who had done so much with me, shared my
first successful climb to a summit, July 1969. At the top of Helvellyn in the Lake
District with, from left to right, Paul Goodbeer, my cousin Stephen Turner,
Robert, Kevin Maynard and myself. (The boy behind the rock was nothing to do
with us!)

(LEFT) The colourful scene in Kathmandu at the start of our expedition provided plenty of material for filming

(BELOW) The first major obstacle, a huge and precarious bridge over the Dudh Kosi, the first of many that I had to negotiate. Waiting forty-five minutes for the film crew before I could cross did not help my nerves!

(OPPOSITE) Namche Bazaar, the Sherpa capital, from where we gained our first good view of Everest. This picture is looking away from Everest towards Kwangde.

(TOP) The trail from Namche Bazaar is hard going as it follows the spurs of the hills towards the monastery at Tengboche and Kala Pattar, behind which rise the snow-capped peaks of Everest (*right*) and Nuptse (*extreme right*).

(ABOVE) The crew from left to right: Mark Stokes, assistant cameraman, Desmond Seal, cameraman, Jane Parfitt, sound, Neil McDonald, producer and (*back view*) Allen Jewhurst, director.

OPPOSITE PAGE

Just as we were leaving the tree line behind, we gained a glorious view of Ama Dablam in the sunlight.

(INSET) The last tea house before Everest, at Gorak Shep. On the left is our sirdar, on the right our cook.

(TOP) The black hill of Kala Pattar, harsh against the statuesque and snow-clad Pumo Ri.

(ABOVE) Yonden Sherpa and myself, triumphant on the summit of Kala Pattar, with Everest (*left*) and Nuptse in the background.

Sunday. It was a very emotional moment as I walked through the final gate. After nine days of all-out effort I had walked almost 100 miles, and I knew that once again I had extended my absolute limits of endurance. I cannot describe the satisfaction and contentment it gave me, yet it was also a sad moment to think that something which had given us so much pleasure was over.

Phil's support had been tremendous. I had really enjoyed walking with him and no praise for him is too high. He had looked after the equipment, helped me on with my boots and whenever there were any difficult stiles or other obstacles to surmount. He had prepared the meals while I rested and often gone on ahead to ascertain the route where this was not obvious. The only tasks I had to perform were to walk and make any final decisions.

Graham and his wife were at Bowness to bring us home. The car was a welcome sight and we went for a quick celebratory drink and sit by the lakeside before making the return journey.

I still had some unfinished business with the Lyke Wake Walk. The psychological problem of distance no longer existed. In June 1979, I teamed up with my friend Keith Williamson, who was interested in the Lyke Wake Walk as a classic route and also wished to do a walk with me. Gail, his wife, dropped us off at Osmotherly on a pleasant Friday morning and arranged to meet us at Hasty Bank the following morning, from which point she would provide support at every road crossing. I personally feel that support detracts from the sense of adventure, but, if it had to be this way then so be it. You still have to do the walking yourself.

The day went fairly well except that progress was probably a little slower than anticipated. While crossing Holey Moor I heard a voice from behind, 'Mr Hawkridge, I presume?' One of the walkers about to pass us had recently attended a talk that I had given in Leeds.

They were soon out of sight, something which makes me acutely aware of my own slow rate of progress. In the late afternoon, the Glider Station on Carlton Bank provided some interest before the more arduous crossing of Cringle Moor in the evening. Exhausted and with darkness falling, we made camp alongside the path in the Broughton Plantations.

The morning brought a rude awakening – in fact many rude awakenings – as hordes of walkers swarmed along the path. The disused railway track seemed relentless and, unsure of the route at this point, we headed for Esklets, which appeared to be a short cut, as it started to rain.

Esklets, I would think, is not of the firmest footing even in good weather, and with the rain this proved to be a boggy and deeply hazardous diversion. The heavens opened as I climbed the steep and muddy bank towards Flat Howe, where Keith was already waiting in the car, having gone on ahead. Cold and wet and having no particular appreciation for this type of terrain, the lure of our mobile support was too much, and I decided once again to accept defeat and retire.

In 1981, Roger Sharples, a friend who was then a senior member of the teaching staff at Moorfield School for physically handicapped children at Preston in Lancashire, wanted to do a walk with me to see at first hand the problems and how I overcame them. His parents, Geoff and Marjorie, who were among my closest of friends, lived in Dent, and I decided it would be a good idea to complete the Three Peaks by the original route from Dent to Littondale.

On Thursday 28 May we met at the Sun Inn in Dent and made preparations for the walk. We were a party of four, the other two being Dave Colsey and Norman Harrison.

The weather was glorious as we left Dent and the only incident to mar our ascent of Whernside was me getting bogged down while crossing a drainage furrow and only managing to extract myself with some difficulty. The weather broke, however, as we left the summit and we attired ourselves suitably and rested as the showers drifted over. Luckily the heavy rain stopped and continued to hold off until we arrived at the Hill Inn in the early evening.

The mists hung around Ingleborough the following morning and our start was delayed as we waited for a break in the weather. By about 9.00 a.m. conditions had improved and the long steep haul commenced. While traversing round to the ridge leading to the summit plateau I managed to slip shoulder-first into a bog. Fortunately the dive resulted in damage only to my pride as I cleaned the dirt and slime from my arm. The boggy section on the descent of Ingleborough seems to get worse with every crossing, though perhaps with the passage of time you forget the severity.

By mid-evening the Crown Hotel in Horton was a very welcome sight. After a short pause it was on to the Pen-y-ghent Café, where they had stayed open especially in order that I might enjoy the luxury of a decent meal.

The following morning my left foot was giving me some cause for concern as I ascended Penyghent, but the route was magnificent and, with four sections where the use of hands on rock was required, my mind was soon on other things. If ever inspiration was needed there was no finer place from which to receive it. With my goal now in sight and still feeling comparatively fit nothing was going to stop me at this stage.

On the summit I was overcome by a feeling of elation and relief that I had once again triumphed over the Three Peaks. Happy memories of my previous four ascents of Penyghent came flooding back as I started my traverse and descent to Littondale. The wild pansies and strawberries were in full bloom, and the occasional frog could be seen making its way through the marshy undergrowth as we finished the later stages of the walk.

The time now seemed appropriate for another attempt at the Lyke Wake Walk and Dave Colsey was interested. We decided on the last week in August 1982, and left Osmotherly on the Monday evening. Cameron Wilson, a trusted and reliable friend, accompanied us for the first part of the walk before returning home with my car. When Dave or I telephoned, he would return to collect us from Ravenscar, or in the event of any difficulties to effect a rescue.

We made camp on a level area, just large enough for the two-man tent and almost on the path itself, above Scarth Wood. For most of the following morning we took shelter under the trees of Coalmire from the torrential rain. By midday, with only four days remaining in which to complete the walk, our schedule, under such atrocious conditions, had become impossible.

On arriving at Huthwaite Green, the rain had ceased, but a very cold wind was blowing. We were wet, morale was very low and we decided to give up and walk to Swainby and safety. Cameron was more disappointed at our failure than I was, but in the true spirit of the walk I had retired with the philosophy that, if I had completed it at my third attempt, then I should be unable to try for a fourth time.

In reality, I was becoming extremely disturbed by my continued lack of success, as were certain friends, who though they believed they possessed the necessary qualities to complete the walk with me, now considered it a serious challenge to themselves to accompany me on a successful crossing, three friends having already failed.

Striking while the iron was hot, I decided to make what would probably amount to my most serious and final attempt the following month. A couple of days before I was due to commence the walk, my mother died, and I delayed my start until after the funeral. My mother had always referred to the Lyke Wake Walk as the walk I could not do, and, with this in mind, I was determined to put the record straight.

What better time to do a walk – and this walk in particular – while I came to terms with the terrible loss? There was no room for failure. My personal pride and belief in my ability to survive and overcome was at stake.

A friend of my sister's, John Fitzgerald, and I left Osmotherly early on a Tuesday morning, 21 September, in gentle drizzle. On the previous evening I had declared my intentions at the Queen Catherine, and obtained permission to leave my car there for the duration of the walk. The staff enquired if I knew just what I was taking on, and what arrangements my back-up team had made. It took some time to explain that you cannot have a back-up team (assuming I could have mustered one) hanging about for four or five days, and moreover this was not in keeping with my reasons for doing the walk, but that I had by now a well-developed appreciation of the North Yorkshire Moors. After hearing me out, they gave me what is best described as a few words of reserved encouragement.

The drizzle stopped and things went smoothly until we were unable to find a path from the Glider Station to the road at Carlton Bank. A descent through chest-high ferns put us back on course, and one or two more tricky descents followed before we made camp in the Broughton Plantations.

The tree-lined path seems longer at every crossing, a feeling which also applied to the bed of the disused railway line. I suppose it is the fact that you are walking on a fairly level uniform surface for a considerable length of time which creates the illusion that previous crossings were less continuously arduous. Or maybe you just know what is coming next: more of what you are already suffering.

By nightfall, we had reached the road by Margery Bradley. Throughout the day we had rationed our liquids, having made inadequate provision for obtaining drinking water in the volume required. My intake of liquid is fairly high due to the prolonged physical effort involved.

At this point John made a short detour to a nearby public house and brought back supplies of lemonade. I immediately consumed one large bottle which, together with the remaining bottle, proved to be the perfect morale-booster.

The following morning the Moor was completely veiled in thick mist and we delayed rising in the hope that things would improve, and also, I have to admit, because of my reluctance to pull myself together. However, despite visibility being down to about twenty yards and the atmosphere really damp, the show just had to go on.

To complicate matters further I was unsure of the route on the remaining part of the walk, and conditions were hardly ideal to be guiding oneself with just a map over boggy moorland.

Initially we followed the road around Rosedale Head before diverting for White Cross and, after crossing and re-crossing the road, to Loose Howe. A line of marked posts eased matters until the mist lifted.

I have my own technique for crossing bogs. Walking sticks can disappear in seconds if not handled very carefully and, of course, in such situations it is every man for himself. At one point, with John at least 100 yards away, I almost came unstuck, if that term is appropriate. Crossing really bad bogs can almost be likened to walking on water, especially at my speed, and a minor misjudgment had me up to my knees in mud. Before I stopped sinking, and without too much conscious thought, I dived for the opposite bank where a superhuman heave pulled me to safety.

At moments like this the fear only strikes you after the event, and I was pleased to be still able to experience the fear! Shortly after this a man who passed us earlier returned to see if I needed any help over the bogs. Finding that I had already crossed them, he expressed amazement before vanishing again over the horizon.

We had a short rest on Shunner Howe before crossing the Blue Man-i'-th'-Moss during which we pressed on regardless of a shower. Although the terrain at this point is very stony – it could almost be described as a lunar landscape – we were making excellent progress, thanks largely to the lemonade!

In the evening we crossed the Roman Road, at which point John went on ahead to make camp before darkness fell. The light was failing quickly as I arrived at the stepping stones, and I negotiated them with little thought of the consequences any error of judgment would bring. I was in a state of collapse, but somehow I knew that this was the turning point of the walk.

Things were going extremely well, and only disaster could stop me now. Although rather ragged and blistered, I was thoroughly enjoying the walk as we pressed on next day towards the Ministry of Defence site at Fylingdales. It has a certain fascination to everyone who passes, and, having often driven past it, I wondered what a walk past would reveal. For some time the 'golf balls' had been a prominent landmark and something to be aimed for, but now I had a feeling of nostalgia as we left them behind at Lilla Howe. From this point it is just a question of keeping going, although one or two surprises were still in store around the vicinity of Jugger Howe Beck.

Throughout the day there had been very strong winds, and on arriving at the Scarborough–Whitby road it began to rain, presenting us with the dilemma of whether to pitch the tent or carry on. If we carried on it was perfectly conceivable that we would finish that evening, but in the dark. We would be wet and there would be no comfortable place to spend the night.

We chose to look for a place sheltered from the strong wind and get the tent up before we got too wet. Luckily we found an ideal place, near the main road at the entrance to the lay-by. We were safely in our sleeping bags at 6.00 p.m. by which time the heavens had opened.

With an early start, we completed the walk at 8.00 a.m. the following morning. It had taken precisely four days from trig point to trig point, but at last I had completed the walk. All tension was gone – until, that is, we encountered an over-enthusiastic dog along the road to Ravenscar.

We had a celebratory can of lemonade at the Post Office before making the full day's journey by bus back to Osmotherly via Scarborough, Guisborough, Stokesley, and Swainby. At the Queen Catherine, where the staff looked in amazement, the landlady, on hearing someone say, 'He looks to be in a bad way,' remarked, 'Well, he didn't walk any better than that before he started.'

THIRTEEN

The Challenge Gone?

After I had climbed Ben Nevis in 1974 the challenge of climbing mountains had gone, and I had turned to tackle long distance walks. I doubted that there had ever been the type of challenge which others imagined there was but, whatever the motivating force was that had made me want to climb progressively higher peaks, I thought I must now be content with what I had achieved. There could be no question of tackling anything higher or more demanding. Ben Nevis had been a very personal affair. Throughout the five years it had taken me to reach the summit, I had never invited anyone else to get involved with the project. It was just between me and the mountain. I had never had any inclination nor desire to introduce a third party. My association with the mountain was a private and intimate one. I had too much respect for it to risk spoiling our relationship.

If I ever climbed alone again then I thought I would have to content myself with lesser peaks. The balance between calculation and risk finally weighed too heavily on the side of danger. The possibility of disaster had always been there, but now it hung over me like a dark cloud. I had come through some tight situations and had several narrow escapes. My good fortune could not go on indefinitely. I was tempting providence, and I had to accept that enough was enough. I did, however, continue to climb with friends and family, including a sponsored (and filmed) ascent of Scafell Pike in the early part of 1975 to help the supporters of Larchfield School raise funds for their hydrotherapy pool. I do not really hold with sponsored walks and such like. There seems to me something morally wrong with asking people to part with money simply because you are prepared to do some activity which either you should be doing anyway or will enjoy. However, I was asked if I would be prepared to help achieve the target, and on this occasion I agreed. I must say that although we successfully completed the climb after ten hours of hard work, the pressure of *having* to succeed in climbing a mountain to raise money was something I could well do without.

Graham later climbed Buckden Pike with me one Sunday morning. I climbed Fleetwith Pike with Phil, and Dale Head twice, once with my father and once with Chris Greenhow. One of my friends from Vancouver was over in Britain, and I took her – at her request – up Grey Knotts. On three occasions I made the gentle climb up Simon's Seat through the Valley of Desolation from Bolton Abbey. I also made the steady walk up Pike o'Blisco from the Wrynose Pass. In July 1978 I climbed Blencathra with my father; at the end of August I climbed Great End from Wasdale Head, and in July 1980 I climbed Esk Pike. I had once again taken my parents to Keswick for their holidays, but my mother's health was failing rapidly and my father stayed with her in Keswick while I climbed alone.

A tour of Eastern Europe in 1977 furthered my experience of foreign travel. On my return I had two things in mind – the Dales Way and America. The Dales Way was possible; it had required a lot of hard work and the ability to come to terms with physical deterioration. A big question mark hung over making a trip to America; I was still mortally afraid of flying. Learning to live with pain, suffering and agony was one thing, but coming to terms with my fear of flying was a completely different matter. There was also, of course, the balance problem.

I understood physical distress and pain but flying was not like that. Once I was aboard, there could be no escape or respite should the stress prove too great. I did not have to fly, I did not need to fly, but it was something I wanted to do to further my personal aims and ambitions. The more I thought about it the worse I felt. I was suffering from a fear of the unknown.

If I wanted to go to America then I had to fly, so I went out and booked an airline ticket. The situation had to be faced and I knew that the time was right to face it. To give the matter a little more perspective, I was going to make the journey alone. Most people can do all sorts of wonderful things when accompanied by friends, associates or relatives, but facing the realities of adventure with a complete lack of emotional support is quite a different matter, and one which can only be fully understood and appreciated by the few who have done it.

I was going to go to America, and this time there would be no package tour. I would be free to travel as the inclination took me. I had no predetermined route or fixed ideas about what I wanted to see. I would just plan my holiday as I went. The uncertainty of my itinerary offered plenty of scope for excitement. There were a few places which I knew I wanted to visit: the Grand Canyon, Yellowstone, Yosemite, Vancouver, Niagara Falls, and the Aztec Pyramids in Mexico City. Provided I could work these places into the schedule everything else I saw would be a bonus. I was to depart on 9 September and arrive back in England on 9 October. I chose a flight by Boeing 747, reasoning that the larger the aircraft, the less likelihood of feeling isolated or claustrophobic should my first experience of flying prove too much. In the event the excitement at the prospect of touring America contributed enormously in helping me to overcome the anxieties I had about flying. It was something that I had to do if I wished to unlock the door to the great adventure which lay ahead, and I did it. America was a dream holiday, and I accomplished everything I had planned to do, including a trip to the Aztec temples in Mexico which had had me worried after I had been advised not to travel to that country alone.

Having completed America, including a week-long tour across Canada by bus, my next ambition was to tour Australia and New Zealand. I hoped that I would make the trip in January 1979 and began to save. However, in the summer of 1978 I started to go out with a girl whom I had known for a number of years, and a trip to Australia became out of the question. I had no wish to go on my own and I could not afford to take both of us. The inclination had gone. It had been replaced by something more important!

On 1 September 1979 we were married, and on the following day we left London Heathrow for America, once again bound for New York JFK and for a similar length of time to my last trip. There were several places that I still wished to visit and some where I would like to return to with my new companion. The trip went well and included a short walk down and through the towering pinnacles of Bryce Canyon.

My wife had lived with a much older woman before our marriage and she was unable to adapt to life with a man, or at least with me. On 8 November her emotional problems came to a head and she left. At her instigation we separated and were later divorced. I was on my own again but I had now left home, and I had to maintain my independence. I had friends and relatives who would help me but I had no one I could run to. If I had, then I never saw them as a possible option – my days of running were over. For the first time in many years my faith was severely shaken as I slowly picked up the broken threads of my life.

By December 1980 I was back on my feet again and ready to face the world, alone if needs be. There were lots of Roman remains in North Africa that I still wished to see, and I booked a holiday in Tunisia. One week at a hotel situated near Nabeul and Hammamet and a further week touring the country by coach.

My visit was a rewarding experience in every way. I loved the atmosphere and the way of life. I never quite knew what to expect next, and each day brought along some new and exciting adventure, I had also acquired a taste for olives and yogurt, two foods I would not have previously fancied!

On returning home I immediately arranged a further tour to Morocco, departing about a month later. If I was going to travel to a warmer climate, then I reasoned, I may as well go while we were in the depths of the English winter.

I flew to Tangier and another North African tour was under way, a fairly demanding itinerary visiting Meknes, Fez, Marrakesh, Casablanca and Rabat, that was nonetheless enthralling, in particular the archaeological and geological wonders I saw, which were always my main reason for holidaying abroad.

By now I had moved to one of the Inland Revenue's new Accounts Office computer centres, at Shipley, where Dave Barnett resurrected my flagging career. I thoroughly enjoyed working for Dave but following the industrial action of 1981 I had the gross misfortune to gain a new boss, notorious throughout the service. I had accrued annual leave with the intention of holidaying in Australia but his first action was to ask me to forfeit this and point out that if I did not he would make life as uncomfortable as possible. I refused. It was not his job to renegotiate or amend my conditions of service. Through the difficult period when my mother was terminally ill and dying I was chastised for taking annual leave at awkward times as I took mornings off to take her to hospital. The argument was that she was not my responsibility. This man was a spectre from my past and for as long as I had known him he had made stupid and uncalled-for remarks about me.

Shortly after my mother died in 1982 I was saved from the depths of despair when he was moved on and replaced by Max Smith. At my annual appraisal interview Max's superior told me that there was bad news and good news, which did I wish to hear first? My annual report, which had been completed by his predecessor, indicated that I could not perform my duties in a satisfactory manner – I should be dismissed or at very least retired or demoted. The good news, however, was that since receiving the report Max had taken to observing me personally to check on the comments made therein and that he could confidently report that I had now substantially improved and there was no longer a serious problem. The truth was that my work had neither deteriorated nor improved and the problem was the reporting officer. As far as work was concerned Max was my light at the end of the tunnel and

I had the good fortune to remain with him until shortly before I retired in 1987 when my condition deteriorated and I found myself crippled with pain resulting from trapped nerves in my upper spine.

The improvement in my working conditions came shortly after I completed the Lyke Wake Walk. It had been my fourth attempt, but now I had no outstanding walks on which I had failed. Yet the long distance walk remained something very special to me. It offers the chance of excitement, occasionally verging on the daring, and the opportunity to test one's dedication, application and endurance to the absolute limits. It is also both a satisfying and extremely rewarding adventure, the mind being enriched by the natural beauty of the countryside and the soul enhanced by the suffering and stress, while being in the close proximity of another person. Two people bonded by a single aim – the walk. It is a shared experience which stays in the memory for ever, an experience shared with all who know or are interested in the walk. The dark cloud of disaster never hung over me on such expeditions.

At first my appreciation of the Lake District and early exploits with mountains had been inspired by the works of W. Heaton Cooper. Once fired, my passion for mountains and their rugged beauty was fuelled by the books of A. Wainwright, a must for any walker, but indispensable to anyone with severe physical limitations. Although Mr Wainwright does not dwell on severities – in fact he openly encourages adventure and more often than not advocates the more exacting and exciting routes – his work is so finely detailed that, with a little practice, one can draw one's own conclusions.

All my outdoor activities have been inspired. It has never been just a question of doing, it has been more a matter of total commitment in pursuit of an intangible goal. The North Yorkshire Moors, the Dales and in particular the Lake District all cover evocative countryside in a continuous band across the North of England. Combined with the rare sense of humour and motivation provided by Mr Wainwright I decided eventually I had to make an attempt at 'A Coast to Coast Walk', a route pioneered by him and clearly defined in his guide book. The ingredients for a memorable adventure were all there.

The Lyke Wake Walk had been immensely enjoyable and John found walking with me a challenge. He was very keen that I should once again test my limits and, provided we started from the West, the Coast to Coast walk should be enjoyable even in the event of us failing to complete it.

The Dales Way had been a long hard push. Every mile I had completed had been one less to do. The weather had been scorchingly hot, the countryside had been at its best and the walk had given me a tremendous feeling of satisfaction and achievement. It had taken 8½ days to complete the eighty-one miles, and at the end my problem had been that my whole body was worn out. I could walk no further. I had reached my absolute limits of endurance on every front. Logically there could be no more as far as distance was concerned; I had reached the end of the road. And the Coast to Coast Walk is 190 miles long.

If I was to progress any further, the one certain thing was that I needed a different approach. I have always walked for pleasure and, if the enjoyment ceases, then so does the walk. My need is to know that I have performed to my capacity, given everything in pursuit of an ambition. I have never aimed to break records, personal or otherwise, but determining that critical point has always been entirely my own decision and I would never walk if I thought it was not going to be so.

I decided that to have any hope of completing the walk – or to keep going for more than eight days – I would need to cover fewer miles a day than I had previously done. On my last outing, the Lyke Wake Walk, I had covered about ten miles a day and this was achieved by pressing on relentlessly throughout the hours of daylight, which were not particularly long in late September. If I allowed four weeks for the Coast to Coast Walk then I would have to average only a little over six miles a day; however, there was the distinct possibility that there would be some enforced periods of inactivity in the event of bad weather. If we did the walk in June then perhaps the extra hours of daylight would go some way towards offsetting this and maybe allow me to spread my effort over a much greater period of the day.

The person with whom I walk is about the most important decision I have to make. He or she must wish to do the walk and be prepared to progress at the same speed as myself; each of us has to be tolerant of the other's ways. It would be hopeless if a walk was terminated because of a silly disagreement, which could so easily happen when two people are in such a confined and emotionally testing environment for a long period. You must also have an honest belief in one another's ability and strength of character.

Surprisingly, most of my walking associates are not 'walkers' by nature, but simply fit people, who, for reasons best known to themselves, are prepared to suffer hardship, put their trust in me and step straight into an adventure. Experienced walkers would be dismayed by my slow rate of progress and would also resent my firm leadership.

My leadership is based principally on the enormous amount of enthusiasm I have for the venture in hand. The goal is there to be achieved, although not at any cost. The walk, mountain or whatever will still be there tomorrow, next week or next year. If we do not observe a strict code of discipline and calculate each risk carefully, then we may not be.

Should the need ever arise for me to be rescued I would probably have a lot of questions to answer and I must, therefore, take every precaution to make sure that barring any unfortunate accident or disaster, it never happens. Although I am experienced I could easily find my right to undertake such demanding ventures challenged. I must always be vigilant, pay careful attention to detail, diligent in my research, thorough in my preparation and prudent in making my decisions.

With our approach agreed and our preparations finalized John and I left for St Bees on 28 May 1983, Spring Bank Holiday Saturday. The weather was not too good and we visited my friend Bill Mason, celebrating his ninetieth birthday, and his daughter Marjorie in Keswick, while stopping to purchase one or two last-minute items of equipment. Arriving at the Coast we unloaded and Ian Davison, a good friend who had travelled with us, returned home with the car. It is not a pleasant sight to watch your vehicle depart while you get into boots and protective clothing in the rain. However, it was comforting to know that for the next four weeks, our transport would be available at a few hours' notice should an emergency arise.

We lingered over a hot drink at the sea front café until the rain had ceased, and the walk commenced in earnest. Within minutes we were crossing the rock-strewn river outlet and climbing the path to the very exposed cliff-top path. The adventure had begun and it was not very long before the short rock climb out of Fleswick Bay was providing the excitement. Beyond the lighthouse the path becomes extremely airy and eventually disappears. Not being heroes, we took to the fields, but the cliff-edge walk had been most enjoyable, with thrift and many other plants in full bloom. It seemed like nature's own hanging gardens, the varying hues providing an ever-changing colourful display.

The Lowther Arms at Sandwith looked too inviting not to call at after stretching muscles we had not used for some time, before camping near Demesne Farm.

The following morning I encountered my first real problem, a pair of enormous level crossing gates on the Whitehaven to Barrow line prominently signposted that they should be closed after use. By whom? They were chained and padlocked with maximum security and could not be opened, so I had to climb over them – and they were a good five feet high.

This was shortly followed by a perilous crossing of a bog which involved swinging down a bank with the aid of a hawthorn tree, landing on a narrow plank which floated on the mud and quickly crossing the six feet or so to the other side – a very risky manoeuvre with two walking sticks. However, although the plank disappeared into the sticky depths, I survived unscathed and was immediately rewarded by the sight of a stoat scampering across the marshland ahead.

We rested for lunch at Cleator before tackling the 1,131 feet of Dent, which, although of only moderate height, took much longer than anticipated. The walk by Nannycatch Beck provided an enchanting highlight to the latter part of the day, one of those never-to-be forgotten idyllic places, so close to the road yet so remote, and was followed by a short rest at the Kinniside Stone Circle before continuing to Ennerdale Bridge where we made camp.

With our food supplies replenished at the village store, we headed for the scenic beauty of Ennerdale Water, Angler's Crag and the valley beyond. On arrival at the pumping station it began to rain and, wishing to remain as dry as possible, we took cover under some trees growing amongst the ruins nearby. The tranquillity of the scene was a complete contrast to our next stop, Angler's Crag. I found the rocky traverse both difficult and frightening. The track had narrowed, becoming almost a rock climb and the drop was fearsome.

We stopped for lunch, high on the outcrop, while I assessed the merits of continuing. What else could we do? It had to be pray and proceed with extreme caution. Fortunately, the most hazardous part, which dipped over the rise concealing the route ahead, proved to be only a few yards long and we were soon out of danger and on to the sparsely wooded lakeside path. As darkness fell we made camp about halfway along the forest road. There were few sites suitable for our small two-man tent and I suspect that if noticed we would have been promptly moved on.

With this in mind we made an early start before the forest workers arrived. The valley was completely shrouded by a heavy mist which periodically turned to rain. Forest clearings appeared like prehistoric landscapes. You could easily imagine some weird monster stepping out of the mist, an illusion destroyed only by discarded petrol and oil containers. The forest road is a relentless drag and, as the mist began to swirl, the sight of Pillar Rock looming imposingly through an opening in the thick veil provided a magic moment.

It had long been one of my ambitions to climb the 2,927 feet of Pillar and as the weather brightened the mountain was revealed in all its splendour. Seeing the steep routes to the summit unfortunately did nothing to hasten any ideas I might have had of attempting it in the foreseeable future.

Out of the forest we were soon passing the Black Sail Youth Hostel – and what finer setting could a building have? At the sight of the arduous climb which lay ahead we were tempted to linger a while and enjoy the magnificent prospect. Happy memories come flooding back whenever I see such mountains as Great Gable, Green Gable and Haystacks. The long steep ascent of Loft Beck awaiting us, we set forth over the glacial deposits to arrive at the foot of the most difficult section. The way ahead would be a long hard slog up the loose and stony track. Two men were at the top just starting on the descent, and very shortly they were making rapid progress as they slid, only partially under control, down the scree. John must not have been thinking seriously about what was happening because, as we looked up, he said, 'It must be much easier up there, look how fast they are coming down.' If that was meant to be encouragement!

The sun was now high in the clear sky and it came as a pleasant surprise to find that a coffee machine had been installed at the Honister Quarry Shop. As the Lakeland tourist trade expands annually it seems that the only unchanged parts are the fells, timeless islands in the tide of man's progress.

At Seatoller I crossed paths with a local friend, Stan Edmondson, who was preparing for an evening's fishing on Buttermere. The well-earned luxury of a meal at the Yew Tree lifted our spirits after four days of walking on a diet of sandwiches. After the meal it was back to the more serious business of making camp, and the site at Rosthwaite seemed conveniently situated.

I had been averaging just over seven miles a day and, with no physical deterioration to speak of, our progress was too good to be true. And so it proved. The heavens opened early the following morning and we were tent-bound until mid-afternoon. I slept through, taking full advantage of this enforced rest. Borrowdale is not noted for being the driest of places, but eventually the rain abated and progress up Langstrath was possible.

The rain made the walk spectacular as the water teemed down

the valley. Mountain streams in spate are always spectacular, but it made the crossing of tributaries, normally only a trickle, quite precarious. The evening walk was very enjoyable and this eased the frustration the earlier rain had caused. As darkness fell we made camp on the level summit of what appeared to be a drumlin around the 1,200 feet mark.

We had not long retired to our sleeping bags when there was an almighty crack. The heavens opened once again and both sheet and fork lightning flashed across the sky, illuminating the interior of the tent despite our two layers of protection. I am not certain how safe one is in a tent with metal poles at that altitude and in those conditions, but as the situation was completely beyond our control there was little point in worrying.

The morning was misty but there was no rain and we made an early start to capitalize on our good fortune. Greenup Edge was not too distant but the going was difficult and, on arriving at the shores of a tarn some way past the summit, I concluded that we had lost our way.

Wainwright's guide is a masterpiece and reasonably easy to follow but it is one thing interpreting it under pleasant conditions or with a familiar skyline and another being forced to make an instant decision in thick mist when the track just peters out at your feet. A second attempt from the point of the disappearing path soon rectified matters, and it was not long before we were sitting out a shower at the head of Wythburn, a long desolate upland valley.

This was a convenient point at which to take breakfast. For me this consisted of a banana together with bread and butter. The only good thing that could be said about the banana, which I believe had travelled – and not too well – from Ennerdale Bridge, was that at least the skin had remained intact. Quite remarkable, considering the pulped state of the contents. However, it was edible and you cannot afford to carry food for miles and then waste it because of its unappetizing appearance. Hunger and necessity make all things possible.

Far Easdale is notoriously wet in normal circumstances, but today conditions were atrocious and it was not long before the water had penetrated our hitherto sound footwear. A party of American walkers taking a rest provided a lighthearted exchange before we descended to Grasmere where I had made prior arrangements with my friends Richard and Jennifer Hardisty to have a bath and wash our used clothing. I was by now in such a state that I was jokingly asked as I walked through the village whether I would be requiring soap or Jeyes Fluid. The crossing from Borrowdale had taken its toll in other ways too. My left ankle was beginning to hurt at a point weakened by the operation carried out over twenty years before, and the soles of my boots were also showing serious signs of wear.

With supplies replenished and spirits restored by the luxurious living afforded us, our start for the Grisedale Pass was delayed by adverse weather and an urge to linger and enjoy the kind hospitality. Eventually we left about noon, once again feeling confident that things were going well. The gentle part of the ascent over, we were just beginning to admire the view when the heavens opened yet again.

We sheltered as best we could but the situation became impossible as the water penetrated our 'waterproof' clothing. I began to feel cold and my joints were stiffening. The only thing to do was press on regardless of the weather. Once over the summit at least we would be descending to the safety of the valley. Perhaps we could reach Patterdale before dark.

Conditions were treacherous underfoot on some of the steep muddy inclines which eventually gave way to a slow but less hazardous boulder-strewn track. I had always promised myself that some day I would visit Grisedale Tarn, but I had never quite envisaged it under these conditions. It rained incessantly and the place had a certain eeriness, with the outline of the Tarn barely visible from the path.

By the time we had crossed the outlet stream – alive with shoals of small fish – I think that we had reached saturation point, being completely soaked from head to toe. There would be no lingering for us at the Brothers Parting, which incidentally was inscribed by a relative of Richard, the friend with whom we had spent the previous evening in Grasmere. He used to ascend there daily, complete with tools and wearing his professional apparel which included a bowler hat.

Ruthwaite Lodge, although picturesque, offered little consolation in the pouring rain. Locked and barred, it seemed to add insult to injury in our time of distress. Sodden and exhausted, we made camp on the first suitable spot which arrived with the tree line. There was still time left to continue further, but we had suffered enough in the atrocious conditions.

We had now been on the road, or should I say fells, for one week and had covered over forty-six miles of difficult terrain in very mixed weather. We were still on schedule, and the short rest for a meal at Patterdale was most welcome as we debated the merits of the weather and the guide book's warning about the next stage. Once we started it would be imperative that we crossed the summit of Kidsty Pike before there was any deterioration in the weather. A sudden lowering of cloud could spell disaster and, although from time to time we had mysteriously been circled by a rescue helicopter, I had no desire to be a casualty.

After lunch the cloud lifted and it had to be a hard push as we commenced our ascent to Angle Tarn, with the wet clothes from the previous day hung out to dry on the rucksack. With only one complete change of the larger items we could ill afford a further drenching until they were in a more serviceable state. Our other equipment was also damp and would be the better for a break in the weather.

Angle Tarn appeared like a jewel set amongst the rocky outcrops and will long be a cherished memory. Little things like this make everything worthwhile. Unfortunately, however, my ankle was giving me considerable cause for concern. We continued without delay across the marshy uplands, knowing that in the interest of safety we had to reach Kidsty Pike before nightfall.

At 10.00 p.m. we were on top of the 2,560-foot summit and hastily descended to the first not-too-exposed grassy hollow to make camp. We had only just bedded down when I heard loud snoring. I thought that John had fallen asleep rather quickly until I discovered it was in fact a sheep, which had taken shelter in the lee of the tent, breathing very heavily.

Next day as we packed up and headed for Haweswater, a light mist was blowing across the top few hundred feet of the mountain. Quickly descending out of this, I realized how fortunate we had been to complete the summit of Kidsty Pike with good visibility the previous evening. Besides having splendid views of High Street the route doubles back along a ridge and is no place for the unsuspecting in poor weather.

We passed several dead sheep, the carcases of which were being ravaged by crows and ravens, and the array of walls rising from the lake cast a ghostly gloom over the area at the head of Haweswater. I was now in great pain with my left ankle, and the unrelenting track which runs adjacent to the lake was soul-destroying.

Step by step a dream was fast fading, and the fine prospect of the Lakeland scenery was equally rapidly giving way to the rolling hills of the Pennines. Past Burn Banks a magnificent glade of bluebells carpeting the woodland floor and two quaint packhorse bridges in the same vicinity provided some compensation for the hardship, and a fitting end to the day.

The following morning I could barely stand, and my ankle was seized up with pain. Only when I walked did it go numb but as soon as I stopped, which I had to do often, the agony returned. Some considerable damage must have been done already and I felt that if I continued much further, I would end up in hospital, and not Robin Hood's Bay as planned.

Shap seemed an appropriate place to terminate this episode and we arrived there after a close encounter with a large bull running with a herd of cows, and the thrilling sight of a golden eagle taking its prey. In 9½ days we had completed approximately one-third of the total walk and had had an exciting and enjoyable time. On this occasion a crossing of the Lake District had to suffice. Maybe with boots repaired and my ankle healed we would return to take up where we left off? The lure of adventure is strong.

The damage took about four weeks to heal, but the effort had been well worth it. My ankle apart, I had suffered much less physical deterioration than on the Dales Way and it had been just as enjoyable. We had crossed five ranges of hills and I knew now what my physical limitations were in terms of distance and the number of days for which I could keep going.

There were few mountains left in the Lake District which captivated me to the point where I needed to climb them, but I still had a yearning to ascend Pillar and perhaps also Fairfield, Crinkle Crags and High Street. One thing was certain though. I had no desire to rush out and climb them alone. I had mellowed – and I no longer needed the solitude as I had before. I still did not like crowds, but I would much rather the ascent of those special mountains was a shared experience.

At the beginning of August 1985 I had arranged to take work colleagues Julie Baker and Carol Taylor (whom I had previously introduced to sailing) to the Yorkshire Dales for the day in order that they could abseil. It had long been Carol's ambition to descend by rope from as great a height as possible and Julie was keen to broaden her horizons on exciting outdoor activities.

At short notice I had to do some work for the Fieldfare Trust (of which I was a founding director, until I resigned, unhappy with the direction it was taking) in the Lake District. Rather than break one of my engagements, it made sense for us all to go to the Lake District. I would carry out my duties for the Trust in the morning and we would go to Borrowdale in the afternoon. This we did, and in the evening I took them to see Pillar. They agreed to accompany me on an attempt to fulfil my yearning and climb it the following week.

On the Thursday evening we drove up to Ravenglass and camped overnight in readiness for a reasonably early start. I had been in two minds as to whether or not I would be able to complete the ascent from Wasdale Head in one day, but eventually I convinced myself that it was possible.

The following morning we booted up outside the Wastwater Hotel and made our way up Mosedale. Although it was not raining the weather did not look too promising. It had rained on most days since early June and we could consider ourselves lucky that it was no worse than overcast, as we made our way steadily up the valley. There was a lot of water in Gatherstone Beck and it took some considerable time for me to pick my way across the swollen stream. There is no hopping from stone to stone for me, I must take the plunge and carefully wade through the water looking for sound footholds in shallow water as I go.

First came the zigzagging path and then the long haul to the top of the Black Sail Pass. The wind was blowing very strongly and a short distance above the pass we stopped for lunch. There was little shelter but we took advantage of what scant protection we could find as we ate and rested. The wind rose to gale force and I was barely able to remain on my feet. As I tried to walk it lifted my sticks, sweeping them away from me.

The situation was not only impossible, it was also becoming dangerous. I began to wonder how I would manage to get back down. I asked Carol and Julie if they still wished to continue to the summit as I would be attempting to make my way back down. Even at that quite modest altitude strong winds are very cold, and it can be difficult to breathe as the rush of oncoming air beats against your face. I put no pressure on them to return with me, the choice was completely their own.

The thought of not making it to the summit was too much for Carol but Julie was by now aware of the toll the icy cold winds were taking. Carol decided to press on for the summit while Julie and I played safe and began our descent. Progress in the strong wind was very hazardous for me, and it was not until we had re-crossed Gatherstone Beck that there was any noticeable respite.

Despite severely frightening herself, Carol made it to the top and, just to emphasize my slow rate of progress, had caught us up by the time we were only midway down Mosedale. I was pleased to see that she had come to no harm since I had doubted her wisdom in deciding to continue, but as I make my own decisions, so must I allow those around me to make theirs too.

Carol had completed the Three Peaks of Yorkshire walk on several occasions and this was the limit of her previous fellwalking experience. As far as she could see there was no way that I would ever climb Pillar by this route. It was much too difficult for me. That, though, was something I would have to find out for myself. Perhaps if she had accompanied me on some of my previous outings she would have been a lot less certain.

The following week I returned with Ian Newman of the Fieldfare Trust but the weather was unsuitable on the two days we had available. Undeterred, I returned a week later with another companion, but we were once more unfortunate with the weather. This time, however, I confess that I lost my nerve on the drive up and would not even have made an attempt had conditions been favourable, although I probably would have tried Crinkle Crags or Fairfield. Was Carol's warning getting through to me or did I just feel that neither the time nor the companion was right to try again?

During the latter half of 1985 I had suffered pain resulting from the trapped nerves in my neck and a general deterioration of my spine. Although this gave me a great deal of discomfort it did not actually stop me from walking, nor did walking seem to make it any worse. My problems were in sitting and in sleeping. Hospital attention confirmed that the problem was there to stay but they were able to alleviate the pain by manipulative physiotherapy. While receiving treatment I sought advice as to whether I should continue with my strenuous walking activities or if the exercise and strain would make matters worse. I was told that most probably the trouble was caused as a result of using walking sticks and keeping fit may well have lengthened rather than shortened my active life. It was therefore up to me to balance any pleasure with the pain it caused and do what I felt was right.

My physical activities throughout 1986 had been extremely limited but I decided to have another attempt at Pillar. I had promised Ian that I would do a walk with him the following year after we had been rained off, and he was able to accompany me at the August Bank Holiday.

I left Wasdale Head at 8.00 a.m., the plan being that Ian, together with his wife (who is a physiotherapist) and children, would catch me up before I crossed Gatherstone Beck. Everything went according to plan, and crossing the beck under normal conditions was a formality. We arrived at the Black Sail Pass without incident and quickly proceeded on to Looking Stead. From here the long steep slog up the most difficult part of the walk began. Progress was laboured and slow, but not impossible, as I fought every inch of the way to gain height. Time had flown and it was already mid-afternoon. The weather looked a bit uncertain and there was still a considerable way to go up the steep, exposed stony track before the summit ridge could be attained. Fearful of the time and an imminent break in the weather, I decided that the only sensible thing to do, once again, was retreat.

Shortly after the Black Sail Pass it began to drizzle and Ian's wife and children returned to the safety of Wasdale Head without further delay. Ian and I struggled on in what was by now heavy rain and strong gusting winds. We arrived at Wasdale Head at about 8.00 p.m., thoroughly soaked and cold. A change of clothes and refreshment at the hotel quickly melted away the feelings of failure. It was now apparent that I could not manage to climb Pillar in one day and would need to return with a different approach if I ever tried again. Looking on the bright side, my neck felt no worse for the effort and this was a relief.

Getting to the top of mountains was never solely a matter of responding to a challenge, it was a quest for adventure, enjoyment and a purpose in life. They provided the physical motivation which added immeasurably to my life. Was there a challenge? The motivating force was still there, the strong desire to realize my potential, and explore my capabilities in some of the most glorious surroundings in Britain.

FOURTEEN

The Way to Everest

I thought – no, I knew, beyond all doubt, that climbing Ben Nevis alone in a single day had been my ultimate performance. Perhaps I could set myself new standards where several-day expeditions were concerned but for a single day outing Ben Nevis was my absolute limit of effort and endurance on every front. I was very happy that I had reached such a level of physical and mental output and living with such knowledge had eliminated all self-doubt. There was no longer any urge to improve and no feeling of regret that I could have done better had I tried. It is wonderfully satisfying to know your limitations and be pleased with them.

I had never thought of myself as being worth media attention and if I had perhaps the media might not have thought likewise. The warden at the Glen Nevis Youth Hostel thought my ascent did deserve media coverage but requested that I avoid it as it could induce others into treating the route with less respect than its hazards warranted. People had occasionally expired on the route and many more suffered accidents. I had no intention of involving the media and the incident slipped by unnoticed except by those few who had actually witnessed it. I had been doing this sort of thing for six years and no one except my immediate family and those who had seen me whilst I was out knew or bothered. This was the way I wanted it. Although it was extremely hard work, I climbed mountains simply for pleasure and not for any other reason. I could never become the world's best but I could realize my own potential and this was all I ever set out to do. It was purely self-satisfaction in the knowledge that I had made my body and mind perform to their limits in achieving a preconceived goal.

Publicity, especially if the true context of events was lost in any uninformed report, would probably have upset me and created unnecessary pressures. Climbing for attention would be a risky business and it was, after all, my life that was at stake if anything did ever go wrong. If I had needed adulation or public approval I am sure I could have found a much less arduous way of attracting it and the story of a handicapped man walking Britain's highest fells would always have its share of sceptics.

The following March, 1975, I was receiving an award from the Civil Service in recognition of the examinations I had passed at night school and for my efforts in climbing mountains, learning to sail a racing dinghy and running a Scout Troop. The press were invited and focused their attentions solely on my ascent of Ben Nevis when in fact the award was mainly for the grade A I had obtained in GCE 'A' level Accounting. I also recorded an interview for BBC Radio Leeds. This was the beginning of a happy relationship I enjoy with my local newspapers and radio.

In 1975 I was also nominated for the Spastics Society Achievement Award and attended the luncheon in London. I received a runners-up medal as my achievements were rated to be about the eighth best of those invited. Most of the seven placed ahead of me were being congratulated for their mental achievements or were well known to those who managed the society. The following year I was nominated for the society's literary award and my piece concerning my walk on the Three Peaks of Yorkshire (subsequently published in the *Dalesman*) was given second place by the judge Robert Robinson. After he read his citation he asked me whether the contents were fact or fiction. My reply was somewhat disbelievingly accepted.

Early in 1978 I was approached by Yorkshire Television about doing a piece for the local news programme, Calendar. A director visited me at home to discuss a possible location and format. To give him some idea of my capabilities I let him see a couple of my cine films. He thought they were really good but believed the public could not take me. He had thought that I would be mentally or educationally subnormal and that someone pointed me in the direction of the mountain and told me to go. The fact that my mountain exploits were self-motivated, highly calculated and carefully planned came as a great surprise to him. He felt unable to proceed further with the venture although he did congratulate me on the quality of my films and expressed his admiration for my efforts. From this time onwards I kept Yorkshire Television and the BBC informed of the long-distance walks I was attempting. I did not want the day to arrive when they could say they knew nothing of what I was doing.

When I published my book *Sticks and Stones* in 1987 the BBC gave me a mention on the local news programme *Look North* and Yorkshire Television wanted me to attend the studio for a live interview. With only thirty minutes to go before I was due to leave home I received a telephone call cancelling the engagement. You can imagine my feelings . . .

That July, a local film company expressed an interest in making a documentary and I agreed to climb Ben Nevis for this purpose. I knew Chris Bonington reasonably well and suggested he join us as my companion and interviewer. During two very warm days we climbed Ben Nevis and the film was shot. (It was, incidentally, a very good film but has never been shown.) The scenery was spectacular with snow to be crossed near the summit, the conversation was interesting and the walk went well. It was while we were on the mountain (thirteen years and one month to the day since my last ascent) that Chris asked me if I had any aspirations regarding mountains left in my life. I replied that I would like to see Mount Everest and that if I ever got the chance I would take a morning flight over it. It came as a shock when he answered that I was perfectly capable of climbing the 18,000 feet to Kala Pattar, a ridge adjacent to Everest, offering perhaps the finest view of the mountain. It certainly overlooked base camp and the south-west face. Hillary's route to the summit would also be visible.

Over the next twenty-four hours we talked about every aspect of such a venture and the likely difficulties. I was taken a little by surprise and much of the conversation did not sink in, but the seeds, of belief and possibility, were firmly sown. The idea would haunt me in the months ahead.

After six months' deliberation I had decided that going to see Mount Everest was something I really had to do but before I made a final decision I went up to see Chris to go over certain details and confirm that my plans were practical. It was 25 February 1988 and all being well this would give me another six or seven months before I went. As usual Chris was working to a tight schedule, having arrived back at Newcastle Airport only that morning, but over lunch we talked about the route, the difficulties as he envisaged them, the length of time he thought it would take me between various points and the equipment I would need.

Over the past six months I had done my research and now we were talking about places and distances to which I could relate in my mind. The thought of Everest created certain tensions, both physical and mental, within me. I desperately wanted to go. In fact, it was something much stronger than that within me; it was as if I knew that I was destined to. I was fearful of committing myself to such a far-reaching decision, and yet I knew that the time was now as right as it ever would be for such an expedition.

Chris was still optimistic about my chances of success at reaching Kala Pattar and felt that with twenty years' experience I knew my limitations well enough to survive. The main problem would be in allowing enough time, that is, getting the distance between each overnight stop right. He believed that acclimatization to the increasing altitude would pose no serious problem as my rate of progress would be such that I would acclimatize as I steadily progressed. Although enthusiastic and encouraging Chris was also pointing out the difficulties and possible pitfalls: the exposed bridges and the place where he had once lost a Sherpa youth who fell off and whose body was later recovered from the river some distance downstream. He was totally honest with his assessment of the situation but remained convinced that my plans were realistic.

My expedition was to be a lightweight two-man trek with just one Sherpa guide and myself carrying the minimum amount of equipment we would require to survive. On the higher slopes temperatures would be likely to drop as low as minus twenty degrees celsius through the night while it could be fairly warm throughout any periods of sunlight. Although I would have liked to have taken a tent, in view of the extra weight this was a luxury we would have to do without and we should have to stay in tea houses which were present along the route and have Gore-tex covered sleeping bags in case of emergency. Food, although simple and basic, would be available at these tea houses.

In an effort to attract sponsorship and keep the cost down Chris agreed to write a small piece about the proposed expedition and the reasons why he felt it was worthwhile, and also drop a line to the manager of Berghaus Ltd requesting that I be supplied goods at a substantial discount. By way of an introduction he sent a letter to a well-respected Sherpa Agency in Kathmandu which he used regularly and gave me details of airline personnel with whom he had direct contact. I left feeling that the decision had now been made, Chris had done everything possible to get me started with the venture and it was now up to me to keep the momentum going and make sure it happened.

The next stage was to organize and plan any preparatory work I intended doing and I returned home via Keswick visiting my good friends Molly Lefebure (the writer) and her husband John. I had been promising to climb a Lakeland fell with them since May 1984 but somehow there had never been a convenient moment. Since I would need to test my physical capacity quite rigorously in the coming months we all knew this opportunity of a day out together could not be allowed to slip by, so we planned to climb Fairfield at the end of June. They were also genuinely thrilled by the prospect of my trek to the foot of Everest.

My preparations for Everest were to be not so much training but more a test of my physical and mental state to make sure that I still had what I thought I had. Because one was able to do something last year it is easy to imagine that one can still reach the same level of performance the next. However, in the case of someone performing at or very near to their limits, this is obviously not always the case. Somewhere in life one has to peak. Where the activity being pursued involves living life at the limits, with death the penalty for any serious misjudgment, it is imperative that this point is recognized and accepted. I could well do without going halfway around the world only to discover that my capabilities were all in the mind, a thing of the past. An historical record of achievement may well instil the mental edge of self-belief but that is little consolation to an ageing body and I was rapidly approaching forty, an advanced age for someone like myself to be still quite so active, I had been medically informed the previous year by the specialist I consulted when I was being incapacitated by the pain of the trapped nerves in my neck; the bones were closed together and physiotherapy could not make it better, only stop it getting worse. As I had to take more and more days off work I decided to retire, though the DHSS specialist (who asked me where my wheelchair was . . .) actually advised me that I should go on working as I was medically unemployable and would never get another job. What else could I do to fill my time? Would I not get bored? I saw a private specialist at the same time who was similarly hardly able to believe I could walk (my hips are locked rigid and it should be impossible). He said, 'Whatever it is that's keeping you so fit I suggest you keep doing it.' My answer, 'I climb a few mountains' was not the one he was expecting! He went on to confirm not only that others who had had the operations that I had were most of them back in a wheelchair by the age of twenty-five; very few were walking after thirty. And I was planning to climb in the Himalayas at forty.

The first thing to do was get my flights sorted out and booked. I reckoned that the best time of the year to do the trek would be October when the weather should be at its most settled and the hours of daylight still quite lengthy – in fact probably on a par with my ability to maintain my daily effort. I was offered an outward flight on 25 September but a couple of days later I was notified that this was overbooked and offered a confirmed booking for 28 September returning on 10 November. Six weeks seemed a reasonable length of time for my expedition. This would allow me a maximum of about thirty-five days to complete the ninety-mile round trek from the airstrip at Lukla to Kala Pattar and back.

The schedule I had worked out with Chris was a fifteen-day walk in, a few days spare at Kala Pattar just in case Everest was hidden behind cloud, and a similar length of time for my return. To achieve this would mean covering about three miles a day, a modest target by my normal standards. On the other hand I would be carrying my share of supplies and equipment and I had no gauge of how I would respond to the altitude (though I remembered my reaction to the comparatively low altitude in the Alps!) or what sort of progress I would make over any very steep, boulder-strewn or icy sections.

I wrote to the Sherpa Agency and also confirmed that Berghaus were prepared to assist with my equipment requirements. Writing to Kathmandu is a bit of a hit and miss affair and apparently my first letter did not arrive but I quickly established a helpful and friendly relationship with Berghaus. I wrote to two other suppliers, Mountain Equipment and Ultimate for assistance and once again received a positive and helpful response. I was now arranging to purchase whatever items of equipment I needed as soon as I could afford them. It was imperative that I obtain them as quickly as possible in order to do some user-trials to test fully their suitability, comfort and usefulness.

Equipment is generally designed for the average or perfect body, and certain items such as boots and rucksacks do not always perform with the advertised or anticipated comfort on an awkwardly stanced figure. Sometimes clothing which seems to fit perfectly well in the shop twists and works its way completely up the body when worn by someone using walking sticks. Items which may seem reasonably comfortable for a short while can become unbearably painful when used for any prolonged period. It was therefore absolutely essential that every piece of equipment I was to take to Everest should be thoroughly tried and tested. I needed to have total confidence that everything I used was the very best available. There was no room for doubt either in myself or anything I used.

I sent lots of letters to potential sponsors: banks, newspapers, supermarket chain stores, sweet and confectionery manufacturers and mail order firms – in fact any company which I thought had a record of sponsoring similar events or whom I believed may be sympathetic towards the type of thing I was attempting to do. Articles were written in the local press and a request for financial assistance appeared in local Chamber of Trade and Commerce journals. I had never previously sought sponsorship but had often been told by people that I should have since they or the companies they were involved with were looking for a person like myself to support. Now I was asking – but I was not receiving any positive response. In fairness, one company did send me £25 as a token gesture with their refusal and this at least covered the postage I had spent on the exercise.

I knew when I made my decision to go to Nepal that financing the expedition could be a rather delicate matter and I had been to see my bank manager to confirm that I would be allowed to cover any shortfall by way of an overdraft. My friendly bank manager was sympathetic and believed I had a secure financial background and the ability to make good any shortfall together with interest on my return. This at least gave me some peace of mind as I began to make financial commitments. I was taking a bit of a gamble but would at least not have to withdraw through lack of funds or loss of financial nerve.

Local newspapers, who had covered many of my past exploits, produced quite lengthy pieces on my proposed Himalayan venture although as one journalist, Jim Greenhalf, later admitted, deep down he was not convinced it would actually happen. He had kept faith with my 'far-fetched' idea only because as far as he was aware I had never previously failed to achieve what I had set out to do. Upon the appearance of these articles I received a telephone call from Yorkshire Television requesting an interview for *Calendar*, the regional news programme. YTV did not have a good record when it came to dealing with me. Since that first visit from a director in 1978 they had contacted me several times and I them but nothing had ever materialized. It was less than twelve months since they had cancelled a live interview with me only minutes before I was due to leave home for the studio. I now gave them a cool response. I asked them if they were really serious and they did not pursue the matter any further.

The local press coverage was followed by interest from *The Guardian* and, after a searching interview, a fair and comprehensive article appeared on 2 April. On reading this a producer from BBC North Television contacted me regarding the possibility of doing a piece for the local news programme, *Look North*. I had previously made one appearance on this programme when I had published my book *Sticks and Stones* and was not exactly enthralled by the result, particularly as although the BBC said they were impressed by the Ben Nevis film I had made with Chris Bonington, they were not prepared to come up with any reasonable deal for it. I told them that I had already refused YTV an interview and felt that I had nothing to gain by giving them one. I could do without being exploited for the sake of television and my reasons for going to Everest were deep-rooted and personal, not simply to seek media attention. My views were reluctantly accepted and I thought the matter closed.

I visited my GP, Dr Richard Lambert, to discuss the practical implications in relation to my physical problems. I had consulted him before I had made my original decision to go and, after declaring that I was mad, he had offered his full support, believing that if this was what I wanted to do then I should proceed. We both knew that with my deteriorating spinal condition I would not be up to such a venture for much longer. Now it was a matter of getting down to actual details and arranging a programme of immunizations, investigating any worrying pains and assembling an appropriate medical kit. Dr Lambert was in my opinion one of the most helpful and knowledgeable GPs I had ever been associated with. Whilst remaining professional our relationship was always one of honest and direct communication combined with humour. I never hid my views or feelings from him and he was open and friendly in his response. I had some very serious disorders but between us we managed to keep them under control and make light of the situation.

With the help of physiotherapy the ankylosing spondylitis in my neck was now under control and the only worrying pain I had was on and around the prominent bone on my right ankle. Dr Lambert's main concern was to make sure that it was not a floating chip off the bone which would most certainly have to be removed for long-term comfort and safety. I was referred to St Luke's Hospital for X-rays and fortunately these revealed nothing out of the ordinary. I could at least now walk on the ankle knowing that although it was a bit painful there was nothing seriously wrong with it. Perhaps the discomfort was muscular and would disappear with exercise.

When I had first started to climb mountains in the Lake District it had secretly been one of my ambitions to climb the top twelve highest peaks, as listed in the Red Guide to the area *Baddeley's Lake District* and three summits remained unvisited. It seemed like a good idea to attempt these as my preparation for the Everest trek. Tenth on the list came Fairfield and I had already made arrangements to ascend this with Molly Lefebure and her husband John. Crinkle Crags, at 2,816 feet, was twelfth and I invited my friend Cameron Wilson and his wife Angela to accompany me on this walk. Previously I had walked over Ilkley Moors with Cameron and since that time he had cultivated a liking for the high fells of Lakeland. Like many others he was none too sure that I would return from the Himalayas and was keen to fit in what could be a last walk.

My final preparation was to be on the eighth highest and probably the most difficult of all twelve, Pillar, the 2,927-foot peak on which I had already made two abortive attempts. With the long walk up Mosedale before the steep haul began, I had discovered (painfully) that the distance was far too great for me to complete in one day. Because of the problems to be encountered and my past failures I had no shortage of friends wishing to join me on this one. It would be as much a challenge for them to ensure my success as it would be for me to reach the top. I had talked over my difficulties with friends who knew the route well. A. Wainwright was convinced that from the form I had shown on the other mountains I had climbed my only real problem was the distance, although the long steep climb out of Looking Stead would be a severe test. I had a good friend whom I first met when I moved to Bradford, David Wright, who was a 'mountain man' in the true sense of the word, and he fancied his chances of success on Pillar with me. We would need at least two days with a possible third if the weather broke, and his positive attitude seemed conducive to a good expedition.

The outline for my physical preparation was now mapped out. Crinkle Crags the first week in June followed by Fairfield at the end of the month and finally Pillar during the first week of August. This would give my mental and physical resolve a fair battering, without – I hoped – overdoing things, and at the same time leave long enough for me to recover fully before I left for Nepal at the end of September. I had to agree that the whole plan was rather ambitious but if I could come through these early tests I should be in a good frame of mind and physically fit for what lay ahead.

The producer at the BBC, Neil McDonald, seemed to have as much resolve as myself since he was back on the telephone wanting to know how my plans were progressing. Once again I was adamant that I could do without his attentions but as a compromise finally agreed to allow him to visit me to discuss the trip and my plans. A meeting was arranged for 20 May.

Neil, who at that time produced the regional news programme *Look North* alternate weeks, is a climber in his late twenties. The previous summer, he informed me, he had climbed Mont Blanc. He knew the Lake District well and we found we had much in common. I filled him in on all the developments regarding my preparations and the trek. He wanted to film a piece for *Look North* on my ascent of Crinkle Crags and proposed Everest trip. Convinced it would be well made I decided I had little to lose, provided I performed as anticipated, and agreed to allow him and a two-man crew to accompany me. I consulted Cameron and he was all for an appearance on television and not in the least perturbed by their presence. I, however, had made enough films to realize that nothing is quite as straightforward as it ultimately appears on the screen and knew every shot has to be worked at, so that the camara crew would be a time-consuming distraction.

Later the same day I was due to meet Mountain Equipment at Stalybridge and Glossop to see equipment and clothing which might be suitable for my trip. Mountain Equipment are internationally renowned for their down sleeping bags, duvet jackets and Gore-tex waterproof suits. I wanted the very best gear available and I believed that they were the people to provide it. They agreed to support my expedition by offering excellent terms on the items I wished to purchase and also producing a sleeping bag with exactly the right amount of down filling to cope with the expected night temperatures, should these not coincide with the specifications of one of their standard models. To this end I provided them with details of the highest point of intended use and the expected time of year in order that their in-the-field expert could advise of my requirements. The staff were very helpful and extremely concerned that I take the right equipment, both to keep the weight to a minimum and to stay alive.

My next foray into the equipment market was a trip to Berghaus at Newcastle-upon-Tyne. Berghaus produce a superb range of rucksacks, boots, warm clothing and other accessories. Once again I was looking for the absolute best in equipment, as my life could well depend on it. I spent a whole morning trying on boots, carrying weighted rucksacks, checking the fit of Polar Plus clothing and looking at other useful items. The shop assistant was very patient and helpful – if slightly taken aback by my reason for needing the goods. I left with what I considered to be the most comfortable and appropriate items but I would have to use them under difficult or more testing conditions before I made any final decisions on what exactly I would be taking with me.

My physical condition was giving me considerable cause for concern. Aches and pains were becoming all too frequent and I was beginning to wonder whether I was not suffering only from a series of temporary minor disorders but had rather deteriorated to a permanent state of decrepitude. At this stage of planning it was not a pleasant position to be in, but only a good walk or two would clarify matters. Towards the end of May I was visiting my father in Leeds and while on a short walk around the gardens of Temple Newsam I realized that things were getting worse. I was hobbling along with great difficulty and in some considerable pain. Realistically I had to admit to myself that I was not walking very well at all and with only four months to go to my departure to Nepal I was becoming increasingly worried.

Two days later the pain in my right hip and groin had reached a point where I was in agony and almost unable to walk at all. I had great difficulty in getting out of the bath. To complete the depressing state of affairs I watched part of the ITV Telethon and realized exactly what type of things companies wished to support or be associated with. Funds were going to some charities of a very dubious nature. Perhaps I should not have let this bother me, but I suppose that deep down one of the many reasons why I was making the journey to Everest was to show quite clearly where my cards lay. If companies did not wish to support me that was their choice; the more difficult things became the more determined I was that the whole thing was going to be a success.

Physically things had become about as difficult as I believed they could get and my first outing was now only one week away. On 7 June I would endeavour to climb Crinkle Crags from Little Langdale. Since we would be starting our ascent from the Three Shires Stone at the summit of the Wrynose Pass it was not to be the most arduous of climbs. I had previously covered the first half of the route when I had climbed Pike o'Blisco some years ago and did not remember any particular problems. Crinkle Crags is a series of summits protruding from a long ridge and one of the reasons I had not already climbed it was that I knew a complete traverse was beyond my capabilities. With this in mind I would have to be content with whatever point I could safely reach provided I sat on top of at least one of the shattered rock domes.

Cameron, Angela and I were to meet with Neil McDonald and the film crew at The Three Shires Hotel the evening before and finalize arrangements for the following day. We had triple cause for celebration: it was Neil's birthday, we were in one of the most beautiful places in Britain and I was about to take my first steps along the road to Everest. To add to the happiness of the occasion I had taken along my dog Megan who was about to scramble and pull her way up her first mountain. Megan is not a dog I would want to let loose on open fells for fear of her chasing sheep or leaping over a precipice and I personally would not wish to handle her on a lead in such a demanding situation. Cameron, however, was able and willing, although perhaps he didn't know quite what he was letting himself in for! I knew her presence would add greatly to the excitement and unpredictability of filming and, besides, I hoped she would really enjoy the outing.

For the walk I wanted to test my new Pulsar 45 rucksack, Scarpa Fitzroy boots and Freestyle walking breeches. I normally walked in my tried and trusted Hawkins Scafell boots. They were really solid and comfortable and suited my requirements perfectly but unfortunately now a discontinued line. I was not happy that my existing pair were sufficiently stout to withstand the rigours of another long walk and needed to find an adequate replacement. The Fitzroy is a full steel plate boot as opposed to half plate of the Scafell but otherwise quite similar apart from being of a more modern construction technique. I cannot use a plastic reinforced sole as it always returns to the boot's original shape. A steel plate eventually adopts the shape of the foot using it; in my Scafells there were permanent bends, which provided the correct support for my feet. I took my Scafells along in case any serious difficulty arose. My rucksack was packed with a load similar in weight to the one I would expect to carry to Everest. The walking breeches were ultra light, comfortable and made of a modern high-specification material which supposedly dried very quickly and offered some protection against cool winds.

We had aimed at a nine o'clock start but with the preliminary filming work and other delays it was eleven before we actually set foot on the fell. The weather was warm and sunny and progress pleasant. The camera crew periodically went ahead and did their filming as we walked past causing us a minimum amount of disturbance. Constantly straining on a long leash, Megan had a whale of a time leaping into every water ditch she could find and splashing her way along, dog-handler extraordinaire Cameron being dragged along behind in involuntary hot pursuit. In all honesty I considered Cameron's offer to handle Meg an heroic gesture. Controlling a determined animal on a long lead is not the easiest of tasks. But Meg was there to have fun too, I was making slow if steady progress and it was a hot day.

Lunch was taken by the shore of Red Tarn. My new boots were hard work (as are most new boots) but perfectly comfortable. The route took us behind Great Knott before climbing steadily to the ridge of Crinkle Crags. At my last place of rest before the summit we were afforded splendid views of Langdale. Neil thought this an ideal spot to conduct his interview since he would not be wasting time unnecessarily and the backdrop was magnificent. He questioned me about my forthcoming trip to the Himalayas and the reasons for undertaking such an apparently demanding venture. I felt the short interview was to the point and went well.

The summit was not too distant but there was a short steep scramble/mini rock climb blocking the way ahead. This type of feature was nothing new to me, however, and with some difficulty I was soon on top of the first Crinkle sharing the experience with my companions. When we arranged the walk Neil had expected me to reach the summit but perhaps had not fully realized the effort it would take actually to get there. The time had flown. It was five o'clock. Common sense dictated there was no time for any further Crinkles; in fact a hasty retreat was called for. The film crew, who needed to return home that same evening, bade us farewell after making sure I had safely descended the steep rocky crags. Quickly they disappeared over the horizon, making me all too aware of my own acutely slow progress.

As the shore of Red Tarn arrived so did the midges. The evening was drawing in as we arrived back at Wrynose at exactly ten o'clock. Megan must have walked many times the distance we had and as soon as the car door was opened she leapt on to the front passenger seat, her usual spot, and flatly refused to move for anything. This was a very tired dog and I felt pretty much the same way myself. Considering the problems I had been having recently I was very pleased with the day out. The only effect was two blisters on my right hand, which fortunately remained intact. I had a slight swelling on my right ankle but this was nothing serious, most likely an aggravation of the problem I had previously had X-rayed by wearing new boots. I would have to check this on my next outing. The new equipment had all lived up to my expectations. Although I had serious reservations about committing myself totally to the boots this was only because of the extra stress the full steel plate and resulting lack of flexibility put on my ankles. The weight was about right and I could walk quite well in them if necessary. They would be ideal for wearing with crampons should these be required on the higher reaches of my Himalayan trek.

The film for *Look North* was edited down to about four minutes and broadcast two days later on 9 June, the same day as I had been invited to a meeting at BBC North (Leeds) to discuss the possibility of them making a full-scale documentary on my Everest trip. Present at the meeting were Roger Bufton, the BBC's regional manager, Allen Jewhurst, a director from Chameleon Films of Leeds, Neil McDonald and myself. Basically we went through my proposals for the trek and Allen Jewhurst outlined the resources and requirements needed to produce a film. My concern in agreeing to make a film was first of all that I should not be used or abused and secondly that the theme and story of the film should be in keeping with my principles and general view of mountains, walking, disability and life. At the meeting it became clear that the BBC were very keen on the idea of making a documentary and that, to my mind, Allen Jewhurst was the right man to make it. He would make the film for the right reasons. It was also apparent that Neil McDonald had every faith in my ability to carry through my plans to a successful conclusion.

I was pleased with the piece for *Look North*. It was filmed well, skilfully edited with appropriate moody music and was a great success. The following morning it was broadcast nationally on Breakfast Television. I had provisionally agreed to BBC North's proposals, subject to their final offer, and it was now up to them to convince the powers that be in London that the programme was a viable and worthwhile proposition. Because of the very considerable financial outlay they would need to have total conviction in the venture and my ability. The film on Crinkle Crags would perhaps go some way towards this. They were obviously hoping for a quick response but as is usually the case in these matters the decision can take a long time to make.

Allen Jewhurst had been to Everest film-making before and had also been to K2 and several other remote – and cold! – places. From this first meeting I could not say whether or not I would get along with him for a prolonged period, but Chameleon had an excellent reputation for making adventure films and track records are really all you can go by. He appeared to know what he was talking about, was familiar with Kathmandu, the flight to Lukla and the route beyond, and I felt his experience would be of considerable benefit to me. The main thing that I was concerned about was that anyone who accompanied me understood one thing – that I would be making all my own decisions and in complete control of any situation arising. Likewise, they would be free to follow their own ideas and objectives. Hopefully there would be no clash of interests and we would develop a good working relationship, but while there were areas in which I was prepared to compromise, there were others where I definitely would not – if they tried to make any decisions regarding my health or capabilities.

Allen's reasons for agreeing to make the film (I do not think he particularly relished the prospect of returning to Everest in the wake of his good friend Joe Tasker's death on the North East Ridge) I believed were sincere. The first thing was the challenge of making a successful hour-long film based on only one relatively unknown person. The second was to capture the challenge and adventure of the expedition of a severely physically handicapped person without dwelling on the disability aspect. In fact once established at the beginning of the film it would then have to be largely ignored or at least taken as read. This was good news for me since once out there we would each be faced with our own difficult although differing challenges: the crew to produce a good film, mine to reach Kala Pattar. No one would be resting on their laurels or just doing a job. Everyone had an equally important task to perform with little margin for error.

On 13 June I gave a talk to the area Scout Association AGM held at Leeds Civic Hall. It went extremely well and I received a fantastic reception, but for the first time I had to answer a battery of questions about my trip from a packed audience. I was never anything but honest but the questions asked gave me an insight into how responsive the general public was to the prospect of this exciting venture and how much interest it had created.

My four minutes on the BBC had created some interest and two large firms of solicitors from Cardiff and Milton Keynes donated £250 each towards the expenses of my trip. The money was a godsend, arriving at a critical time when my finances were strained to the limit.

An ascent of Fairfield with Molly and John was arranged for the last Sunday in June and just a few days prior to this the pain in my right ankle improved drastically – overnight. The problem completely cleared up. Although the ankle had shown no adverse reaction from my day out on Crinkle Crags this was marvellous news.

Since the day I first underwent surgery thirty years ago I have been prone to aches and pains appearing suddenly and without warning for no apparent reason. This had been one of them and like most of the others it had eventually gone in the same way it came. All I can do with such pains is to try and ascertain the medical reason for them. If there is no logical diagnosis or apparent risk of serious lasting damage I believe I must persevere and continue to live life in the manner which I choose, trying whenever possible not to let the trouble discourage me. Which is not to say that I do not monitor every disorder and treat it very seriously, but life has to go on and I reckon I might as well give it a hefty push in the direction I want it to go. The cure to most disorders is usually either rest or exercise and unless medically advised otherwise I endeavour to try various combinations of both.

I arrived at Molly and John's in Newlands on the Saturday evening ready for an early start next morning. Our plan was to park near the Swan Hotel in Grasmere and make the very steep direct ascent of Stone Arthur before heading via Great Rigg to Fairfield. We discussed every option to the route and prepared for the day ahead before retiring early. It would be a long hard day and I decided not to experiment with any new equipment. An all-out effort would be required if we were to have any hope of success.

The weather had been warm and dry since the beginning of June and the overnight rain was welcome as it would consolidate the ground, but we could do with it clearing up before we commenced the steep climb. It had reduced to a steady drizzle as we arrived in Grasmere and a visit to our mutual friend Heaton Cooper seemed a good idea while we waited hopefully for it to clear. The rain ceased and the clouds began to disperse as we left the car, booted up and began our walk up the lane. The track up Stone Arthur came into view. It appeared long, steep and completely unrelenting as it cut its way directly upwards through the bracken. I assessed the alternatives and decided that since the direct route should be just within my capabilities the severity would be preferable to some lengthy less exciting detour up the valley. At some stage the height had to be gained and I reckoned we might as well attain it as quickly as possible.

The track went on and on upwards very steeply. Conditions underfoot were difficult with many areas of loose stones to ascend. I was at my limits of what I could manage and there were few places where we could safely stop for a rest. The most encouraging factor was that it was easier and safer to keep going upwards than it would have been to turn around and descend. In no time at all we were being afforded splendid views of the valley below. About halfway up the 800–foot climb I had one difficult moment when I half lost my footing on a tricky section of steep scree but John was immediately on hand to assist. Molly was scouting on ahead and periodically returning with words of encouragement. We rested and took lunch just below the 1,652-foot rocky summit of Stone Arthur.

The strenuous part of the climb now past it was just a case of making steady progress over the upland ridges ahead. We arrived on the summit about four o'clock and then beat a hasty retreat down Greenhead Gill. To descend by the same route as we had taken on the way up would have been most unwise. The way down Greenhead Gill was not clearly discernible being heavily overgrown with fern fronds, but Molly, who has an intimate knowledge of the area, went on ahead finding the easiest route for me. Once in the Gill bottom a decent track was located and I wearily made my way back to the car. I was very tired. It had been a long hard day and a severe test, but I was suffering no ill effects. Fairfield, Molly and John had given me a most enjoyable day and with the physical improvement I was now looking forward with eager anticipation to Everest.

A two-day ascent of Pillar would finalize my preparations. A magazine, *Outdoor Action*, had asked if they could accompany me on the first part of this walk to do an interview for an article. David Wright and I were to be joined by two brothers, Giles and James Manchester, friends and neighbours of David. They were keen fellwalkers with some climbing experience, in their early twenties and fit enough to carry most of the equipment we would need for our overnight camp. In the event of a break in the weather or serious difficulty on this more arduous climb the extra numbers would add to the safety.

By 27 July there was still no news from the BBC and it would soon be time for me to confirm my arrangements if I was to be departing for the Himalayas on my own. Another problem had also arisen, swelling in my legs was becoming increasingly troublesome. This had developed for no apparent reason. It was over a month since my outing on Fairfield and I had done nothing which might upset my physical state. The previous week I had been to Cambridge researching my family tree but had undertaken nothing at all strenuous. The next few days were to be a nightmare as the swelling in my legs became acute and my knees stiff and painful.

Whatever it was that was causing the swelling it was general since it was affecting a considerable part of my body. After an agonizing weekend I was at my doctor's first thing on Monday morning. The problem was diagnosed as a water infection which was causing excess fluid retention. A specimen was sent to the laboratory to confirm this and the problem treated with antibiotic tablets. Within days the infection was cleared and abdominal swelling gone but my legs were still retaining fluid and my knees stiff and painful. Yet I still had an appointment with Pillar – if I was in any condition to keep it.

I could manage to walk but that was about all I could do. I was unable to get in the bath or pick myself up if I fell or got down on the floor. I could not kneel at all. My knees had insufficient bend and the kneecaps too tender to bear any weight. However, I decided to proceed with the trip to Pillar partly because of the other people involved and also because if this disorder had occurred while I was walking in Nepal I would have still had to continue, if only back down, which could be a fifteen-day trek.

After recording an interview for Radio Leeds I left for Wasdale Head, taking Giles with me. In the Climber's Bar at the Wasdale Hotel we met up with David, James and the journalist and photographer from *Outdoor Action*. As a trial for the Himalayan trek I slept out in the open on the shores of Wastwater. I had not yet purchased the actual sleeping bag I would be using but by placing my existing goosedown bag inside a waterproof bivi-bag I would get a fair idea of what it would be like. Although the ground was stony I was comfortable enough to sleep. Through the night it showered several times but I managed to remain warm and dry and sleep on.

For this walk I was trying out a new pair of Scarpa Alp Attack boots, they being much less rigid than the Fitzroys. Once again my Scafells would be going along just in case the Scarpas proved unsuitable in any way. On the long walk up Mosedale I did the interview and posed for innumerable photographs. By the time we reached Gatherstone Beck it was midday and time for the journalist and photographer to leave us. The steep climb to the Black Sail Pass lay ahead. The exercise was keeping the swelling in my legs to a minimum and the stiffness in my knees was slightly easier, but still a problem. After a short way up the steep section I realized the boots were not giving me the necessary support on the soles of my feet and changed into my Scafells. The Scarpas were extremely comfortable to wear but too light and soft to provide the considerable degree of support and protection my weak, delicate feet and ankles needed.

By the time we reached Black Sail Pass the weather was beginning to close in. David and Giles went ahead to find a suitable spot for our overnight camp while I rested and chatted to James. By four o'clock the wind and rain had arrived and we were safely camped alongside a tarn below Looking Stead. My legs were showing no serious ill effects but I was pleased to be in my sleeping bag resting and enjoying one of David's special curry recipes followed by fruit cake and banana custard. It was unlikely I would be enjoying such fine fare along the road to Everest but the inclement weather I could do without.

The most difficult part of the climb was still to come and I had left our picturesque camp site by seven o'clock the following morning and was quickly past Looking Stead and on my way up over the first massive outcrop of rock. Progress was slow and hazardous as I worked my way upwards through the morning mist. I was grateful for the close attentions of my companions as I skirted fearful drops and climbed over large rock step after rock step. Openings in the cloud were now appearing and with any luck the cloud would be dispersed by the time we eventually reached the summit.

At the top of the first rock band I had reached my previous highest point on the mountain. The second rocky outcrop was climbed and the way to the summit now lay through a gateway of rock down which poured a pile of loose stone scree. This was the type of terrain which thrilled me and as it loomed out of the mist there was nowhere on earth I could have been happier. Beyond this the summit still lay shrouded in mist some way along the ridge in the distance but progress was steady and around half past eleven we were at the summit taking our photographs. The cloud was clearing, intermittently exposing wonderful views and then closing in again. The descent back to Wasdale Head was to take another nine hours of sustained effort.

Pillar is probably the most difficult mountain I ever climbed and I was fortunate to share the experience with such good company. If the deterioration of my legs proved to be permanent it may have to be the last but as my forty-third peak in Britain and the fulfilment of a twenty-year ambition to climb the twelve highest summits in the Lake District I could not hope to bow out with a more distinguished and satisfying performance.

At least my legs seemed to have benefited from the effort. The exercise reduced the swelling and increased the range of my knee movement but my knees still remained stiff and painful. The improvement, however, was short lived and I quickly slipped back to my previous state, and the painful decision whether or not to continue with my Himalayan plans loomed large. Provided I got no worse I knew that although in pain I could still ascend over rough steep terrain, so long as there was someone present to assist me get up and sit down. There were several weeks to go before my departure and with medical attention I was optimistic there was still time for the situation to improve.

I was due to confirm my bookings on 8 August but the BBC thought they were close to being given the go ahead and asked me to put off finalizing matters as long as possible. The long-awaited telephone call came on 16 August and a delighted Neil McDonald from the BBC unofficially confirmed that the budget for the film had been approved and travel arrangements would now be dealt with by them. I now knew that if I went ahead with the trip there was no room for failure. The film would bring both advantages and disadvantages. I would have the benefit of the crew around me, Chameleon's expertise in the field of travel and Allen Jewhurst's knowledge of the locality. On the other hand I would lose the total flexibility that going alone would bring and I would be under increased personal pressure to accomplish what I had publicly stated I intended to do. Yet that should give me the edge necessary to succeed if at all possible, and the BBC's involvement also meant that I could now completely devote myself to getting fit. Some pressures had come and other pressures had gone.

FIFTEEN

To Everest
the Hardest Way

A meeting was scheduled with Chameleon to iron out the final details. The travel plans were to be organized by Diana Penny of Bufo Ventures and her Sherpa husband Ang Zangbu. A provisional itinerary had been prepared and we were due to fly out to Kathmandu on 19 November and return on 24 December. The five weeks was a week less than the time I had anticipated it would take me based on Chris Bonington's advice. The planned route included a couple of short detours for scenic filming and I immediately ruled these out as being impractical. I think that when Diana and Ang Zangbu first saw me they considered ruling the *whole* trek out as being impractical. Any faith they had was quite simply based on Chris Bonington's recommendation and the BBC's desire to proceed with the venture. But faith they had.

Although I was sceptical about any form of rigid itinerary I agreed to what seemed like the least demanding schedule. I knew I would only ever be able to do my best and would not be capable of walking or covering specified distances to order. The plan therefore was really only a rough guide setting targets to be aimed for. As the trek progressed beyond the 12,000-foot point the altitude gained each day would become more important than the distance covered, it being medically wise to ascend no more than a net height of 1,000 feet a day. There were also some rest days included in the schedule and I would have to consider forgoing these should I fall too far behind target.

Moving the expedition forward almost two months to November and December would reduce the hours of available daylight in which I would be able to walk. The weather, however, should be much more stable and drier at that time although night-time temperatures somewhat cooler. Throughout the nights we could expect the temperature to drop to around minus twenty degrees celsius on the higher reaches. There was also the prospect of walking and camping on snow and ice for a period of about seven to nine days as we progressed beyond the 14,000-foot mark. In fact the previous year a very heavy overnight fall of snow (about six feet I believe) had trapped many trekkers on these higher parts putting their lives in considerable danger. Some Sherpas, who I presume had not been adequately clothed and tented, succumbed.

While out in Nepal we would have at least three days spare before and after the trek, time necessary to confirm all flight bookings out of Kathmandu. You have to register at the airport three days before the journey is due. On our arrival we would be using these days for filming the build-up to the trek. On our way home we could use this waiting period to pursue another activity if we so wished. The general consensus of opinion was that a trip to the Chitwan National Park, to the south-west of Kathmandu, would be the most enjoyable. The BBC, however, did not feel that the budget would run to this. Another option was to take a two-day white water rafting trip down the Trisuli River. This seemed an exciting if rather daring prospect and, against my better judgment I felt, I was coaxed into agreement.

Yorkshire Television were once again asking for an interview for their regional news programme, *Calendar*. My being a daring sort of chap they thought it a good idea if they lowered me down the 300 feet of Gaping Gill on a caving club's bosun's chair. They had got it wrong. I am not a daring sort of a chap. I believe that I know my limitations; what I do is take highly calculated risks in order to fulfil ambitions which involve a considerable degree of personal physical input. Being showered with a downpour of cold water while suspended on a thin steel wire hung over a great chasm was never one of my ambitions. Perhaps I may have found this acceptable had it been a small part of a much greater adventure but under these circumstances I felt it was not a true reflection of the activities I undertake and I declined the invitation.

For the purpose of an interview I agreed to climb Beamsley Beacon, a rocky moor north of the Ilkley–Bolton Abbey road. Despite the trouble I was having with my legs the terrain posed no serious problems and apart from the sound recordist having difficulty with the breezy weather filming went smoothly. The piece was completed with the use of some slides of Chris Bonington and myself on Ben Nevis and broadcast five days later on 26 August. It was long overdue for ten years had now elapsed since YTV first approached me regarding a piece for *Calendar*.

My collection of clothing and equipment to take with me was now beginning to take shape. I had a Redline down sleeping bag,

Annapurna duvet jacket, Freestyle breeches and Kongur Gore-tex waterproof suit from Mountain Equipment. The purpose-built suit seemed a bit of a luxury but I felt it could well mean the difference between life and death at 17 or 18,000 feet in the event of adverse weather. My final choice of tent was Ultimate's The Tent, a well tried and tested mountain tent of traditional design. I would pack everything into my Berghaus Cyclops Expedition II rucksack for the journey out there and then carry my immediate needs in a Dart 25 daysack. The most comfortable warm clothing I could find was Polar Plus, also by Berghaus.

The only boot I knew for certain that I could comfortably walk long distances in was my pair of Scafells, a model Hawkins no longer made. My existing pair had been resoled once and were moderately worn. I contacted Hawkins to ask if they would be prepared to make me a new pair at whatever cost. The pattern or last was apparently no longer in existence and further production was not possible. A couple of weeks later however I received a telephone call from the manager to say that a pair of size 8s, now obsolete stock, had been found in a store room and that they would let me have them free of charge. This was great news but unfortunately because of the now delicate state of my ankles I was not able to walk them in. I tried but it was impossible. I would have to take my tried and trusted ten-year-old pair after all and hope that they held out. They looked as if they might provided I was not walking over sharp rocks for long distances, but to be on the safe side I would take along my once-worn pair of Scarpa Fitzroys which I knew met my strict requirements despite their extreme rigidity and would also come in useful if I had to wear crampons at any point.

The problem with stiffness and swelling in my legs was getting worse if anything. Water tests were now showing up nothing. The next step was to send a blood sample for analysis in the hope of detecting an underlying cause. This was taken on 1 September. I tried taking mild diuretic tablets as prescribed by my doctor to see if the problem could be alleviated that way.

I took a week's holiday in the Lake District, staying with a good friend in Keswick, while I waited for the results of the test. Megan would have to go in kennels when I went to Nepal and I wanted to spend some time alone with her before the summer was out. Retrieving a piece of driftwood from Derwentwater and chasing a ball on the beach at Seascale are two of her favourite pastimes and I was glad to see her active and having fun. The Lake District was also a good place for me to purchase some extra pieces of specialized equipment that I would need: an ice axe and ice hammer with fittings; crampons; ice screws; new rope; lightweight karabiners and abseiler; climbing harness; warm gloves; sunglasses and total block sun cream for protection against the glare from the snow and ultra violet rays. Attention had to be paid to every last detail.

I already had good climbing gear but modern materials make for a considerable saving in weight and perhaps improved performance. I wanted absolutely the best available that suited my requirements and was not prepared to make do with anything just because I already possessed an item that approximated to my needs. The expedition demanded total commitment all the way and not simply when it was convenient. Motivation and inspiration come from many sources and narrowing any likely causes of failure down to the human element goes a long way towards creating the feeling that it is really up to you and you alone. Extra ounces in themselves seem to mean very little but if you have to carry them to the point of exhaustion while depending on them for your survival, that is a different matter. Although one obviously hopes it will never come to this the possibility must always be considered.

The blood test proved to be clear and still there was no explanation for what had gone wrong with my legs. I had strongly believed it was due to some type of internal chemical imbalance but there was now no evidence to support this theory. The next course of action was simply to increase the amount of exercise I took. While I was at the Health Centre I booked to have the first part of my cholera, typhoid, polio and tetanus immunizations on 26 September.

Ironically it was at this time that for insurance purposes I had to provide a doctor's note to say that I was medically fit to undertake the trip. Apart from the problem with my legs (and I could still walk), I was physically fit and my doctor was happy to state this. Our Nepalese visas and trekking permits had been applied for and everything now seemed to be in order.

I had my first lot of immunizations and was pleasantly surprised to find that although they brought on a fevered feeling for a few hours they were almost painless. I had deteriorated to a state where only twenty hours a day rest with my legs raised higher than my heart was preventing swelling and serious damage. With less than eight weeks to go before my departure I needed some improvement, and quickly. I had tried everything I and my GP could suggest and there remained only to see a specialist. Despite the unwanted experimental surgery that I underwent as a child and its resulting problems I still have to wait three months or more for an NHS appointment. I chose to go privately as I always have done when I believe the problem needs urgent attention.

An urgent appointment was arranged for me to see my regular specialist (NHS or private). I asked him if he thought there was anything he could do to help me in the seven weeks remaining to me. He knew my medical background and the proposed Himalayan venture fascinated him. I think he thought I was absolutely crazy but believed there was a certain sense and truth to it. Seven weeks he said was a reasonable period in which to get some improvement although the problem could be the onset of muscular arthritis and I may never again be restored to my former self. He placed me under the care of St Luke's Hospital physiotherapy department.

One thing was now very clear. If the deterioration was permanent this was going to be my one and only chance of ever seeing Mount Everest under my own steam. There is nothing like having all one's eggs, in fact life, in one basket for focusing the concentration and effort. If everything had not been booked and arranged I would not have contemplated going in my present condition, but other people whom I greatly respected were now involved finan- cially and otherwise and any change of plans did not affect only me. It was something which I really wanted to do, I could still walk and hopefully there would be some improvement with physio and hydrotherapy.

At the beginning of October Sir Edmund Hillary, the man accredited with being the first to reach the summit of Mount Everest, was giving a talk in Leeds and the BBC arranged for him to do an interview with me for *Look North*. We met in the picturesque surrounds of Golden Acre Park on the outskirts of Leeds. As a child I clearly remember the remarkable events of May 1953 and feeling fiercely proud that it was a British expedition that had made the final breakthrough. I had never for one moment thought that some day I should be treading some of the same ground. I had not been an aspiring child. I simply progressed one step at a time discovering new horizons as I went.

Sir Edmund was folklore and it came as a pleasant surprise that I should get to meet the man. We talked about the Everest area and the route to Kala Pattar, the temperatures that could be expected and the improvements that have taken place in equipment since 1953. On camera he was enthusiastic and full of encouragement but privately he reckoned I had little or no chance. The steep climb to Namche Bazaar would prove an impossible obstacle, he thought. In places the track was no more than a narrow ledge and many sections were boulder strewn, not to mention some of the precarious bridges spanning rapidly flowing rivers of icy-cold glacial melt waters.

I think Sir Edmund thought he had been conned into some sort of practical joke or that I was completely ignorant of what I was letting myself in for. Initially his doubts caused me some concern but on such a short formal meeting perhaps he was having difficulty in reconciling the handicapped person he could see before him with my twenty-year history of pursuing similar activites. In an effort to help him fully grasp the situation I presented him with a copy of my book *Sticks and Stones*. Although still somewhat sceptical about my sanity and prospects of success it did seem to go some way towards relieving his general disbelief. For me it was a privilege and honour to meet the great man himself. Maybe the very idea of a quite severely disabled person about to undertake something which seemed impossible, something that was considered demanding and hazardous enough for the average able-bodied individual, was just too difficult to understand.

My physiotherapy began at St Luke's. Whatever the course of treatment there remained only six weeks and two days in which to get results. I quickly learned it would be Sara Dennison who was expected to find the improvement. After being assessed, the first action was to reduce the swelling with the use of Flotron equipment, a pulse-inflated splint which works by a series of compression actions. The session was completed with a massage aimed at removing any remaining fluid and encouraging the muscles actively to return the waste products to the body as they occurred.

Improvement had to be monitored carefully. With the swelling being physically removed it would be easy to imagine that things were getting better. The pain was acute. The muscles in the back of my legs felt like strands of barbed wire. Every time they moved it was almost as though a string of razor blades was being dragged through the flesh. My knees were very stiff and would not bend without yet more pain. Sara was optimistic, though, that we would soon get some definite signs of improvement, and her positive attitude helped maintain my enthusiasm. Her heart and soul went into every session of treatment and I lived with the belief that no one could have done better, whatever the outcome. I was quite simply receiving the best treatment available.

A week later I was showing sufficient improvement to add hydrotherapy to the other treatments. My hydrotherapist was Denise Gledhill and her strict discipline – making sure the pool exercises were executed correctly – was initially very intimidating. A more trusting partnership developed once she realized that I always put everything I had into the programme, shirking nothing. The water was at about body temperature and the exercises were extensive and demanding. The pressure of the water prevented further swelling while the heat relaxed the muscles reducing the risk of injury. When progress was made more air was added to the floats on my legs in order to maintain the degree of effort required.

To get the maximum amount of benefit one had to have an appetite for hard work, and I was at the hospital at 8.30 prompt every morning. Improvement was slow but steady, the sharp points being slowly relieved from the barbed wire feeling. The resulting 'taut wire' sensation was still very painful but a step in the right direction.

The vaccine for my meningitis inoculation had now arrived. It was a course of three injections to be given at fortnightly intervals. The second part of my cholera, typhoid, polio and tetanus was due, which would then leave only an injection of gamma globulin to protect against hepatitis and a further tetanus after my return home. Just as well that I had every confidence in Sister Atkinson's ability with a syringe . . .

With only four weeks left to my departure I thought I had better take a short walk to ascertain my current ability. I enlisted the support of David Wright and we went for a walk by the River Aire at Thackley, a local beauty spot. One day the following week I was due to give a talk at Tonbridge in Kent for the Spastics Society and I reckoned that if I could manage to use the London Underground things would be looking much brighter. Although it was hard work I made the journey all right, suffering no serious adverse reaction.

Work on the documentary was to start the following day with an afternoon filming session at St Luke's Hospital. The next morning we were due at Chris Bonington's home at the foot of the Northern Fells in the Lake District. Neither the BBC nor Chameleon had been aware of my deterioration until the previous week when I had signed my contract. Although it was for only the nominal sum of £50 plus the travel expenses I had not seen fit to discuss my problems with some organization with whom I did not have an agreement or any firm understanding. I was both emotionally and financially very deeply committed to the venture and if at all possible I intended to go through with it. Without any legal basis to our relationship there was little else I considered they needed to know. I fully intended getting to Kala Pattar whatever, and that I believed was sufficient information for them to make their own decisions regarding the making of the film.

As the director jokingly told me later, while we were on the trail, my trek would make a good story whether I cracked up, fell off the track and died or made it to Kala Pattar. The latter outcome would not necessarily even create the most impact for the viewers. However, if I was to have a nervous breakdown or fall into the depths below could I make sure they were filming at the time. Of course it was just a joke and he most sincerely hoped that I would make it to Kala Pattar, but there was a lot of truth in what he was saying. His film was about human endeavour and the fact that we were going to Everest, although providing a spectacular backdrop, was incidental.

The time for departure would soon be here. Days seemed to fly by as I made my final preparations. With two weeks to go I asked if my morning visit to the hospital could be followed by another in the afternoon. Between visits I had to make some effort at fitting in a short walk or working on my exercise machine. The additional session allowed me to work at becoming more mobile in the knowledge that Sara was there to relieve the tension from my taut calf muscles and smooth away any swelling afterwards. Improvement was slow but positive. The severe pain behind my knees was gradually easing. The 'taut wire' feeling was giving way to the more normal pain of stiff swollen joints.

Any uncertainty about my condition had now gone for I could tell by the way it was also affecting my arms and neck that it was here to stay. It was too late to worry about whatever had brought it on. My problem was to get it under control and learn to live with whatever I had left. The rules of the game may have changed but there was still a game to be played and won.

Bon Voyage, Good Luck and cards simply offering Best Wishes arrived from many friends, relatives and well-wishers. My family were prepared for what I had decided to do. I was deeply touched when I discovered that my father, in response to scepticism expressed as to my chances of success, stated that I had never failed in what I had chosen to do before, why should I now?

As my packing got under way some last minute additions had to be made: a new torch, drinking-water bottles, cup and plate and other small items. My medical kit had to be kept to a minimum and yet still provide some form of cover against every foreseeable problem. I just managed to keep my main rucksack down to the airline regulation weight of 20 kg plus my daysack as hand luggage.

The most difficult part of the expedition was now upon me. Megan had to go in kennels and I had to make a new will. Megan and I had been together for five years and apart from the occasional short stay with her mother we had never been parted. Megan joined me when I was at a very difficult period in my life and her companionship means a great deal. There is no way you can explain to a dog that you are going away for five weeks and should anything go seriously wrong will not be returning. She would get used to her new surroundings in a day or so; it was really I who would be missing her and I suppose feeling a little guilty about the apparent desertion. In the event of my not returning I had made adequate provision for her but this was little consolation to the whining animal as I said goodbye. This was a distressing moment which put life into true perspective and reminded me of the treasures 'I valued most. At this moment I knew that whatever happened I had to survive.

I returned to an empty home to spend my last night alone. The call of Everest was strong and I knew that whatever the heartache it was a road I had to follow. Something deep from within drove me on. My condition had deteriorated rather rapidly from the days only four months ago when I reckon I could have taken the trek in my stride. The dangers were still the same, but now I was walking with great difficulty. I dreaded the return of the awful pain in my left ankle that I had felt on the Coast to Coast Walk. However, the problems seemed to add an extra dimension to events – perhaps fear and uncertainty. It was not simply a question of putting in a good performance, more than ever I needed to find that extra something: a source of drive and acceptance that comes through the soul, a resignation to the fact that there is a goal to be achieved and life beyond does not exist. Some may call it total commitment and single-mindedness. Maybe the less understanding, bloody-mindedness. Whatever, I needed to find this strength and inner belief which comes through faith and understanding. I would have only this one chance to get to Kala Pattar and every ounce of energy in my body and soul was focused on this desolate hill high in the Himalayas. I prayed to God that he would give me strength to do what I had to do, and to accept any consequences, good or bad. Perhaps my physical decline was all part of something far greater than I could ever hope to understand and would not reduce my chances of success. Destiny once again awaited but this time the outcome would depend greatly on my own actions.

SIXTEEN

The Ultimate Adventure

The film crew and I were to meet at Chameleon's studio in Leeds at 7.30 a.m. on the Saturday for an 8 a.m. departure to Heathrow. The team consisted of director Allen Jewhurst, cameraman Desmond Seal, sound recordist Jane Parfitt, and assistant camerman Mark Stokes. Producer Neil McDonald from the BBC had left for Kathmandu the previous Wednesday in order to arrange for our filming permit and liaison officer and iron out any problems there might be. The proposed itinerary was as follows:

Saturday 19 November	Depart London Heathrow 1630 for Dhaka via Paris
Sunday 20	Arrive Dhaka 0955, depart for Kathmandu 1500, arrive 1610
Monday 21– *Wednesday 23*	Filming in Kathmandu
Thursday 24	Morning flight to Lukla (9,350 ft), walk to Phakding (8,701 ft)
Friday 25	Walk through Benkar and Chumowa to Jorsale (9,101 ft)
Saturday 26	Steep climb to Namche Bazaar (11,306 ft)
Sunday 27	Rest day in Namche Bazaar to acclimatize
Monday 28	Walk through Sarnassa to Pungo Tenga
Tuesday 29	Steep climb to Tengboche monastery (12,687 ft)

Wednesday 30	Walk to Pangboche (12,798 ft)
Thursday 1 December	Walk to Dingboche (14,337 ft)
Friday 2	Rest day at Dingboche to acclimatize
Saturday 3	Walk through Pheriche to Dughla (15,069 ft)
Sunday 4	Walk to Lobuche (16,174 ft). Expect snow from here
Monday 5	Walk to Gorak Shep (17,008 ft)
Tuesday 6	Difficult climb up scree to Kala Pattar (18,192 ft)
Wednesday 7	Descend to Gorak Shep
Thursday 8	Across the Khumbu glacier to Everest base camp
Friday 9	Spare day
Saturday 10	Return to Gorak Shep
Sunday 11	Return to Dughla
Monday 12	Return to Pangboche
Tuesday 13	Return to Tengboche or Pungo Tenga
Wednesay 14	Return to Namche Bazaar
Thursday 15	Descend to Jorsale or Phakding
Friday 16	Climb to Lukla
Saturday 17	Morning flight to Kathmandu
Sunday 18– Monday 19	In Kathmandu (spare in case flight from Lukla is delayed)
Tuesday 20	Early morning departure for Cheraldi on the Trisuli to start two-day white-water rafting trip via Fislingtar to Muglin
Wednesday 21	Leave Muglin for Kathmandu
Thursday 22	In Kathmandu

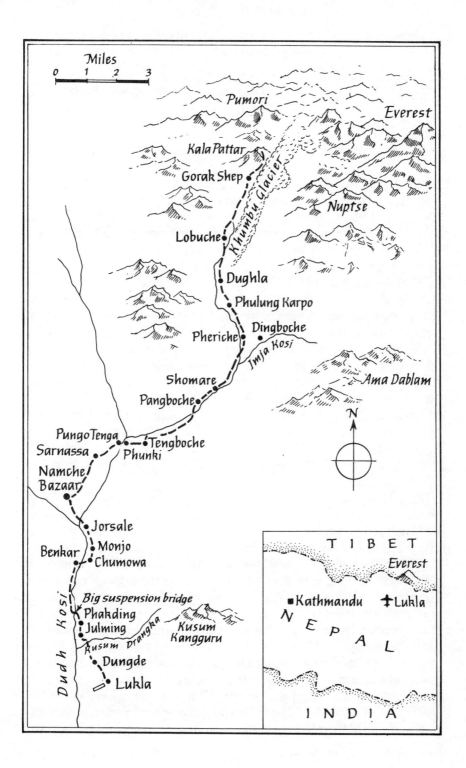

Friday 23	Depart Kathmandu 1710 for Dhaka, arrive 1840
Saturday 24	Depart Dhaka 0015 for London Heathrow via Dubai and Paris, arrive 1030

Filming began at Heathrow where I ascended an escalator several times while the cameraman captured different angles with each ride. Luggage was checked in and I waited nervously. I have never been at my happiest or most relaxed when flying and such a long journey held many fears for me. It had been over seven years since I had last flown in an aeroplane, but fortunately I was travelling with others who were not afraid or at least not showing any signs of disturbance.

The Biman Airways DC10 lifted off easily and very shortly we were in Paris. Here the plane was loaded to capacity with the last few passengers searching frantically for empty seats after a mix-up with the allocation of seat numbers. It was a good flight and the night lights of Istanbul standing astride the Bosphorus looked spectacular as we made our way east. As dawn came we were over Northern India on our way to Bangladesh, the Himalayan peaks dominating the skyline in the early morning light. Two large mountains were constantly clear above the cloud. One of them had to be Mount Everest and I was thrilled to capture my first view of it. It was, however, a little daunting to think that we were flying at around the same altitude as the distant summit and that I intended to climb to almost two-thirds of the way up it.

The flooding in Bangladesh, caused by deforestation of the neighbouring Himalayan foothills, was to be seen everywhere as we lost height before landing. I had not expected the land to be so green and intensely worked. The flight on to Kathmandu was in a much smaller aircraft and the way the young pilot handled it convinced me he was a either a recent recruit from the Royal Nepalese Air Force or he drove a sports car. Just as I was becoming worried, however, I inadvertently bit into a piece of uncooked chilli pepper from the in-flight meal and that took my mind off everything else.

The land in Nepal is inhabited and cultivated to its upper practical limits and the aerial view of the hillside terracing gave me an astonishing first sight of the country. The Nepalese were obviously a very resourceful and industrious people to survive such a lifestyle.

With our filming equipment, customs clearance was a lengthy

process. We were staying at the quite modest Blue Diamond Hotel in the Thamel area of the city and the drive there was through both narrow dusty streets and modern wide malls, an exotic mixture of the old and new. The snow-clad Himalayan mountains lay to the north, just visible on the distant horizon.

Kathmandu was a city of corner shops. Everywhere there were traders trying to sell something: meat, fruit and vegetables, confectionery, ornamental carvings, carpets, books, local handicrafts and souvenirs; photography equipment, restaurants, clothes and day trips, trekking and safari tours and white-water rafting expeditions. The scene was colourful with cycle rickshaws, motorized three-wheeler rickshaws and an assortment of dilapidated cars wending their way through busy streets. Around every corner was an unexpected and sometimes unbelievable sight. Sacred cows wandered along alleyways looking for vegetable waste while packs of roaming dogs scavenged through piles of rubbish in search of their next meagre meal (maybe an ecology-conscious refuse disposal system, aimed at minimizing the risk of disease?). The city was a hive of activity until eight o'clock in the evening when everything suddenly closed, leaving the place a ghostly void.

The first three days were completely taken up with filming. The idea was to capture some of the main sights and sounds of Kathmandu. The temples, market places, shops, transport and people. I soon learned that my Sherpa companion for the film was to be Yonden, a 34-year-old local man who was a translator for the head lamas, besides being the proprietor of a carpet business. Chosen both for his photogenic appearance and his ability to speak good English, he was descended from a traditional Sherpa family who had long been deeply involved with the Buddhist religion. His father was a lama and Yonden hoped that he too would qualify when he could find time to complete his studies and periods of devotion. Together with his Indian-born wife and two young daughters he lived in a small neat house in Kathmandu taking care of his elderly parents and unmarried sister.

He was keen and helpful. Perhaps too helpful. It was difficult for him to understand that I was there to walk to Kala Pattar. He had been to the Everest base camp once before and therefore knew roughly what to expect. Severely disabled people were not uncommon in Kathmandu but as I was to find out later there are none or very few in the Himalayan foothills. Yonden's attitude was conditioned by experience. Nepalese people spend most of their time earning a living, and the average life expectancy is only forty-five. The thought of a physically disabled person having the time or will to pursue such an apparently worthless and dangerous undertaking, with no tangible result, was unimaginable. The whole exercise was incomprehensible, and the goal highly improbable, to Yonden but he had helped in the making of films before and was pleased to be engaged with such a high profile on this assignment.

I needed Yonden's total commitment and support and privately offered him an extra payment of £50, equivalent to nearly two months' wages, if I was to make it successfully to Kala Pattar and survive the return. This proved to be no incentive at all since he did not think I had any chance of getting there, and I later had to offer the bonus on condition that he simply made every effort to make sure things went as smoothly as possible. There was a distinctly positive response to this second offer making the payment a worthwhile proposition on my part. With this deal I became, in effect, his co-employer, probably his major paymaster, and he treated me with the appropriate respect. Had I made the trip without the BBC this was the way it would have been from the start. I would have been in full control paying for whatever services I required. Monetary reward for efficiency and goodwill is a great motivator where people are searching for ways to improve their standard of living.

The filming in Kathmandu was sometimes laborious, with Allen wanting several takes to get shots just right. Many of the sequences would probably never be used but with the possiblity of my getting out to Lukla and walking only a short distance before I retired in distress he felt he needed something on celluloid at an early stage. Making a film also meant that a story with a continuous thread had to be woven into events. For someone suffering from stiff and swollen legs and wishing only to see Everest at close quarters this became something of a nightmare. My personal relationship with Allen was good and, maintaining faith in him as a first-class filmmaker, I endeavoured to give him my full co-operation. He knew things were difficult and whenever practical released me from scenes immediately I had played my part.

My most frightening scene was a shave by cut-throat razor administered by a street barber. I felt quite uncomfortable as the blunt blade scraped over my face. He produced a leather strop and sharpened the instrument. I felt a little easier until he suddenly grabbed hold of my throat in order to shave the region around my neck. This was too much and I declined his invitation to continue further, promptly paying him and retreating into the watching crowd. I have never had a complete cut-throat razor shave and could do without taking my first in primitive fashion on a street in

Kathmandu with a cameraman only inches away. I think this particular piece of action was dreamed up by the film crew as some sort of practical joke just to entertain them and test my nerve.

Early one morning we climbed the 365 steps to the 2,000-year-old hill-top temple of Swayambhunath to see the sunrise. Large numbers of Buddhists were worshipping at one of Nepal's oldest shrines before they went to work. Walking around the central stupa they spun the numerous prayer wheels and made offerings of food or flowers at shrines as they went. The sight of the sun slowly appearing over the distant hills, gradually lighting up Kathmandu and the surrounding valley, still thinly veiled by wispy sheets of the early morning mist, was worth every part of the effort involved. A resident population of monkeys entertained us with their antics. At Pashupatinath, the holiest of Nepal's Hindu shrines, several pagoda-like buildings were decorated with hundreds of erotic wooden carvings which Yonden said were illustrations to the Kama Sutra – the Hindu equivalent of a stained-glass window illustrating a scene from the bible in a Christian church, I presume. It was also to this site that people brought their dead to burn and as I made my final preparations for the hazardous trek ahead the sight of two young bodies burning on funeral pyres brought home the reality of life and death.

The forty-minute flight by a twin-engined nineteen-seater plane to the mountainside airstrip at Lukla was a worrying prospect. The journey is reputedly the second most dangerous scheduled airflight in the world, a thought which did nothing to ease my fear of flying. We were at Kathmandu airport early and taking breakfast while we awaited our departure on the first flight. At this moment I was overcome by my first bout of diarrhoea and although it was probably the result of something I had eaten the previous day I could not discount the idea that fear was playing some part. This was not a good moment to be stricken by such an unpredictable and embarrassingly uncomfortable condition. My first problem was to get to a toilet and urgent investigation revealed that there was only one on the premises and this was in the departure lounge. To get there I had to leave the restaurant (which was upstairs) and enter the airport by another entrance, queue at a check-in, have all my documents inspected and stamped before finally locating the place I was in despterate need of. By some miracle I made it and the cubicle was free. This was the best omen I could have hoped for.

A further visit and it was time to board the small blue and white twin-prop plane. My adventure was about to begin in earnest and how I coped with this first serious challenge to my courage could be a sign of how the rest would go. Take-off was fantastically smooth and the flight a marvellous experience I have to confess I thoroughly enjoyed. The view of Everest carrying a faint halo of cloud was spectacular and touchdown on the twelve-degree-angled dirt-track runway perched on a high ledge above the steep-sided valley was a great feeling. A great feeling that the first part of the journey was over, that I had triumphed over the unreasonable fear the thought of the flight had provoked – and that my bowels had remained stable. Wrecked blue and white fuselages and wings were dotted around the airstrip but fortunately I was not aware of these until after the landing. It had been like coming in to land on a ski jump in reverse 9,000 feet up on a mountainside. The trek would soon be underway.

The first thing was to acclimatize to the altitude while our sirdar sorted out equipment, staff and team of yaks. Lukla is at an altitude of 9,200 feet, and although the effect of rising to this height quickly is normally considered to be minimal, I knew from past experiences in the Alps that the amount of energy I use to walk would soon have me in serious difficulties. Altitude sickness is an ailment for which there is no reliable form of treatment. The symptoms are a headache, dizziness and sickness, and the result can be sudden death. It is not something to be taken lightly. I would be taking every reasonable precaution to make sure I was not afflicted and letting my body gradually get used to the rarefied atmosphere was a start.

Lukla airport consisted of the runway, a turning area and the control tower. When aircraft were due to arrive or take off people and stray dogs were cleared from this fenced area. The trek would begin with a crossing of the airstrip before we followed the valley north-wards, gradually descending to the river. The track was good and the first noticeable occurence was that the local people came out of their homes and stared, eventually making a tut tut tut noise as I walked past. Whole families lined the single street villages. Men and women looked amazed while children pointed fingers and made remarks. Yonden believed that they had probably never seen a physically disabled person before and the tut tutting sound meant they were sympathetic. Some asked Yonden where we were making for and his reply would produce a look of bewilderment and total disbelief. They obviously intended no harm or malice and I was not offended by their curiosity. The Nepalese, despite their level of poverty, are very largely a scrupulously honest people with good intentions and it is difficult not to be won over by their genuinely sincere natures.

The first night's camp was scheduled for Phakding and the porters and yaks set forth in advance to prepare for our arrival. I made steady progress and was pleased that I could still manage to walk after a week without physiotherapy. My knees were stiff and climbing even small steps was difficult but, for this first day at least, the trail went downhill. I was accompanied by Allen and as darkness fell it became apparent that we were not going to make it to the camp. There was an immediate solution to the problem – stay at the nearest tea house, and this we did. Other members of the crew came back to find us, bringing news that camp was still a long way distant. We were only at Dungde. A bigger problem had also arisen. Part of the filming equipment had not arrived on the flight with us and would be needed before the trip was through. Lithium batteries, I believe, used for filming at cold temperatures. Neil was assigned the job of sorting this problem out and returned to Lukla where he could send telephone messages back to the ever-reliable Diana Penny who fortunately had remained in Kathmandu. The missing case was located and forwarded on the next flight.

With the help of Imodium tablets my diarrhoea was under control, which I was very pleased about since the visitors' quarters were in a large upstairs room and the toilets outdoors. The food on offer at the tea house was a mixture of boiled rice and small pieces of dark green cabbage. We decided to try this more out of a feeling that we had to eat to sustain ourselves, rather than out of hunger or temptation. I was pleasantly surprised to discover that Pepsi Cola, Fanta orange and Cadbury's chocolate were also available – the price being governed by market forces. Such morale-boosting luxuries were to be available at other tea houses all the way to Gorak Shep, although sometimes the supply was erratic and the price rose steadily with the altitude.

The second day of the trek was now upon us. The altitude was posing much less of a problem to me than I had imagined it might; perhaps the respect I was treating it with was paying dividends. The route continued downhill, passing through some of the many small settlements scattered along this hospitable broad ledge on the eastern side of the valley.

The crew had returned from the camp at Phakding and by the time I arrived at the first bridge, a large ornamental wooden structure like something from a Chinese willow pattern design, they were ready to film. The bridge crossed the Kusum Drangka, a small tributary of the Dudh Kosi near Julming and from it was a superb view of Kusum Kangguru at the head of the valley. The snow-covered mountain dominated the skyline and to the fore was an array of marvellously coloured trees, in varying hues of green, orange and brown. These were the sights that inspired me, the main reason I was here. The scene before me only fuelled my desire and determination to see my ultimate goal further. The bridge was a little rickety but not too difficult and I slowly made my way across, feeling happy that we had now descended to the valley bottom and would soon be climbing again. Somehow, walking downhill did not seem conducive to achieving our target of climbing to over 18,000 feet.

Throughout the afternoon I steadily gained height, only to descend again in the evening to Phakding. It had taken me 1½ days to reach the place I was expected to reach in the first afternoon. Either I was falling way behind schedule or someone had got the planning wrong. The porters were delighted at having a day off and, given the chance, would continue to press on knowing that it would take me two days to catch them up. For them it made for an easy life, but it was causing me very serious concern for it was a situation which could not continue if I ever hoped to reach Kala Pattar. It was still early days though, and all I could sensibly do at this stage was resign myself to pushing on as best as possible.

The following morning I was keen to get underway and, accompanied by Yonden, was walking at 8.00 a.m. We had not gone far when we bumped into Al Burgess, one of the well-known mountaineering twins from Holmfirth and a fellow Yorkshireman. Allen knew him well and this was an appropriate moment to film an interview. He was full of encouragement but could not believe the enormity of the task I had set myself. For the first time I could ask someone who still had the trail fresh in his mind what the route ahead was like. His reply was that there was a clearly defined track and that yaks were capable of following it as far as base camp. Despite the difficulties there was no reason, he thought, why I should not make it if I stuck to this track and remained able to keep going long enough. He wished me every success and we bade each other farewell.

Yonden and I were making good progress, walking on ahead of the group. We turned a bend in the trail and in front of us appeared an enormous suspension bridge hung high across the Dudh Kosi River. I knew we had to cross it but in desperate hope and disbelief I queried this with Yonden. His answer unfortunately confirmed that I was right. Somehow I had to get across the eighty-yard span of swaying planks suspended from wires. As we got closer it became apparent that apart from the structural wires the bridge had no other protection at the sides. Between the wires were open gaps and towards the centre the main wire was only about two feet from the walkway itself.

I was terrified at the thought of stepping out on to the unstable and unprotected bridge. The film crew were still some way distant, back up the trail, and there was no sign of them. I should have to wait for their arrival before crossing or they may insist that I did the crossing again for the camera. We sat down and waited. The passing of time did nothing to alleviate my fears which increased with the sight of each successive crossing I watched. The bridge definitely swayed and if more than one person was on it at a time there was also a tendency for it to bounce up and down. (At this point there are a great many trekkers and porters on the route. Beyond Namche Bazaar the number drops sharply.)

After about forty-five minutes the film crew arrived and decided my crossing would be too spectacular to miss, especially if anything was to go wrong. We would, however, have to wait a short while longer until the sun moved around to bring ideal lighting conditions. The more I looked at the next eighty yards strung out precariously in front the worse I felt. I decided that I would rope up and have Yonden following closely behind, hopefully in a position to clip me on to a side wire if I faltered or fell. The bridge was six planks wide but towards the middle a couple of them were broken.

When the moment of reckoning was upon me, I had to be decisive. At times like this I endeavour to maintain a tranquil state by praying for the strength to face whatever may lie ahead. I was as ready as I would ever be and, with Yonden left in no doubt about his task, I set forth. I knew that I had to concentrate completely on what I was doing and at all costs keep moving forward. If I was to stop, that would be the end. I had to fix my eyes only on the decking immediately in front of me to maintain momentum. The flimsiness of the bridge and the drop below to the swirling rapids of the Dudh Kosi were irrelevant. The only thing which mattered was my balance and the positioning of my feet and walking sticks. Steadily I made my way out on to the narrow strip of wood, past the point where the initial drop appeared and then towards the middle with the side wires gradually decreasing both in height and in the amount of protection they afforded as I went further and further forward.

Yonden was giving instructions but I did not want to listen and kept shouting for him to concentrate on what he was doing with the rope and karabiner. He had this crazy notion that if I focused my field of vision on the other side of the bridge and did not look down all would be well. How on earth he thought I was going to know where to place my sticks I can't imagine, when one minor error would have had serious consequences. The gradual descent to the centre complete there now remained only the task of getting back up the other side and off. My prayers were being answered for the strength to keep going came from somewhere. Slowly the other bank was coming within reach.

I stepped off the bridge thrilled that I had managed to cross without incident. At that moment I reckoned that the crossing was the most nerve-testing thing I had ever faced and overcome. It is hard enough to endure a nerve-racking experience; it is even harder coldly and calculatedly to proceed knowing that you must continue if the experience is to end. I was not being thrust into an irreversible situation. I had chosen to do this and for all I knew things could get much worse around the next bend. The decision to continue was always mine and the responsibility in the event of a mishap likewise fell upon me. I was choosing to challenge my mental and physical limitations in pursuit of what I felt was a worthwhile goal and my personal boundaries were expanding with every day and obstacle that passed. Daily I was learning more about the real person within, and was content (if a little apprehensive) each evening as I retired to my sleeping bag. Content because I had given all and, although tired, had come safely through another day, and apprehensive about what was to come.

We had now crossed to the western side of the valley and the land was much more savage. The steep-sided mountains swept uninterruptedly down to the river. The track was narrow, sometimes skirting the top edge of very high vertical walls cleanly cut by flood waters sweeping round bends in the river. With trepidation I walked along the edge of these fearful drops unroped. The path was about three feet wide and above, to our left, rose a hillside of loose stones and boulders. Should these precariously perched lumps of rock decide to re-arrange themselves we would undoubtedly be crushed and swept away in the landslide. True to form the route continued as a series of ups and downs. No sooner did we gain height, perhaps 500 or 1,000 feet, than we descended to the valley bottom again.

Our rescheduled destination was Jorsale but we were not yet at Benkar, the next river crossing, and darkness was falling. Once again the team had gone on ahead but not too far this time and camp was made just across the river. I was walking with Allen when news came back of a horrific bridge around the next corner. Several trekkers experiencing difficulties had had to get on their hands and knees to cross the large wooden cantilever construction which carried no side fencing at all. Allen definitely wanted to capture my efforts on film and as the light was failing rapidly he decided that he and I would once again stay at a tea house, there being one only a few hundred yards before this nightmarish obstacle barring the way ahead.

Tea houses offered good cover from the cold nights at a cost of only a few pence. Invariably there was an open fire with the smoke usually drifting upwards before leaving through a hole in the roof. Reasonable food, sometimes such luxuries as Sherpa stew or hard-boiled eggs, were available very cheaply and also, as I have described, bottled drinks and confectionery at the going rate. The sleeping area however was communal and everyone had to be quite close together with simple wooden boarding for a bed. This in itself was no problem, but the altitude caused many trekkers to suffer from nasal and other breathing complaints and in the dry smoke-laden atmosphere the place sounded like a battlefield for snorers. There was also the problem of being woken by the flash-lights of those suffering with lax bowels, which was an all-too-common occurrence. I had no grounds for complaint for I was frequently one of the offenders on both counts, but I much preferred the clear cold air and quiet solitude of my tent whenever possible.

A few hundred yards down the trail and my nightmares of the bridge materialized. The glacial melt waters of the river poured thunderously down a narrow gorge in the valley. The bridge is obviously positioned at this point because the crossing is narrow. Beyond the battered remnants of a previous bridge stood this new construction, a high platform with no side stanchions. I visualized that I would walk straight across it before I had time to become gripped with fear. The distance along the top was not far although the drop to the noisy waters below did not look too enticing. A closer inspection revealed the bridge to be a little narrower than I had expected but, even worse, the climb up to the aerial platform was fraught with danger. It was up over a series of round split tree trunks with small gaps between each one; gaps large enough to allow my walking sticks a clear passage. I was not about to tempt providence by stepping out over such an unforgiving drop with these treacherous traps lurking beneath my feet. I decided to rope up and crawl across, dignity on this occasion taking second place to safety.

I felt quite at ease crossing by this method since once prostrate there is no longer any risk of falling and it is simply a question of shuffling forward and concentrating on the job in hand rather than any would-be danger below. For the purpose of film-making though it is not simply a question of performing a feat before the camera. Whenever possible there has to be dialogue and, however much engineered, the more natural and meaningful this is, the better. Throughout each take I had to endeavour to keep talking. While I was roping up Allen had the brilliant idea that I should tell Yonden that if I was for any reason to fall off he should throw himself over the other side and thus we would both be saved (presumably he would mount a rescue!) as we hung like stirrups from the planking. It was a theory I prayed would never have to be executed, but it suited me to have Yonden under instruction in the hope that he would concentrate on his immediate duty, leaving me free to concentrate on mine.

It did not work. Yonden was still full of helpful advice and I had to shout to him that I had the situation under control. As we neared the far bank I became aware that I was holding up a train of heavily laden yaks and was pleased that the herder had waited for me to descend at the other side before driving them across. Along the trail I lived with the fear that if I did not get out of the way in time I would be trampled underfoot or pushed off a narrow ledge by a train of yaks, so I was constantly aware of the need to get to a safe place if I heard the sound of a jingling bell or the voice of a herder in places where there was insufficient room for them to safely pass by.

The route was now a continuous series of rock stairways ascending and descending their way up the tree-lined valley, sometimes curving in an attempt to follow a contour as a tributary stream was crossed. I was behind schedule and pressing on as quickly as possible so as not to lose further ground. Today I was supposed to be enjoying a rest day in Namche Bazaar, but the mountainside settlement was about 2,500 feet higher and still some way distant. Past Monjo the route should have recrossed the river but after changes in the landscape following ravages by the swollen Dudh Kosi a new trail had been opened up on the east bank. This was good news since we had been receiving reports of some very hazardous obstacles to be overcome on the western side. Returning trekkers who stopped to talk to me had grave doubts that I would reach the foot of the steep climb to Namche Bazaar let alone the town itself.

By late evening we were safely camped on a sandy bank on a bend in the river below this steep climb. If I could make it to Namche Bazaar the following day I would only be one day behind schedule. Climbing steep hills is what I enjoy most and I went to sleep relishing the prospect of getting to grips with the barrier ahead. Few people thought that I would make it but by tomorrow evening either they would be proved wrong or I would be on my way home. Whenever I came up against any difficulty the answer was simple – either I overcame it or I returned home. It really was as straightforward as that, but I considered the latter measure was perhaps equally as drastic as any decision to continue. The climb to Namche may be steep and perilous but it was a regular route and I believed that if others could make it I could also.

Before the steep climb began there was first the little matter of crossing the most precarious bridge yet. There was nothing spectacular about this piece of civil engineering. In fact quite the reverse. It was simply three tree trunks spanning the swirling rapids. Some well-worn cross planks were nailed on to these main beams to give it some extra width and where there were none, loose stones were placed between the spanning logs to fill the gaps. The overall width of the structure at this point was about three feet. It was eight o'clock in the morning and there was no time to stand on ceremony. A hard day lay ahead. We were not filming and therefore it did not matter if anyone was with me on the bridge. Neil took my sticks and walked in front of me while I put my hands on his shoulders. Allen followed closely behind ready to steady me in the event of anything untoward happening. Without too much concern we proceeded to cross. Since there would be no more filming of bridges I would follow this routine at future crossings. A day later I was shocked to learn that an Australian man had reputedly fallen and died at this bridge a few days earlier.

The track to Namche zigzagged its way up a cliff face somehow managing to cling to the steep rock and earth. Quickly we gained height and by the time we were about 1,000 feet above the river we arrived at what was to be the crux of the ascent. The path narrowed down to a sandy ledge about nine inches wide and over the edge was a precipitous drop down to the river below. Many prayer flags adorned the area and I understand these were in memory of a Frenchman who had earlier fallen from the ledge. These tales of horror are difficult to substantiate but I would imagine they are highly probable. These were the only two recent accidental deaths reported although another seven had reputedly died from altitude sickness and one of these we were to witness the following day.

The sandy ledge had to be passed and I had two options. I either made my way along and up it or I climbed over a smooth rock angled at about fifty to sixty degrees on the top side of the track. I opted for the rock climb on the grounds that if I slipped off I still had the nine-inch ledge to fall back on, provided of course I did not slip straight over it. Although the fingerholds were sparse and not over-generous in size, the angle of the rock was easy and my only concern was the abyss below. Because the incident was to be filmed Yonden would be immediately behind me and ready to wedge my feet if necessary. Neil, no mean climber, positioned himself near the drop to provide extra cover. Slowly I moved up over the smooth rock, having great difficulty in finding suitable fingerholds. Those I did locate were covered with a layer of very fine sand and it was hard work to maintain my grip. As I held on precariously with one finger a wasp buzzed around it. This was all I needed: to be stung in the one hold separating me from the 1,000-foot drop below. And as I neared the top, straining with every ounce of effort to keep going, I met the camera about twelve inches or less from my face . . . Once committed to the rock, however, the only way off was by keeping going upwards.

The dangerous part of the climb to Namche behind us, I turned a corner and Everest suddenly came into view, an unexpected bonus. Framed by the trees, it dominated the distant skyline, a fine halo of cloud pluming over the summit. This was one of the moments I had waited for, my first uninterrupted view of the highest peak in the world; a just reward for the morning's uphill slog. Further reward waited around the next corner in the form of a tea house. The proprietor was a Sherpa who had accompanied Reinhold Messner on his Everest exploits and thus could afford such a prestigious development. A bottled drink and Five Star bar were in order. Five Star bars are best described as small Mars bars and together with small bars of Cadbury's chocolate are the main confectionery items freely available in Nepal.

The steep climb over, the afternoon was a long steady pull up to Namche Bazaar, the Sherpa capital and trading centre. The team went on ahead leaving Yonden, the liaison officer and myself to follow at our own pace. The liaison officer was struggling and indicated that he intended to go no further than Tengboche. After the early struggle I had had with my legs they were now beginning to move much more easily. They were not swelling and the range of movement in my knees was steadily increasing. Yonden's attentions were no longer necessary. In difficult situations his help was greatly appreciated but he found it hard to restrict the assistance to my moments of need especially if we were filming. Eager hands would get hold of me or lift my feet over obstacles, but to avoid any misunderstanding or problems I diplomatically let him get on with it, although at times I found it a little overbearing. He meant well and was trying to do a good job of looking after me. The air was now much more rarefied but I was coping quite well and if I forwent my acclimatization day in Namche I would be only one day behind schedule. I knew this would be a risk but I felt fairly fit and I hoped that with my very slow progress upwards I would get away without that acclimatization day. Further encouragement came with the news that there were hot showers available at our campsite and for the equivalent of fifty pence one could feel clean and refreshed. After five days of all-out effort in the warm dusty atmosphere this was a most welcome prospect.

Namche was a place to buy authentic souvenirs of the region and the busy streets were lined with shops selling all types of goods, each trader proclaiming that his wares were genuine or that his prices were the best. The place reminded me very much of Stornoway in the Outer Hebrides or Lerwick in Shetland – though of course Himalayan style. A business, social centre and complete civilization in a remote area.

The climb out of Namche was another steep affair but my spirits were high after making up some of the lost time. The schedule, although not completely inflexible, needed to be followed fairly closely. There were only the rest days, which were really necessary for acclimatization, and the trip to base camp which could be used for other purposes. Already small parties of trekkers were returning without having reached Kala Pattar or base camp. Often the failure had been due to the slowest member of the group holding up the rest so that time had run out. This could very easily happen to me if I lingered too long. I already realized that a rest day would be a luxury, perhaps with disappointing consequences. On the other hand altitude sickness could be far worse.

Towards the end of the pull out of Namche I began to suffer from a headache, the combined effect of extreme effort and the altitude. The trail now faithfully followed the 3,500 metre contour line in a north-easterly direction. Around spur after spur it went forward in the form of a narrow path perched high on a steep hillside. On average it was about three feet wide but in places at the extreme point where it went around spurs it narrowed down to only inches. In a couple of points the path disappeared completely for two or three feet and the only foothold was a stone protruding from the hillside. The ground fell away steeply and any mistake would not be forgiven. This was true of most of the route to Sarnassa. For the first time we were in open country and the sparse shrubbery consisted mainly of berberis from which Yonden ate the little red berries. The film crew were shooting some long-range shots today and I was accompanied only by Yonden until the late afternoon when Allen joined me.

From Lukla to Namche there had been a beautiful small grey and white yak following our other beasts but today it was no longer with us. The lunch consisted of delicious roast beef and for several days we enjoyed beef again. It seemed likely that we had brought our meat along on the hoof and the young animal had been butchered in Namche, which came as an unpleasant shock, but the meat was an improvement in the menu and we did have to eat. Maybe this was not the same creature but we would never know for certain.

My headache was persisting and this was now accompanied by a feeling of sickness. The altitude was affecting my nasal system and I was clearing away phlegm and blood by the handkerchief-full. When I lay down I found it difficult to breathe. I was suffering from mild altitude sickness and together with the phlegm problem I felt very ill. A local youth employed as a cook boy on the Korean Ama Dablam expedition was being brought down from base camp with altitude sickness. He had been carried thus far down, but as he came past us he was – with some assistance – walking. Quickly he and his helpers vanished around the next spur. Shortly afterwards word came back that he had dropped dead. This was more than hearsay and not encouraging news. The Ama Dablam base camp was at no great altitude, perhaps 15 or 16,000 feet, and I was aiming for over 18,000 feet.

I did not make it to camp that evening and had to stay in my ill state at a tea house on the outskirts of Sarnassa. The proprietress, whose Sherpa husband had climbed Everest twice, detailed another six recent deaths in the area from altitude sickness. The building was still under construction and once again being financed by a Sherpa's exploits on Everest. The rest of the team went on to camp and I was left with the resident family and an American couple. I was feeling very poorly and unable to eat. The pungent smoke from the open fire hung heavily in the air and I was experiencing considerable difficulty in breathing. I was fearful of my physical condition and for the first time wondered if I would survive the night. The fact that my disability is the result of brain damage played on my mind. I was being encouraged to eat but could not face food and was content just to sip liquids, an essential requirement at altitude.

Nights were now very cold with temperatures falling below zero, and in the morning there was ice out of doors. My headache had eased and I felt a little better. Neil and Yonden arrived back at the tea house early to check on my well-being. I was ready to continue with the trek but felt in a very bad mood. I just wanted to be alone and I found walking with Neil and Yonden almost intolerable, but as we progressed the feeling of wanting solitude gradually eased. In the late afternoon I made it to our camp at Phunki situated at the foot of the steep climb to Tengboche.

I had recovered from the mild dose of altitude sickness and was going well although I was now two days behind schedule. The next few days would be crucial but where steep climbs were involved I usually reached my target destination. The fact was that my progress on near level ground was little better than on the more severe steep terrain and this was where the average trekker covered distance quickly. The schedule planner had not taken this into consideration. Perhaps they thought I would not make it all the way to Kala Pattar and therefore the schedule would ultimately be irrelevant.

Apart from suffering from a bout of diarrhoea the climb to Tengboche was fairly straightforward, there being few, if any, places where the steep tree-lined trail was exposed to sheer drops. I made it to our camp which was situated immediately in front of the monastery in time for lunch. I spent the afternoon visiting the famous Buddhist religious centre and filming scenes which might fit in with the audience I was due to have with the lama the following morning. I retired to my tent early to get as much rest as possible, update the tape-recorded diary I kept for the film and prepare for the day ahead.

My audience with the lama was early in the morning and Yonden and I were soon walking through the rhododendron forests on our way to Pangboche. In places where the morning sun did penetrate the shrubs there were icy patches on the ground. The trail was level and there were several settlements in the clearings. The land was obviously very fertile because, despite being at an altitude of around 13,000 feet, the agricultural farming was intense. The highlight of the day's walk was the crossing of a suspension bridge hung high across the Imja Kosi River. The rickety bridge, which fortunately had meshing on the sides, linked the route across a gorge. I would not like to estimate the height of the drop beneath it, suffice to say it saved a long steep descent and subsequent ascent.

Towards the end of the day I was beginning to struggle. The sole of my right foot was hurting badly. Allen had walked with me since the crossing of the bridge but now I was accompanied by our cameraman, Des.

I had by now worked out where I stood with each member of the party, and my working relationship with each was different. Neil looked after me, making sure I had whatever I needed. He helped me into my sleeping bag and tent, helped me get up and put my boots on; whenever I had a practical problem Neil dealt with it. Despite some differences in our social attitudes, we got on very well. When I was in a dangerously exposed part of the route I needed Allen around. He was totally dependable and, reassuringly, although he did not appear strong, he was physically very solid, strong enough to lift me should the need arise. We had some frank and honest exchanges but I had the greatest respect for him and enjoyed his company. At difficult moments I found inspiration from my association with him, as I did from that with Des. Being cameraman meant that Des was occupied for most of the day and it was usually only in the late afternoon when he would walk back from camp to accompany me for the last hour or two. Today was one of those days and I needed his inspiration more than ever as I hobbled along very tired and concerned about this sudden pain in my foot.

As darkness fell we arrived at our camp at Pangboche. Neil quickly removed my boots. The pain was centred on the ball of my right foot and I instructed him to massage it in an attempt to disperse the tension. Throughout the past nine days my feet had been firmly encased in boots and, apart from this pain which seemed to result from the continuous pressure, they were showing no signs of serious wear. Neil worked his hands over my foot and ankle bringing ecstatic relief from the intense pain. The instant response eased my worry and concern considerably. This was a problem I should have to monitor very closely in the days ahead, if necessary stopping to treat it at the first sign of any serious threat.

Yonden had been taking a close interest in the trouble my foot was causing and the following morning greeted me with, 'Good morning Mr John. How are your balls today? Do they need massaging?' His command of English was excellent and he had learned a new term . . . I looked down at my feet and replied, 'Not too bad, thank you. I'll see how they go.'

Today our target was Pheriche, which at 14,000 feet would be a critical point on the route. A long hard day lay in front of us, for it was much further than any of the previous distances I had covered in one stretch and we were at an altitude whose effects would soon become very noticeable.

The first settlement we came upon was at Shomare, where I managed to purchase a tin of pure orange juice, a remnant from an Everest expedition, and this little luxury boosted my morale no end as the heat from the mid-morning sun beat down on us.

Although it became very cold when the sun went down the temperature through the day was high enough to warrant wearing nothing warmer than a T-shirt.

In the early afternoon I was accompanied by Yonden. The going was fairly easy but the altitude was beginning to take its toll. I was tired and under pressure, knowing that I had to make every effort to reach Pheriche if I was to keep alive my dream of reaching Kala Pattar. Yonden was also suffering. At testing times like this I needed solitude and silence. Yonden, however, being a Buddhist, began repeatedly to chant 'Om Mani Padme Hum' which, translated, means 'to the Greater Glory of God'. This sounded to me like 'Oh Mammy take me home', which did nothing to lift my spirits.

By mid-afternoon we had been joined by Neil for the gentle walk across open hillside terrain. We had now left behind the tree line and the scenery was much bleaker. Conditions underfoot could not have been better but the thin air was biting hard into my physical resources. Every movement was laboured as I pushed myself on, nearing exhaustion. I rested for short periods each time I was unable to walk any further. As we headed for the final ridge before dropping down to Pheriche darkness was beginning to fall. Pressing on became a matter of urgency and I did the best I could.

With the onset of dusk came a sudden drop in the temperature. For the first time it was bitterly cold and wearing of a duvet jacket became essential to survive. Pheriche was still some way distant down the hill over a bridge and along the valley, at my rate of progress probably about an hour's walk. Des and Jane came out from camp to meet us with flashlights and some extra items of warm clothing. I was almost in a state of collapse but their arrival lifted my spirits and fortunately the way ahead was downhill which alleviated the altitude problem a little. We crossed the wooden bridge whose alarmingly dilapidated condition became obvious when the handrail came loose from the main structure as I grasped it. In my exhausted state walking by torchlight along the rutted track to Pheriche in the freezing conditions was as demanding as anything I have ever known.

I had to make it to Pheriche. The alternative to summoning my last reserves and pushing on to the very last was to be carried by our porters. Disappointedly I reckoned I could accept this in a life and death situation or perhaps if the crew had wasted too much of my walking time throughout the day filming. This would only be a last resort, and maybe a decision that would have to be made by those around me rather than by myself. While I could keep walking without endangering the lives of those accompanying me I was determined I would. The moral and ethical side to what I was trying to do was of paramount importance to me: if I did not wish to accept the risks, endure the hardship and give it everything I had then I should not be there. These were all part and parcel of wishing to see Everest at close quarters. Somehow I had to find the strength to keep going and eventually I staggered into Pheriche and the comfort of my tent.

My right foot was once again troubling me and Neil gave it his immediate attention. The 14,000-feet mark is a critical point for acclimatization and we were scheduled to enjoy an essential rest day at this point. I had now been walking for ten days with little respite and if I continued without the rest and acclimatization period would be only one day behind schedule. Whether to rest or press on was a big decision, as both alternatives had their respective problems. I could not afford to lose a day, but neither, and perhaps more importantly, could I risk ignoring medical advice and not acclimatize. Missing the recommended rest day at Namche Bazaar had caused me problems enough, at 14,000 feet the altitude might be even less forgiving. I discussed the possible consequences from the filming point of view with Allen and decided that I would take a rest day and hope also that my foot benefited from not having to support my weight for the next thirty-six hours. Pheriche was the site of the last medical outpost and I had expected to pay a precautionary visit to check on my well-being but a doctor was not at the moment in residence.

We had not been at Pheriche long before we bumped into André Peeters, a reporter for a Belgian newspaper. He was returning from base camp where he had been covering the Belgian winter attempt on Everest. At 8.00 p.m. he was scheduled to make radio contact with Maurits Vreude, the expedition leader at base camp, for an update on their progress. Word of my progress had gone before me up the valley and he was aware that I was in the vicinity. Pleased that we had met he wished to interview me and as a bonus was prepared to let me speak with the Belgians over his radio link. The temperature was well below freezing when contact was established and the handset crackled as by trial and error we found the best direction in which to hold it. High mountains lay between Pheriche and base camp and whatever signal we were receiving was being deflected around these. I heard that the attempt was being made via the normal route and I was interested to learn what progress had been made. A way had been built through the icefall with camps one and two installed and camp three reached. The mixed group of Belgian and Polish climbers hoped to reach the summit around Christmastime.

The rest day was used to do some filming in my tent. Interviews would be required for the documentary and this seemed like a good time to get them out of the way. The altitude brought emotion close to the surface and talking about personal issues would be very difficult. The crew would also have to be accommodated in the confined candlelit area of my tent, an intimidating stage from which I would have to relate my intimate thoughts and feelings. I wanted as few people around as possible and Allen agreed to limit these to himself and cameraman Des, the rest being sent for a walk. Allen conducted the interview, set up the lighting and took care of the sound recording while Des did all the camera duties. I was wedged carefully into position with three candles only inches away from me and a pressurized paraffin hurricane lamp beneath the camera providing the extra light required for filming.

The interview was not something I wanted and I had made my feelings known but Allen was adamant that it would be an essential part of his film and I agreed only as a goodwill gesture towards him. I felt very strongly that the BBC were not paying an appropriate fee for this type of inner searching. However, Allen and Des were now trusted friends and formed a large part of the inspiration behind my continued efforts; they were not the BBC and I had my responsibilities to them as self-employed people whom I now considered loyal friends. My co-operation was their living and, for them, I opened up my innermost self before the camera. I satisfied my own conscience with the thought that if for any reason I was not to survive the difficult days ahead then maybe what I had committed to celluloid would help those I left behind to understand the reason why it was a necessary part of my life.

All too quickly it was time to get back on the trail. I felt much better for the rest and the pain in my right foot had eased. Maybe my body had acclimatized to the altitude but I was finding it difficult to walk at my normal speed. I could only maintain any degree of effort for a short distance before I had to stop and recuperate. As we walked through the last of the high yak pastures the terrain was bleak and cold. Today the route crossed several fast-flowing streams, the margins of which were iced leaving only a narrow channel of water in the centre. Walking over the ice-covered stones was a precarious balancing feat. At times I had to walk through ankle-deep water careful that I did not let it go over my boots while praying that they remained waterproof. Icy-cold wet feet was not a prospect I looked forward to. We arrived at the now uninhabited summer village of Phulung Karpo and the way through involved following the bed of a shallow stream closely walled at either side. Shortly there would be the steep climb to Dughla but for now I could enjoy the sight of the odd yak grazing peacefully on the sparse vegetation while I stopped to eat my own frugal lunch.

I looked forward to the ascent in front knowing that it would be taking me in the right direction – towards Everest. If all went well Kala Pattar and my dream of Everest was now only a further three days distant. The effect of the altitude would become tougher to deal with. Maybe too tough if I lacked the necessary physical and mental resolve. I would soon know the answer to this and many other things about myself. My commitment would be tested to the full if I had to face serious adversity – such as a break in the weather, or a landslide. Already I was bringing up so much phlegm and blood during the night that since Pheriche I had given up trying to sleep. If I went to sleep I awoke with a nightmare and was left gasping for air. My heart would beat rapidly, I did not know where I was and often imagined I was on the verge of death. Obviously I was not dying but the sensation was extremely frightening and unpleasant and best avoided if at all possible. The only way to do this was to lie awake all night, resting rather than sleeping. To while away the hours in the sub-zero temperatures I read, under candlelight, *Illusions (The Reluctant Messiah)* by Richard Bach, interspersed with long spells of contemplation and trying to keep warm. Usually around 4.00 or 5.00 a.m. I would fall asleep for an hour or so knowing that I would be awoken by our porters before I had time to become restless.

The climb to Dughla was enjoyable but at 15,000 feet hard work. Once over the ridge it was only a short descent along the side of a glacial moraine, across a short narrow wooden bridge and up a steep climb through the settlement which consisted of only about three dwellings. It was dark by the time I arrived and the temperature had fallen below zero. I was feeling positively ill with my respiratory problems and wanted only to get to my sleeping bag. Allen, however, had other ideas and wanted to film some interaction with the local people: Yonden and I playing cards, Ambuti, our Sherpani, cooking, and the local folk singing. In the smoke-filled atmosphere, filming of the arranged set pieces was an ordeal which I could have well done without. We were, though, there to make a film and despite feeling very tired, unwell and freezing cold, I somewhat reluctantly co-operated.

We were now high among the mountains and the following morning the view was quite spectacular. The route ahead lay across what could best be described as a lunar landscape with a track gently rising over featureless scree. To the other sides, however, stood lofty snow-clad pointed peaks. We were now looking down on the snouts of several glaciers and the fact that our route was clear of ice was due only to it being in direct sunlight. The track is obviously situated where it is because it favours the best weather conditions. Today, according to the schedule, we could expect our first encounter with snow as we headed for Lobuche at 16,000 feet.

After the initial steep climb, which ended on a ridge strung with memorials to Sherpas and other mountaineering folk who had died in the vicinity of Everest, came our first distant view of Kala Pattar. A small dark ridge in front of the majestic Pumo Ri. Today the wind was gusting strongly and had lifted particles of sharp sand directly into our faces on the exposed uphill pull. The upland valley was a cold and desolate place as we crossed to the western side, a boulder-strewn glacial moraine with frozen waters covering much of the lower ground. I was walking with Neil and the temperature dropped to well below freezing as we approached Lobuche in the late afternoon. The fall in temperature came so suddenly as the sun disappeared it was rather disconcerting to think of the consequences had warm clothing not been available.

Lobuche is a developing site with many new buildings. Waste is disposed of in a heap to one side of the settlement and a pack of lean dogs scavenge for food. Dogs in this part of the world do not seem to harass people like they would in Britain. They are not noisy and excitable creatures, presumably because they have to concentrate all their efforts into finding food to sustain life. The only problem they caused was that throughout the night they sheltered alongside our tents trying to gain entry at every opportunity. I discovered one had managed to get inside the fly sheet and was curled up against the end of my tent. This was not a healthy situation since these mange-ridden animals could be rife with disease and would probably bite if provoked or cornered.

An American journalist returning from base camp was in Lobuche and she wished to interview me about my life and the expedition. In the cold candlelit confines of my tent this proved to be a lengthy and irksome undertaking as she wanted to know every last detail. The questioning lasted almost two hours as she recapped and double-checked her notes. Had it not been for the constant sound of conversation the crew might have wondered what we were up to.

The push to Gorak Shep would be a long hard day and Yonden and myself got off to an early start leaving Lobuche around 8.00 a.m. The way was easy but I found that I could only walk about six to ten feet before I was out of breath. Relentlessly I pressed on, walking until I could go no further then resting just long enough to recover before pushing myself hard again. In the still cold morning air we saw something move among some nearby rocks and for a moment I thought we were about to encounter a Yeti. A closer look revealed it to be a small sleek white creature. A snow leopard, according to Yonden. This sighting was a rare and unexpected treat.

For the first time on the trek the weather was overcast and threatening. The expected winter snows had not yet arrived, which was a blessing, but the prospect of climbing Kala Pattar only to have the view of Everest obscured by cloud was not encouraging.

About midday I arrived at the foot of the day's steep climb which was to be up and over a massive moraine, towards the top of which we spent some time filming. This was to prove a crucial loss as the day progressed. Struggling in the rarefied atmosphere I was feeling very pleased with myself as I crossed the highest point of the trail to Gorak Shep. I was stunned when I turned a bend to see in front of me the largest pile of broken rock and ice I had ever seen in my life. The fairly even track meandered through it hugging the contour line as far as possible. In the distance it disappeared over a small rise, presumably then descending to Gorak Shep.

I was once again walking with Neil and we both knew my chances of getting to the other side of this massive heap of shattered stone and ice that evening were very slim. I would either have to spend the night upon the moraine or accept a lift from our porters. For the moment though my concern was to get as far as possible over this impossible obstacle. If, in the interest of safety, I was to be carried then for my own satisfaction I wanted to be helped as little as possible. Underfoot the going was tough as I stepped from boulder to boulder, my progress being so steady that I was no longer having to rest because of the altitude. Darkness was closing in and the temperature falling rapidly as I battled on as best as I could. I was making inroads into the moraine, slowly closing the gap between myself and the distant ridge but knew that when darkness fell I would not be able to see where I was placing my feet and sticks on the precarious footholds. For the first time I was in serious trouble – unless I accepted help. Considering the safety not only of myself but also those around me I decided that it made sense to let the porters carry me over the remaining ground to camp.

Being carried on a porter's back is an uncomfortable and at times frightening experience, but fortunately these strong fit men make rapid progress as they almost leap from rock to rock, even while skirting precarious drops. Working as a relay team they reached camp within about twenty minutes. I reckon that it would have taken me all of half a day to cross the moraine without this help. Only 1,000 feet higher, across the sandy bed of a dry lake to the north of our camp, stood the extremely inviting ridge of Kala Pattar. Still the snows had not arrived and I retired to my tent a very happy man. My only fear was a sudden change in the weather, and provided this was not too severe I doubted even that would stop me now. My sights were firmly fixed on Kala Pattar. It was 7 December and since 25 February I had lived only for this moment.

I would have to put all my efforts into climbing Kala Pattar as quickly as possible knowing that I had to descend the same day. Another 8.00 a.m. start was called for but today I was setting forth with great enthusiasm. This moment was something that I could not have imagined fifteen days ago, when I had set off from Lukla. I had desperately wanted to make it but had been under no illusions about my chances of success. For two weeks I had lived life one day at a time, often at my limit of endurance and sometimes wondering if there would be a next, but now the moment of reckoning was here. I was in no doubt that it would all be worth it. I could never have committed myself to such a project had there been any doubt. The day was fine with clear blue skies and the winter snows, now weeks overdue, had still not arrived. The view of Everest would be superb and I set forth in the belief that some unknown power from above was looking after me.

Maybe it was, but I had just crossed the dry sandy lake bed when I slipped on a sheet of ice. The narrow strip of ice-covered ground barring the way to the foot of the steep climb stretched for about fifteen feet at the point where I chose to cross. Fortunately the damage was minimal, with only some skin quite deeply cut but cleanly removed from my right knuckles. The first part of the climb was up a very steep zigzagging sandy stairway. After this the gradient gradually eased until it gave way to something comparable to an open fellside covered with very sparse vegetation. This final part of the trek could not have been easier except for the fact that we were now at over 18,000 feet and the altitude was really knocking hell out of me. In the cold thin air I was reduced to taking only a few steps then resting to get my breath back and recover before repeating the operation all over again. The altitude was making me feel very emotional and I could not think about anything relating to those whom I had left behind in England without wanting to break down and cry. Under the circumstances it seemed better just not to think but steadily progress towards my goal.

From Gorak Shep Everest had been largely hidden from view behind Nuptse but now, as I neared the top of Kala Pattar, the mountain began to reveal itself in its full splendour. From the

18,145-foot summit of Kala Pattar the 29,028 feet of Mount Everest towered in all its glory. I fixed my eyes firmly on the great black pyramid which loomed another 11,000 feet above me, and nothing else in the world seemed to matter. The surrounding peaks were all white but Everest is so high most of the snow is blown off. This was my pilgrimage for those who had bravely gone before me. Kala Pattar was the limit of my ability but for George Leigh Mallory and Andrew Irvine, Mick Burke, Pete Boardman and Joe Tasker, Everest was their final resting place and I was here before the highest point on earth paying my respects in person. Somewhere up there the Belgians were still making their attempt.

It was 2.00 p.m. by the time I had reached the summit of Kala Pattar and I had decided that I must begin my descent no later than 3.00 p.m. Going downhill would neither be as time-consuming nor as laborious for the decrease in altitude would help considerably.

I am proud to be British and from the onset of the trek had proclaimed my intention to fly my Union Flag from this remote hill almost halfway around the world. This was my small contribution to the true British spirit of adventure and endeavour. Yonden had taken along some prayer flags to raise.

Accompanied by Allen and Yonden I descended reasonably quickly, feeling that I had been very privileged to enjoy the magnificent view of Everest afforded from Kala Pattar. In the failing light the setting sun was reflected against the still visible part of Everest, a glorious and fitting conclusion to my day with the mountain. We were alarmed to hear avalanches crashing down the face of Nuptse and with each thunderous crack I feared for the safety of the Korean expedition attempting to climb it. By the time darkness fell we were just recrossing the narrow band of ice before heading across the dry sand back to camp.

Gorak Shep consists of one well-equipped tea house, occupied only when the weather is tolerable, and a camping area. My arrival back was a time for celebration and the team had prepared a special meal – the last course of which was a boiled cake!

I had fulfilled my ambition and there now only remained the problem of getting back to Kathmandu. It had taken me fifteen days to get to Kala Pattar and I had lost two stone in weight along the way, though considering the situation we were in, the food was really quite reasonable. Shallow-fried sliced potatoes, boiled rice, hard-boiled eggs, porridge, muesli, yak cheese, bread, tinned sardines and tinned fruit with custard. Over the next four days we made our way thus fuelled back to Pheriche from where Yonden and I, in the interest of medical safety, were flown by helicopter back to Kathmandu.

SEVENTEEN

After Everest

Once back in Kathmandu I quickly recovered. The spare time I had while I waited for the return of the crew was a welcome break. Since my departure from Heathrow I had been under constant pressure to do this, that or the other for someone. When a film revolves totally around one person it makes for little respite for the person concerned, and if the crew were working then there was a very good chance that I was also. My main complaint was that this severely restricted the opportunities I had for taking photographs, which to me was equally as important as the documentary. After filming was completed my physical resources were not up to revisiting locations and the lighting and action which had earlier captured my imagination would probably have passed. If the trip held any disappointments, having the crew obstructing otherwise interesting scenes and views was the only one. I was not taking anything like the number of colour slides I wanted for future lectures and talks.

Now I had only our location manager, Diana Penny, for company and I was able to visit sites in a leisurely manner. Diana's intimate knowledge of the area and understanding of local customs and practices was a great help. Our visit to Bhaktapur, Dakshinkaali and the temple at Bodhnath provided me with the diversion I needed after the intensity of filming in the foothills of Everest. This unscheduled holiday was a bonus that would leave me with some very happy memories of Nepal, and gave me a chance to shop, see the local way of life as it really is and visit neighbouring places of interest; time to unwind, recover, visit Yonden and his family and meet my companion for the next part of the expedition, Sue Aitken.

Sue is an Australian whom we met on the trek to Everest. She is an experienced white-water rafter and qualified lifesaver. On hearing of our forthcoming two-day trip down the Trisuli River she expressed a wish to join us. We needed an extra and her qualifications fitted the bill perfectly. It would look odd if I was to appear in the dinghy alone but it would look equally out of place if the film crew were to suddenly put in an appearance before the camera.

I was uncertain about the rafting and needed the moral support and confidence I hoped Sue would provide.

While shopping in Kathmandu I bought some books on Nepal in an effort to learn more about the country and its people. To my surprise I read a piece on rafting on the Trisuli River which best summed up what lay ahead. It was by Amin, Willetts and Tetley from the book *Journey Through Nepal* and read as follows:

The most popular 'put-in' place for the Trisuli rapids – with colourful names like 'Snail's Nose' and 'Monkey Rapid' and graded from easy one to dangerous 10 on the Colorado River scale – is Charoudi, a small one-street hamlet with a wide, sandy beach where the dinghies are laid out, with paddles and life-jackets, awaiting the 0800 hour arrival of the river adventurers.

It's not just the raging torrent which the challenger has to conquer. Beneath the surface lurk deep potholes into which the current races to circle vertically in a fatal vortex. On the surface, there are deadly whirlpools. Hidden rocks and boulders just below the surface form the third potentially fatal hazard.

Drifting down the river is at first euphoric, the giant walls of the gorge seeming to disappear in the infinity of the sky; on other sections these close so narrowly that the volume of light diminishes. There's exhilaration in the toss and bounce of the 'Tina Devi Rapids', almost placid, a minor grade two.

But now there's a more menacing roar ahead, where the gorge narrows and the road winds along a ledge a hundred feet above the river. The Gurkha crew is cautious. The dinghy is manoeuvred into the bank by a U-bend and they scamper away over the rocks to study the situation at the notorious 'Up Set Rapids'. In spate it's a feared and fearsome stretch of white water and even now its thunder is filled with menace.

They run back, lithe, fit and fearless. The dinghy is pushed off and bounces into the main stream, racing around the bend. Ahead the water boils and crashes over the rocks.

The leader screams a battle cry. The paddles dig deep into the foaming river as the dinghy is caught and tossed like a frail matchstick and the waters roar in over the side.

Newcomers bounce into the middle of the dinghy caught in a kind of heart-pounding trance, adrenaline flowing, as the dinghy dips into a deep and powerful pothole and miraculously bounces out clear of the spray and suddenly it's in the powerful but calm swirl of the current downstream. The crew let loose an exultant victory scream. Exhilaration returns.

In a rare tragedy three months before, the crew lost one of their colleagues, downstream at the Mugling Rapid, when the current tossed him overboard into a pothole. He had no lifejacket and his body did not surface until three days later. River rafting can be deadly. But usually it's tremendous fun.

There's a picnic lunch just before the next rapids, called the 'Surprise'! Afterwards they arrow through the narrow cleft between the foam-battered rocks with an ease born of experience.

Most rafting expeditions take two or three days to cover the Trisuli, down beyond the raging Mugling rapids, under the elegant Jholunge Pul suspension bridge, and on to Chitwan.

This was certainly some introduction to what lay in store and did nothing to allay my mounting fears. The crew returned from Lukla on schedule with the news that the winter snows had arrived immediately after my departure. Some of the team's luggage was due to arrive from Lukla the following day but after a heavy overnight fall of snow all flights were cancelled. I had been very fortunate indeed with the weather. I had originally hoped that I would get the chance to climb an icefield within the vicinity of Gorak Shep and was fully equipped for the purpose. The omission was I felt a loss to the film, but in reality the problems of too much snow and ice could have proved insurmountable.

Whatever difficulties I had encountered on the way to Everest the rapids of the Trisuli were to be a whole new experience and a completely different source of danger. The journey to Cheraldi was by minibus and along roads I had never seen the likes of before; a four-hour drive along open narrow winding roads sometimes skirting the edge of a precipice or on an unsurfaced track where a recent landslide had covered or removed the original road. Many heavy wagons used the route and passing them as we inevitably did was often hazardous.

The bus pulled up alongside a large sand bank by a bend in the river. I slid down the steep loose sandy bank and made my way towards the river. The water level seemed good, neither high nor excessively low. The Trisuli at this point is already a powerful river, wide, deep and fast-flowing, heavily coloured by millions of minute particles ground from the rocks over which it had thundered and forced its way. It was easy to see that this water was in a hurry to find lower land, the more gentle open spaces of the plains beyond. Nothing was going to stand in its path. The gradient of the watercourse was such that the river had cut deeply into the land and now flowed through high walled gorges. On the inside of wide sweeping bends pleasant banks of sand had accumulated but otherwise the water ran swiftly between the confines of large rocks and boulders scoured smooth by the constant attention of this ever-moving gigantic force.

The two dinghies which were to be our means of transportation downstream for the next forty miles or so were inflated and our food and equipment for the expedition were loaded into waterproof canisters which in turn were secured aboard the rafts. Sue joined me and we made ourselves comfortable on the rear wall of the dinghy. Our oarsman for the journey was Robin and he was assisted by two other crew. Emergency procedures were gone through, everything given one last check and away we went. As we glided slowly downstream one could not have imagined a more pleasant way to spend a December's day. Robin was very experienced at rafting down the Trisuli and knew exactly which line he wanted to take as first we went down a series of long gentle rapids. These were exciting but not the heart-stopping torrents I knew the river held in store. 'Surprise' rapids appeared as we rounded a bend. Lunch was a most enjoyable affair as we ate good food and recounted the exciting moments of the morning.

No sooner had we got back underway than we again pulled into the shore. This time it was for Robin to inspect the notorious 'Up Set' rapids before we descended through them. 'Up Set' is about grade six or seven on the Colorado scale. A narrow gorge lay ahead and Robin, together with the film crew, climbed the rocks to view the river from above. I knew 'Up Set' rapids were something special but surely we would not venture through unless all seemed well. I should have suspected what lay ahead when Allen decided that our shoot through would be filmed on two cameras. Never on the whole trip had the team utilized both cameras before. Perhaps it would just provide spectacular viewing. I thought no more except to make certain that my handholds were all they should be.

We set off once more and very soon I could see the roaring waters boiling and thundering their way ahead. Water crashed all around swamping over the sides of the dinghy as we shot downstream. Giant boulders channelled the water into steep powerful glides and in places obstructions hidden beneath the surface forced the water to erupt violently. The river in front was much lower than we were and this could only mean that a very fast descent was imminent. Suddenly all was revealed as we shot over a thunderous drop – perhaps eight or ten feet. I hung on grimly as fear rushed through my body. The situation was out of control. As the dinghy bucked forwards out of the drop it lifted on the crest of a mighty wave and buckled. When it flicked straight again Sue and I were thrown backwards into the raging torrent. Disorientated and uncertain as to what exactly was happening I hung tenaciously to my rope handholds, but my head was submerged beneath a mass of foaming water and looked like staying there. I made a conscious decision to release my hold on the rope and as I did swirled free. At that moment I knew that I had parted company with the craft and was underwater in the rapids.

It is difficult to put a time span on what is happening at a moment like this but despite my lifejacket I was still not surfacing. I thought that this was it. I was about to die. There was little I could do except try to stay calm and pray for the strength to face whatever was about to come. My head momentarily popped above the water, I gasped for air before being quickly swamped beneath the next wave in the rapids. Once again there was little I could do except pray but now I reckoned that if I was lucky I would surface again and maybe I would be able to ride out the rapids. I had taken in a lot of water and was really in no state to think further than my next breath! This time I was not under very long before I surfaced again. I felt Sue grab hold of me and shout to stay calm. The knowledge that I was no longer alone gave me one of the greatest feelings of reassurance I have ever experienced in my life. Although unable to do very much about the situation Sue was not panicking and her calmness gave me some degree of confidence.

I was travelling downstream in an upright position, which was not very safe if my legs were to hit a submerged rock. The water was cool rather than cold and this helped considerably as we floated downstream out through the last part of the rapids. The aim is float feet first in a horizontal position and this we did, Sue guiding us as best she could from behind, while my mind was occupied with the thought of whether or not we would manage to get ashore or be rescued before we came to another rapid. We were drifting through a gorge and gradually getting closer and closer to the massive rock wall. I reckoned that to get hold of the bank would be a good move but Sue had other ideas, for below the surface of the water the rock wall was heavily undercut and if we were to get too close and be swept under the overhang we would most certainly not re-emerge alive.

So now we were endeavouring to pull away from this additional hazard. Sue steered us away slightly back towards the middle of the river when Robin, rowing frantically, suddenly appeared along-side us and we were quickly hauled aboard by a very relieved raft crew. Not, however, as relieved as I was. For the moment I was safe again and extremely pleased still to be alive.

At the next sand bank we put ashore to make sure that all was well, deal with our wet clothing and film an interview while I was still in a state of shock and the incident fresh in my mind. The truth was that I could have retired from white-water rafting right there and then. From the practical side, however, we were nowhere near a road and there was really only one way out of the situation – to continue downstream in the dinghy. Allen had made a canoeing film on the Trisuli before and assured me that 'Up Set' was about the worst we could expect to encounter. In fact on his previous trip one of the canoes had broken in exactly the same turbulent water as where I made my unscheduled exit. With a considerable degree of apprehension I reluctantly got back in the raft. From now on my heart was filled with fear each time we approached the thunderous sound of frenzied water that heralded another set of rapids, for I knew all too well the consequences of any mishap.

Evening camp came as a welcome respite. Our site was a large sandy raised beach surrounded on three sides by the river. The proximity of nearby settlements was proclaimed by two long suspension bridges hung high over the river, one now dilapidated beyond use. Looking upwards in wonder at these flimsy feats of engineering I felt grateful that I did not have to cross either of them. There had been nothing quite as alarming as these along the trail to Everest and I did wonder whether or not I would have made it if there had been.

Our trip ended the following lunchtime but not before a shoot through the treacherous 'Pinball' rapids. The raging water looked as severe as 'Up Set' to me as we drifted gently into the first glide. We had passed the point of no return and all hell was let loose as the dinghy was battered from rock to rock. I got what I hoped was a secure hold and prayed that this time I would make it safely through. Suddenly there was a loud crack. One of Robin's oars had broken and now we were completely at the mercy of the water. The buffeting became worse as we spun our way uncontrollably through the tempestuous stretch. A spare oar was lashed to the side of the dinghy in case of such an emergency and the moment we came out of the chaotic turmoil it was released and pressed into service. I was very pleased – and relieved – as we pulled ashore for the last time. In retrospect I have no doubt that the white-water rafting trip was a worthwhile and mostly enjoyable experience but it was definitely one I should be very cautious about repeating.

We left Kathmandu on 23 December and arrived home the following evening. Friends had collected Megan from the kennels and she was waiting to greet me at the door. Being reunited with my dog was the best possible Christmas present I could have wished for and after five minutes it was as if we had never been parted. I wondered why I had ever worried about leaving her.

Philosophy and Reality

Simply to recollect some of the factual events of the latter half of my life, giving the reader only a brief insight into my philosophy of life, would be to opt for the easy way out. Having arrived at this point you would not expect this of me and you would be right. However, you are probably not quite sure what to expect. Nothing in life should be taken for granted. There is one certain fact about disability: it shows no discrimination and it overtakes everyone in one form or another should they live long enough, and so – to some sooner than to others – beware! Whatever your attitude towards the handicapped, as likely as not it will be reflected upon you should that day arrive. Can you cope?

Philosophical acceptance and a realistic attitude are the real keys to successful living in the face of adversity. It is no use me pretending that I am anything else other than physically sub-normal, handicapped, disabled, crippled, call it what you will. Whatever descriptive term you apply, however, it does not change one bit any problems I may have. The first thing I learned to do was to shut all thoughts of disability from my mind. Henceforth it exists only in the minds of those with whom I come in contact. All right, I am severely limited, but who is not? Everyone has limitations and I am no different. My limitations are immediately apparent to anyone meeting me – perhaps other people's are not. But this does not mean that they are not there and in their own way they are as real as any I may have.

Because my limitations are so real I am compelled to face up to the reality of the situation and in so doing I have the chance to know, understand, and come to terms with them. As the saying goes, 'A man has got to know his limitations', because if he does not then he is a menace both to himself and to others. Knowing and accepting one's limitations adds greatly to the joy of living and, in many ways, I am thankful that I have had the opportunity to discover so many of my own. It eliminates self-doubt and this must be the first major step towards living constructively.

What have been the challenges in my life? What are the motivating forces? My early life under the ever-watchful eye of authority may not have been all it might have, but away from the close scrutiny and infliction of physical torment and official cruelty I constantly searched for the elusive pleasures which would bring satisfaction to my life. At no time did I ever doubt that somewhere there were moments of supreme happiness and peace waiting to be discovered. I was, perhaps, the eternal optimist, but not fool enough to believe that spiritual riches would come my way without my first finding the way, nor that the search would be anything other than long and hard. But I knew that I had to keep going until I found it.

A turning point came out of a small but memorable experience during one of our childhood holidays when my father took my brother and myself on Filey Brigg one morning. I had pestered him for several days to take us on the Brigg, a narrow strip of rocks stretching about half a mile out to sea. The walk along the beach from Filey was quite lengthy and then there was a rather haphazard concrete footpath over about another half mile or so of rocks before the actual Brigg was reached. I knew that when we reached this point that I would be lucky to get any further but would have been well pleased with getting so far. My father, however, decided that I was not going to miss out on the excitement and he picked me up and hopped from rock to rock along the outstretched arm of massive seaweed-strewn boulders. Sometimes the gap between stones was quite considerable and we had to make almighty leaps. I was, to put it mildly, more than a little apprehensive as I flew through the air on his back. However, I committed myself to his expertise (as later I did to the porters on the way to Gorak Shep) in the belief that he knew what he was doing and that all would be well. I had faith in him, he had never let me down before. The experience was exhilarating and the exceptionally fine aspect of the spot made me realize what I would be missing in life if I did not learn to negotiate such places under my own steam. And I did. I taught myself to walk. By dint of the literally thousands of hours I spent kicking a football against a wall I regained balance and strength. There was no short cut. My admiration for Norman Hunter and his colleagues provided the ground work for quite another area.

As a fifteen-year-old my ambition was to live as near normal a life as was possible. I had no wish to bury my head in the sand, to pretend all was well, or to continue living life as I had done so far. There had to be much more. Some drastic changes had to be made.

Despite the fact that every part of my body is affected by my disability, and this is clearly visible to the onlooker, I wanted to be accepted as being normal by society. Unfortunately this could never be and this was the first thing that I had to come to terms with. The hardest thing for a handicapped child or teenager to come to terms with is the pointing fingers and unnecessary comments. Since I am different from the majority of people and do walk very awkwardly, perhaps the attention others give to this is not wrong. Perhaps they mean no harm. Maybe it is I who am over-sensitive; excessively self-conscious. Whatever the reality is, it is not important, but it is crucial that I come to terms with the situation. Alternatively I could hide myself away or take refuge in a wheelchair, but in doing so I would be the loser.

I did not know what I was capable of but I knew that I was no loser. Maybe I was born to struggle, but not to accept defeat. I am British; English and furthermore a Yorkshireman. For generations men had died fighting for their honour and country, they had given their lives for what they believed in, often showing great courage in doing so. No one's life should be a waste, neither theirs nor mine. I had a tradition to follow, standards to live up to; determination and commitment burned within me. I had no wish to fight wars. Fighting is for fools and those well paid for doing so. My fight consisted of upholding my strong principles. Nothing was going to stop me doing what I thought was morally and justly right. There was no doubt in my mind at all, I was always going to stand firm for that in which I believed. Deep within each of us lies an understanding of right and wrong; we may try and kid the world about our motives but we do not kid ourselves. We must be honest with ourselves, because if we are not honest with ourselves, who can we be honest with?

I needed self-respect and reason to believe in myself. However far I progressed educationally I was taking the easy way out. I was not mentally sub-normal, just physically handicapped, and, because of the limitations this imposed on my social and other life, it was too easy to channel all my energies into learning. I had few distractions and sufficient intelligence to be able to both apply myself and enjoy it. The few girls whom I could have gone out with felt sympathy for me and this was something I could well do without. Understanding, yes, but sympathy, definitely not.

I hated strenuous physical activity without a purpose but I needed sport and recreation, even though my choice was very limited. At school I was quite competitive against other handicapped children but that brought little self-respect in the big wide world. I object to competition on any basis other than equal terms.

237

With careful choice there are enough things that almost everyone is capable of doing without resorting to inventing new games or making new rules for those who cannot. For the mentally able such things do little for one's self-respect and I cannot see how they can help you achieve equality in society, if that is what you want.

The fire raged within me and I needed positive outlets, though the operations on my legs had effectively put paid to any faint hopes I may have nurtured of participating in competitive physical sports. Fishing was my first constructive outlet and although it may appear leisurely I can assure you that under the circumstances in which I went it was anything but.

Walking and climbing mountains brought me self-respect. I could only really have respect for myself when I knew that I had given everything in pursuit of a demanding goal. It gave me a new-found inner strength. I felt better acquainted with myself and less ashamed of what I saw in the mirror. I believe in the power of God and the solitude of walking alone, enhanced by my tired state, gave me the opportunity to think clearly, get my life into better perspective. There is a reason for my life. Perhaps I will never be fully aware of just what it is, but I never doubt there is a reason. I always have faith and optimism for the future.

Everest was the apogee of my climbing achievements. Apart from suffering with bowel infections I had come through the trip pretty well. The swelling in my legs had gone and the exercise had jolted the muscles into functioning again. The muscular arthritis was still with me and likely to remain for the rest of my days. The skin and flesh on my lower limbs was irritated and rather delicate, most likely a legacy from the months of persistent swelling. On my return I went for an urgent medical examination to check on my physical well-being and discovered that for the time being my deterioration had stabilized and I would just have to learn to live with the increased pain and loss of mobility. In this situation my trek to see Mount Everest was the best possible thing I could have done and will certainly go a long way towards cushioning any curtailment in my active life. I have pursued my love of mountains to its ultimate, and live with no regrets. My subsequent RADAR/ Access 'Men of the Year' award came as a pleasant but unexpected honour and it gives me great encouragement and hope for the future to feel that my efforts in life have not gone unnoticed.

I am often asked whether I would do the trek again. Ask Sir Edmund Hillary or Chris Bonington if they would climb Everest again. Although I only went to just over 18,000 feet the dangers for me were such that I would not *dream* of doing it again – even if my physical condition were any longer to permit me even to contemplate the thought. Satisfaction and contentment come from having given everything in the pursuit and realization of an important ambition, in succeeding once against the odds when the price of failure could be high, when a momentary lapse in concentration disastrous, illness final.

What plans do I have for my next adventure? None. I once harboured the idea of walking across the Grand Canyon but the prospect no longer seems quite so appealing as it did a few years ago. I have been to the Grand Canyon twice and walked in Bryce Canyon. Perhaps this has helped to satisfy my yearning. I was delighted to be invited to lead a climb up Slieve Donard in Northern Ireland on 9 June 1990, which at 2,796 feet is the highest mountain in the province. It was not particularly difficult or hazardous underfoot but literally uphill all the way, and, in all honesty, after $16\frac{1}{2}$ hours of sustained effort on the first day (my second longest day's walking ever, following my $17\frac{1}{2}$ hours on Ben Nevis back in 1974) I was virtually in a state of collapse. However, I completed the ascent the following morning without any physical deterioration to speak of and thus fulfilled a long-held ambition to climb the UK's four highest peaks: Ben Nevis, Snowdon, Scafell Pike and now Slieve Donard (and raised £17,000 for Phab N.I., the physically handicapped and able-bodied society, in the process). I would like to go to Australia and walk around Ayers Rock before climbing it. And I would like to visit the mountainous Inca sites of Peru. I feel no desperate need to do these things, only the sense that if the opportunity were to present itself I would give it very serious consideration. If you are patient, the right time, if there is to be one, invariably comes, and with the right attitude all things are possible.

Climbing taught me that as we respect others for their principles, effort, and courage in the face of adversity, so we can learn to respect *ourselves* by knowing that we have the ability and commitment to go to the limit and stand alone when necessary. We can face the harsh realities of life with only the support of our own personal beliefs.

Yet the greatest challenges in my life have been those resulting from my endeavours to live a normal life. Often I have worked for people who made a meal of my disability or attitude. A more enlightened superior once succinctly summed up the situation when he remarked that I was a problem, as big a problem as he wished to make me. However, he thought that I had performed my duties better than many and did not find me a problem at all.

Because of my unwavering principles I am a reflection of those I work for. If they make the rules up as they go along or are inconsistent then I appear to be a problem. It comes back to my theory about rules of the game. I will not play games to a constantly changing set of rules. It is too easy to apportion blame down the line without bothering to get to the root of the difficulty.

I hope I have made it clear earlier that I did have some very good working relationships with superiors. Perhaps these too were people with honest beliefs and principles. They understood the unspoken rules to the game of life. When a physically handicapped person requests that they be treated no differently from anyone else they do not mean they wish to be set a series of ridiculous hurdles which they will find great difficulty in negotiating. They mean they would like due consideration to be given to their physical limitations without having this point dwelled upon. There are horses for courses, and this is what good management is about. One may be able to climb 'Everest', but not on a daily basis.

At one time I believed that perhaps if I could understand the psychological reasons for other people's patterns of behaviour it would help me to cope with trying situations. However, I came to the conclusion that psychology is a form of rationalization. It might explain the reasons for certain human responses to given situations but it neither changes this behaviour nor helps with accepting the problem which is being analysed.

Philosophy, on the other hand is about taking a realistic look at yourself in situations when everything is not going as smoothly as it might. There does not have to be an answer. It is an attempt to achieve a greater understanding or appreciation of yourself. If you cannot understand yourself and honestly and openly account for your own actions then how on earth can you ever hope to understand anyone else, let alone try and explain the reasons behind their actions?

The human imagination often far outstretches the body's physical abilities. We see so much action on television and through other media that if we are not careful we begin to imagine ourselves excelling in very tight situations, and, even worse, we criticize others when they fail in difficult or unco-operative circumstances. If we are going to be critical of others then let us get our own performance right first.

Throughout life a person usually develops in three directions: physically, mentally and spiritually. First the body develops and becomes mobile; the mind then begins to increase in awareness and absorbs information; finally we learn to understand life and humanity. If all these faculties are developed, the being grows into a complete person. However, it is possible that we may find one or more of these aspects painful or disturbing and thus we choose to opt out. The important thing, I think, is that we spend time developing each aspect to its potential and not just those which we enjoy most or those at which we are best.

The most neglected area is spiritual growth and it is surprising how life changes as this develops. It has no limits, and we never grow too old to make progress. Unfortunately, whereas physical and mental development are an essential part of living, understanding life's greater meanings is not, and many people do not start to give it consideration until they are forced into doing so. Serious self-analysis or soul-searching can be a very painful business.

My attitude towards living life is based on the following: flexibility, opportunity, responsibility, commitment and enthusiasm. Without being forceful an adherence to these principles results in a FORCE to be reckoned with! By coincidence, or perhaps not, the sequence of letters is also my order of priority.

It is of little use my either dwelling on the past or what might have been. I feel no bitterness towards the surgeon who operated on me, because I have had a good life, despite my disability, and I cannot say what would have been the case had I not had those operations, how my ability to walk would have lasted. What I quarrel with is the *way* it was done, the way my parents and I were not told just how experimental the surgery was, the way I – although young, admittedly – had no say whatsoever in the matter. The real injustice is that there was so little 'after-sales service'. After the age of fourteen I never saw the specialist unless I was in terrible pain or I paid. Even though the pain was a result of an NHS operation (which they had been very quick to rush me into hospital to do) it can take over six months for me to see a specialist, unless I pay. However, I adopt the attitude that I will meet each situation as it arises with the resources – monetary and moral – I have at my disposal. I must always be responsible for my actions whatever they are and whoever they affect. Without commitment I could not believe in myself. Without enthusiasm life might as well not exist. It is the key to everything. Patience is enthusiasm and commitment controlled while responsibly waiting for the right opportunity to present itself.

The FORCE principle has been a very important factor in my pursuit of physical activities where there has been an element of danger. I have always had to operate to a strict code of conduct. It has been great fun, but it was also a very serious business. It was my life that was at stake and I never forgot that. I had nothing to prove by taking foolish risks and I certainly had no death wish.

I was born handicapped and therefore I have never been able-bodied to become disabled. I have never had to strive to restore that which I once had. I have never had to try, as it were, to recapture my youth. I have never had anything to prove either to myself or anyone else. I resist all challenges others throw at me, trying instead to do what *I* think is right and morally proper for me. I am not easily led or dissuaded. I make my own decisions and, although I am by no means a recluse, I go my own way should this be necessary. I do not allow people to take advantage of me but I do go to great lengths to support the things in which I believe.

As a result of all this I do not conform with what society expects of a person like me; I am a controversial character. I *am* a problem – a thorn in the side of hypocrites and the self-centred. I understand the difference between those who give and those who take, those who achieve under their own steam and those who use others, and these are dangerous things to recognize in the world of the disabled and physically handicapped. I believe that each individual should give of his best and be satisfied with the level achieved. As another saying goes 'you only get out of life what you put in'.

I would like to think, however, that in some small way I have been an inspiration to some genuine and sincere folk – especially those who have turned to me with their trust and enough faith to believe that I would be able to help them.

As I said in the introduction, I am no hero. My achievements are extremely modest by most standards. But what I have done is to live life with the courage of my convictions, hopefully tempered by good sense, and decide for myself the things which I could and would do. At times my life was definitely an uphill struggle but I can honestly say that it was all worthwhile – I have no regrets. When I look around I realize that life has been very kind to me. I am an extremely fortunate person. I have *lived*.

Index

Adel Woods, 18, 22
Aiguille du Midi, 140
Airton, Miss, 17
Aitken, Sue, 229–34
Allerton Girls High School, 59
Alps, 139–40
altitude sickness, 208, 218
Angle Tarn, 168
Angler's Crag, 164
Angling Times, 81
Appletreewick, 146
Athlone, 84
Atkinson, Joan, 54–5
Ayers Rock, 239
Aysgarth Falls, Yorkshire, 59

Baker, Julie, 169, 170
Ballinasloe, 84, 85
Barnett, Dave, 160
Barra, island, 108
BBC, 174, 179, 181, 185–6, 187, 191, 192, 196, 198, 201, 223
Beamsley Beacon, 193
Beckstones centre, 122
Ben Nevis, 124–7, 129–35, 136, 143, 157, 173, 175, 179
Beningborough, 79–80
Benkar, 201, 212
Berghaus Ltd, 176, 178, 182, 194
Bhaktapur, 229
Black Sail Pass, 170, 171, 190
Blencathra, 158
Blue Man-i'-th'-Moss, 155
Boardman, Pete, 228
boat journeys, 107–8
Bodhnath temple, 229
bogs, crossing, 155
Bolton Abbey, 146, 158
Bonington, Chris, 120, 175–6, 179, 192, 198, 238
Borrowdale, 165, 166
Bourton, Hazel, 143
Bowfell by the Band, 104
Bowness, 145, 150–1
Branch College of Commerce, Leeds, 63, 66, 67–70

Branch College of Engineering and Science, Leeds, 70
Bridlington, 45–6
British Isles tour, 107, 110, 111, 112
British Rail, 71, 82–3, 85, 86–7
Broughton Plantation, 151, 154
Bryce Canyon, 159, 239
Buckden Pike, 158
Burgess, Al, 210
Burke, Mick, 228
Butler, Miss, 37

Cairn Gorm, 129
Calendar, TV programme, 174, 179, 193
Canada, 159
Carl Side, 94–5
Carn Dearg, 124
Chameleon Films, 185–6, 191, 192, 198, 201
Channel Islands, 112
Cheraldi, 202, 231
Chumowa, 201
Civil Service Award, 174
Clark, Miss, 31–2
Clark, Professor J. M. P., 37
Clark, Peter, 101
Clark, Stephen, 25
climbing, 119–21
Coalmire, 153
Coast to Coast Walk, 161–9, 200
Cod Beck, 82
Colsey, Dave, 153
Concannon, John, 102
Coniston, 104
Connell, Peter, 60, 61
Cooper, W. Heaton, 99–100, 120, 161, 168
Corpach, 124, 126, 131
Cow Close estate, Leeds, 24–5
Cringle Moor, 151
Crinkle Crags, 169, 171, 180, 181, 183–5, 187
crutches, using 50–1

Dakshinkaali, 229
Dale Head, 158
Dales Way, The, 145–51, 158

Dartford Tunnel, 112
death, phobia of, 33, 49
Dennison, Sara, 197, 199
Dent, 150, 152, 164
Dentdale, 147, 148
Derwent, river, 79
Derwentwater Boat Club, 117
Derwentwater, fishing on, 118
Dhaka, 204
Dingboche, 202
disability: coping with, 235; limitations of, 46–7, 235, 236–7
Dudh Kosi river 210–12, 214
Dughla, 202, 224
Dungde, 209
Dungeon Ghyll, 114
Duxbury, Mr, 64

Eiger, 139, 140, 142
Elmete Hall, Leeds, 64
Esk Hause, 97, 99
Esk Pike, 158
Esklets, 151–2
Exide Batteries, 88

Fairfield, 169, 171, 176, 180, 181, 187–9
Far Easdale, 166
Farnley Loco Angling Club, 79
Fieldfare Trust, 169
Filey Brigg, 73, 236
Finch, Philip, 143, 144, 145, 147–51
fishing, 72–82, 92
Fislingtar, 202
Fitzgerald, John, 154
Flamborough, holidays at, 19
Fleetwith Pike, 158
football, 88–90, 109–10
FORCE principle, 241
Fort William, 126, 130–1
Frayling, Nicholas, 108
Fylingdales, 155

Gaines, Bob, 26
Gaines, Brian, 86
Gaping Gill, 193
Gardiner, Ian, 14
Gatherstone Beck, 170, 171, 190
Giles, Johnny, 89
Gilwell Park, Epping Forest, 111
Gipton Estate, Leeds, 110
Gledhill, Denise, 197
Gorak Shep, 202, 225–6, 227, 228, 236
Graham, Miss, 31, 34
Grand Canyon, 239
Grassington, 147
Great End, 158
Great Gable, 96–7, 99–100, 103–5
Great Rigg, 187
Green Gable, 105

Greenfield, Frank, 62
Greenhalf, Jim, 179
Greenhead Gill, 188
Greenhow, Chris, 117
Grey Knotts, 158
Grey Rigg, 150
Grisedale Pass, 167

Hadrian's Wall, 111
Hardisty, Richard, 100
Harriet Trust, 122
Harrison Stickle, 113–15
Haston, Dougal, 120
Haweswater, 168
Hawkridge, John: childhood, 4–57; holidays, 19–22; at Larchfield, 4–17, 28, 29, 30, 31, 33, 60; in callipers, 10–11, 15–16, 32–3, 35, 50; at Potternewton, 17, 28–34, 52, 58–60, 62–3, 64–7; Cubs, 31–2; hobbies, 11–14, 23, 60–2; eleven plus exam, 37, 44; experimental surgery, 1–3, 35–43, 47, 48, 52–7, 63–4, 79, 91, 241; pain, 46, 48–9; crutches, 50–1; Scouts, 52, 110; fishing, 27, 62, 72–82, 83–5, 90, 92, 106, 238; at College, 66–70; with British Rail, 71, 82–3, 85, 86–7; Inland Revenue, 88, 100–2; football, 86, 88–90, 109–10; first fell walk, 94–5, 238; travel, 106–8, 110, 112, 137–40, 142–3, 158–60; as Scoutleader, 110–11, 112, 121, 174; sailing, 112–13, 115–19, 174; climbing, 119–21; fellwalking, 136–7, 140–2; voluntary work, 121–3; on Ben Nevis, 129–35, 136, 143, 173; marriage, 159; Kala Pattar climb, 175–228, 238–9; Trisuli rafting, 229–34; and challenges, 235–9
Hawkridge, Sam, 18
Hebrides, touring, 108, 125
Helvellyn, 97–8
High Street, 169
Hill, Mrs, 31, 62–3
Hillary, Sir Edmund, 196–7, 238
Hogarth, Miss, 5–6, 12–13, 60
Honister Pass, 93, 99, 104
Hornsea, 60, 61, 118
Horton-in-Ribblesdale, 141, 142, 143, 144
Hubberholme, 147, 149
Hunter, Norman, 89, 236
Hunters Lodge, 79
Huthwaite Green, 153
Hyatt, Mr, 64, 65

Ilkley, 21, 145
Imja Kosi river, 219
Ingleborough, 141, 143, 144, 152
Inland Revenue, 87, 88, 100–2, 160
Interlaken, 138, 139
invalid carriage, 91–2
Ireland, holidays, 83–5, 106, 108
Irvine, Andrew, 228

Jack's Rake, 104

Jewhurst, Allen, 185–7, 191, 201, 206, 209, 210, 212–13, 214, 215, 218, 223, 224, 228, 232, 233

Jorsale, 201, 202, 212

Journey Through Nepal, 230

Jugger Howe Beck, 155

Kala Pattar climb, 175, 176, 178, 196, 198–9, 200, 202, 209–28, 217, 219, 221, 224, 225, 226, 227–8; equipment, 178, 182, 184, 185, 190, 193–5, 199; financing, 179, 187; food, 216, 220, 228; immunizations, 195, 198; journey to, 204–8; preparations, 175–83, 189, 192–200; schedule, 192, 201–4; sponsors, 178–9, 187

Kathmandu, 192, 193, 194, 201, 202, 204–7, 229–30, 234

Keswick, 93–4, 96, 97, 98, 99, 158, 194

Khumbu glacier, 202

Kilburn, Mr, 69

Kinniside Stone Circle, 164

Knaresborough, 21, 76–7, 78, 81

Kusum Drangka, 209

Kusum Kangguru, 209–10

Lake District, 92–5, 96–9, 106, 107, 112–15, 127, 131, 161, 169, 180, 194

Lambert, Richard, 180

Langdale, 107

Langdale Pikes, 107, 113

Langstrath, 165

Larchfield School, Harrogate, 4–17, 28, 29, 30, 31, 33, 35, 60, 157; closure, 121–2

Ledgard, Samuel, 28

Leeds United FC, 86, 88–9, 90, 96

Lefebure, Molly and her husband, 176, 180, 187–8

Leigh Mallory, George, 228

Leighton, John, 116, 119

Littondale, 152, 153

Lobuche, 202, 225

Loft Beck, 165

Look North, TV programme, 179, 181–2, 185, 186, 196

Looking Stead, 181, 190

Loose Howe, 155

Lough Ree, 84, 85

Lukla airstrip, 178, 201, 202, 206, 207, 208, 231

Lyke Wake Walk, 144–5, 151–2, 153–6, 161, 162

McDonald, Neil, 181–2, 183, 184–6, 191, 201, 209, 215, 216, 218–19, 219–20, 222, 225, 226

McLellan, Robert, 7, 14, 23, 32, 35, 60–1, 65–6

Marguerite Hepton Orthopaedic Hospital, Thorp Arch, 36, 37–43, 53–7

Matterhorn, 140

Maynard, Kevin, 97, 98

Megan, dog, 183–4, 185, 194, 199–200, 234

Messner, Reinhold, 216

Methley, weekend camp, 52

Monjo, 214

Mont Blanc, 140

Moortown, Leeds, 18, 24

Mosedale, 170, 181, 190

Mount Everest: base camp, 202; climb to, 209–28, 238; journey to, 204–8; sight of, 175, 204, 216

Mountain Equipment, 178, 182, 194

mountain-climbing, as solace, 100–1

Muglin, 202

Mugling Rapid, 230, 231

Mull, island of, 108

Mullingar, 83, 85

Namche Bazaar, 196, 211, 214–17, 218, 222

Nannycatch Beck, 164

Naylor, Mr, 69

Nepal, 179, 183, 193, 194, 204, 216, 229, 230

Nepalese people, 204, 208

Nettleton, Mrs, 17

Nidd, river, 76–7, 78

North Africa, 159–60

Nuptse, 227, 228

Old Farnley, 24, 25, 26–7

Old Man, 104

Orkney, 110

Osmotherly, 151, 153, 154, 156

Oughtershaw, 148

Ouse, river, 79–80

Outdoor Action, 189, 190

PACE group, Leeds, 122

Pagdin, Mr, 30, 59, 66

Pangboche, 202, 219, 220

Parfitt, Jane, 201, 221

Parker, Mrs, 31

Parkinson, Miss, 17

Pashupatinath shrine, 207

Patterdale, 167

Pavey Ark, 104, 113

Peeters, André, 222

Pennine Way, 148

Penny, Diana, 192, 209, 229–30

Penyghent, 141, 143, 152

Perry, Mr, 31, 52

Phab N.I., 239

Phakding, 201, 202, 209, 210

Pheriche, 202, 220, 221–2, 224, 228

philosophy, 240–1

Phulung Karpo, 223

Pike o'Blisco, 158

Pike o'Stickle, 113, 114

Pillar Rock, 165, 169–72, 181, 189–91

Index

Pinball Rapids, 234
Potternewton Mansion School, Leeds, 17, 28–34, 52, 58–60, 62–3, 64–7
Pumo Ri, 225
Pungo Tenga, 201, 202
Pyg Track, Snowdon, 128

RADAR/Access 'Men of the Year' award, 238
Ribblehead, 143
Rillington, 79
Rosthwaite, 165
Ruthwaite Lodge, 167

St Luke's Hospital, 196, 197–8
Sanderson, John, 115
Sarnassa, 201, 217, 218
Scafell Pike, 98–9, 104, 124, 127; sponsored filmed ascent, 157
Scale Force, 97, 119
Scarth Wood, 153
Scilly Isles, 112
Scotland, tour, 107–8, 125–7, 129–35
scouting, 110–11, 112, 117, 119, 187
sea cadets, 112–15, 116
Seal, Desmond, 201, 219, 220, 221, 223
Sedbergh, 149, 150
Shap, 169
Sharples, Roger, 152
Sherpa Agency, Kathmandu, 176, 178
Shetland Isles, 110, 135
Shipley, Yorkshire, 160
Shomare, 220
Simon's Seat, 158
Skiddaw, 94, 95, 96, 98–9
Slieve Donard, 239
Smart, Mr, 16
Smith, Max, 160
Smith, Ronnie, 36
Snowdon, 127–8
Sollitt, Chris, 60, 61–2
Southern, Mrs, 58
Spain, 137–8, 139
Spastics Society, 199; Achievement Award, 174
Spennithorne, 80
Stickle Gill, 104, 113
Sticks and Stones, 174, 179, 197
Stone Arthur, 188–9
Sty Head, 97, 99
Suck, river, 84, 85
Surprise Rapids, 231, 232
Swale, river, 81–2
Swayambhunath, temple, 207

Swinson, Des, 101
Switzerland, 138, 139–40

Tasker, Joe, 186, 228
Taylor, Carol, 169, 170–1
Taylor, Fred, 81
Tempest, Mr, 52
Tengboche monastery, 201, 202, 219
Thackley, 198
Thackwray, Graham, 116, 119, 143, 144, 145–6, 151, 158
Thackwray, Miss, 17
Thirsk, 82
Three Peaks of Yorkshire walk, 103, 141–2, 143–4, 152–3, 174
Three Shires Stone, 183
Tina Devi Rapids, 230
Topcliffe, 81–2, 83, 85
Trisuli River, 193, 202, 229–34
Turner, Kenwyn, 103
Turner, Stephen, 97

Ultimate, 178, 195
United States, 158–9
Up Set Rapids, 230, 232–3
Ure, river, 80

Wainwright, A., 161, 166, 181
Walker, Dick, 81
walking sticks, type, 51–2
Wasdale Head, 96, 105, 158, 170, 171, 172, 189, 191
Waterloo Lake, Leeds, 116
Wharfe, river, 76
wheelchair life, 45–6, 50
Whernside, 141, 142, 143, 144
Whillans, Don, 120
Whitby, 59
White Stones, 94
Williamson, Keith, 110, 151–2
Wilson, Cameron, 153, 180–1, 182, 183–4
Worthing, 95–6, 107
Wright, David, 181, 190, 198
Wrynose Pass, 93, 183, 185
Wythburn, 97–8, 166

Yockenthwaite, stone circle, 148
Yonden, sherpa, 205–6, 208, 210, 211, 214, 216, 217–18, 219, 220, 221, 224, 225, 226, 228
Yorkshire Dales, 59, 169
Yorkshire Television, 174, 179, 193

Zangbu, Ang, 192